Blue Skies

The Autobiography of a Canadian Spitfire Pilot in World War II

D1416877

Blue Skies

The Autobiography of a Canadian Spitfire Pilot in World War II

BILL OLMSTED
DSO, DFC and BAR

Stoddart

First published in 1987 by
Stoddart Publishing Co. Limited
34 Lesmill Road
Toronto, Canada
M3B 2T6

Second Printing 1989

CANADIAN CATALOGUING IN PUBLICATION DATA

Olmsted, W.A. (William A.)
        Blue Skies

ISBN 0-7737-5213-7

1. Olmsted, W.A. (William A.). 2. World War,
1935-1945 - Personal narratives, Canadian.
3. Canada. Royal Canadian Air Force - Biography.
4. World War, 1939-1945 - Aerial operations,
Canada. 5. Fighter pilots - Canada - Biography.
I. Title.

D811.048 1987   940.54'4971'0924   C87-094258-1

Cover design: Brant Cowie/ArtPlus Limited
Cover illustration: Peter Mossman
Maps: Derek A. Bonnett
Typesetting: Jay Tee Graphics Ltd.

Printed and bound in Canada

*To all the men of the 442
and all others who served
their country in the air*

CONTENTS

ACKNOWLEDGMENTS

I wish to thank those who gave me support and encouragement during the many months I have spent writing this book. Dal Russel, whose leadership as CO of 442 Squadron and as wing commander of 126 Wing, was a constant inspiration to me. My tentmate and close friend, Calvin "Pep" Peppler, had a sharp eye for detail that has saved me some embarrassment.

My editorial consultant, Diane Mew, gave me much-needed direction at the very beginning. The staff of Stoddart Publishing were always helpful and cooperative. I am thankful to Charles Pearse, formerly on Intelligence Staff of 126 Wing, for his careful criticism and that extra push.

Above all, my wife Mary patiently read and re-read the manuscript, and the book is as much hers as it is mine. The contribution of my son, Richard, to polishing my sometimes awkward style is, I am sure, appreciated by the publisher.

FOREWORD

The tragic death of Bill Olmsted, author of this extraordinary book, BLUE SKIES, which took place only a short time ago, leaves me almost speechless.

Bill had told me of his attempt to produce his memoirs as a fighter pilot which concluded with the period of D-Day and the activities of 442 Squadron of which I was Squadron Commander when he was posted to this unit. Bill was with and commanded 442 Squadron until he became tour-expired in December of 1944.

Bill was a courageous leader with a great affection for those under his command, both pilots and ground crew. He was a great inspiration to those who flew with him. He will be greatly missed by all those who were fortunate enough to be associated with him during his lifetime.

Dal Russel, DSO, DFC and Bar
May, 1987

CHAPTER 1

OFF TO WAR

November, 1939 — August 1942

My connection with the wartime air force began on a night in November, 1939. The radio was blaring, and I was hunched over the notes from my lectures with reference books piled precariously on the outer edges of my large table-desk. The upcoming Christmas exams were fast approaching, requiring my usual cramming. My study was really the family room, large and cosily furnished, which my parents allowed me to appropriate during critical study periods.

I was in my sophomore year at McMaster University in Hamilton. Having worked hard all summer, I had accumulated sufficient funds to allow me to continue my college education, saving my family an expense they could ill afford. I had just turned nineteen years of age, stood six feet one inch tall, and weighed a skinny 125 pounds.

My father was a self-educated civil engineer who had acquired the skills needed to register in a number of professional organizations. His expertise was acknowledged in the construction industry, but the Depression had been very difficult, forcing the family to become separated frequently as he managed projects in distant locations. I had lived in many different cities and towns throughout Canada and the United States, which had improved my knowledge of geography while disrupting the rest of my education. Sometimes I jumped a class ahead in a new city, only to fall back a year on our next move. We had averaged about one move a year to this point in my schooling.

One result of my nomadic education was to stimulate a strong desire for scholastic success. I intended to become a lawyer, any kind, following in the footsteps of my namesake and Dad's younger brother, Uncle Alf. Uncle Alf had been killed in action

1

on October 30, 1917, at Passchendaele, in one of the bitterest campaigns of World War I. He was an officer in the Fortieth Battery, Canadian Field Artillery while Dad served in the Thirty-fifth Battery. (Mother also lost a brother, Uncle Stanley, killed in action on September 28, 1918, during the final successful Allied penetration of the heavily fortified Hindenburg Line.)

My father had served throughout World War I, surviving many bloody actions which, to my knowledge, he never, ever mentioned. He won the Military Cross in one battle and was severely wounded in that same engagement. Following lengthy hospitalization he returned to the front, ending the war with a captaincy in an artillery battery. During the interval between the two wars he belonged to the Royal Canadian Legion and any military reserve unit based in the areas where he happened to be working.

War in Europe was declared on September 3, 1939. It was a Sunday. The next day my father went to the local armories on James Street, Hamilton, to volunteer for overseas duties, even though Canada would not officially declare war for another week. He was soon accepted in a reserve unit, as a major, although his age denied him active service possibilities. He knew, however, that his training and experience would be useful in developing raw recruits, and he was particularly pleased to be working in an artillery battery.

A Canadian Officers Training Corps (COTC) had been quickly instituted at McMaster, and I became one of the early recruits, although my motive was not a driving surge of patriotism. Many of my friends had volunteered, forcing my hand since I wished to be with them. I found the military lectures boring; parades and marching were particularly repugnant. Army units, maneuvers, saluting, and especially the commands formed an entirely new and strange language. My interest was never stimulated, but even the few months I spent so half-heartedly in the COTC would mean a great deal to my future career, something I did not foresee.

The radio continued to blare, now with a midnight newscast. My father had just returned from the Armories and entered the family room to catch the final part of the newscast. "A pretty big war," he commented. He was noted for his succinct statements.

My reply was equally brief. Instinct told me that Dad had something on his mind. I kept my eyes on my books.

"You're not doing much to help the war effort," he added after a long pause. My retort outlined my involvement with the COTC.

After another pause he asked "Why don't you join one of the services, full time? Volunteer for the branch that suits you best."

"I would like to join the air force," was my rejoinder, "but Mother would be unhappy if I joined up in the middle of my school year and later had to leave home."

His next comment was typical and unforgettable. "Where does your duty lie? To your mother or to your country?"

With those brief comments I was stirred to action. During the ensuing week, I presented myself to the Royal Canadian Air Force recruiting office on James Street. Why the air force? Well, over the years I had spent long hours building small model airplanes of every description, which may have stimulated a desire to fly as a pilot. Some inner force convinced me that if I worked hard enough, my dream of flying would materialize.

After long months of indecision and frustration, I received my official documents and travel warrants early in August, 1940, with instructions to report promptly to No. 2 Manning Depot, Brandon, Manitoba. As the Battle of Britain intensified in the air over England, I was at last on my way, facing a very uncertain future. I was excited and thrilled, but also concerned that somehow I might fail as a pilot or inadvertently do something that would disappoint or dishonor my family.

I boarded a regular CPR trans-Canada train, delighted to find that I would travel in comfort and some style. As the train progressed westward, new recruits joined it at each major stop until perhaps one hundred of us arrived in Brandon, a city of 18,000 set in the rolling prairies west of Winnipeg. Brandon was quite prepared to receive large numbers of raw recruits since it had been selected years before to house Camp Shilo, an army training area which regularly held 10,000 men. We new inductees were probably much less prepared to accept what Brandon and our new careers held in store.

Our quarters and all related facilities at No. 2 Manning Depot were housed in the Cow Palace, a huge barn of a building used for cattle auctions, horse shows, fairs, and new air force recruits. With a high-trussed ceiling above and a concrete floor below, our new home magnified every noise, and the accumulated odors were stale and pervasive. We numbered about twenty-five hundred men; we slept in metal-tiered bunks that had to be kept impeccably neat at all times. Painfully we made the transition from civilian to military life, quickly learning that as Aircraftmen, Second Class (AC2), we were the lowest forms of life, made to be verbally abused by drill instructors who used the most crude and graphic — but effective — language we would ever hear. We became used to lineups and endless waiting — waiting to use the twenty-four toilets, waiting to wash, waiting in a shift line of twelve hundred men for meals three times a day, waiting for pay parade or sick parade. We also waited for the innumerable shots we received as protection against tetanus, the plague, and other strange maladies. I was in A Squadron, Flight Two, with a commanding officer who made regular and frequent bunk inspections. Once we had made our bunks and tidied our belongings, we stood at ease for an hour and then at attention for fifteen minutes while the inspectors made certain that each man was properly dressed and that each bunk and kit passed a very strict scrutiny.

We learned to march. We learned to drill, to salute properly, to become regimented and obedient. From raw, unruly recruits we slowly developed some semblance of military bearing. We endured route marches and long cross-country runs (always after supper) with ambulances bringing up the rear to collect collapsed drop-outs. Everything was done to a meter: rise and shine, PT, breakfast, drill, lunch, drill, dinner, route march, and then bed, so tired that the orchestra of noises created by twenty-five hundred men bunked in one enormous room couldn't stop deep sleep from taking over.

On October 5, thirty-six of us were posted on guard duty to

the small city of Portage la Prairie where No. 7 Air Observer School and an Elementary Flying School were being constructed. Construction had been under way for just seven weeks, leaving the barracks only partially built, without doors, windows, electricity, heat, or washroom facilities. The enormous wood and timber hangars were framed and sheathed, but also far from complete. Some dynamite had been recently discovered at the base of several columns supporting the massive roof trusses of one hangar, and sabotage was suspected. Hence we were called to provide protection day and night for all the buildings against further sabotage.

It was at Portage that we established friendships that were to endure throughout the war or for as long as we remained alive. We were a small autonomous unit, self-administering and self-motivating. We had no senior officer; only a sergeant and two corporals, temporarily promoted from our ranks, who provided some direction and authority. We developed a closeness and unity of spirit and drive which would endure as our careers progressed.

Our tiny group included Don Laubman,[1] a tall, lean Westerner, with unruly hair, a ready grin and laugh, and the piercing eyes of a hunter. An exact opposite in many respects was Bert Houle,[2] older than most of us, with a short, squat, extremely powerful body and a black scowl which supported his air of authority and purpose but belied the brilliance of his university-trained mind. Bert was a take-charge guy and our paths were to cross many times in the future. Peter Wilbey, a young Englishman, was intent in following in the footsteps of his father, a very senior Royal Air Force (RAF) officer. And Ambrose Warnick, from Hamilton, one of eight siblings serving in the armed forces, was to provide humorous situations reminiscent of his exact look-alike, movie actor Mickey Rooney. Ambie had the same size, physique, and facial features of Rooney and the same ebullient manner. This frequently landed him and others in hot water with each situation usually being solved by his singular personality.

We were the first uniformed men to serve in Portage, and our youthfulness, high spirits, and especially our blue air force uniforms, black though they became with prairie dust, made us appear unusual and attractive. For their part the population showed us in words and deeds the true meaning of "western hospitality."

On November 6, 1940, as the first snow fell, we boarded a train for No. 2 Initial Training School (ITS) in Regina. It was there that the serious work of becoming aircrew really started. Our responses to school classes and tests would be carefully monitored to tag us as prospective pilots, navigators, bomb aimers, or air gunners.

I was assigned to K Flight, No. 2 Squadron. It was our Portage group kept intact, all sleeping in one huge room. We took classes on every conceivable subject, whether germane to flying or not, including law and discipline, accounting, hygiene, wireless, link trainer, and mathematics of every description. The weather became bitterly cold, yet we marched for two hours each morning and each afternoon in minus ten degree Fahrenheit weather, often suffering minor frostbite or chilblains. The days were so full and seemingly endless that bedtime provided a very welcome respite.

In addition to obtaining satisfactory marks in all examinations and passing a very strict medical, the final direction of our futures depended to a great extent on how well we performed during a twenty-minute interview with the Commanding Officer (CO). I did reasonably well on all the tests, but my best performance occurred during the interview. It turned out that the CO had been with my father in the World War I and insisted on talking about Dad during my visit. He assured me that I would be recommended for pilot training, which removed for the present my anxiety and doubts.

My good fortune continued when I was posted to No. 15 Elementary Flying Training School (EFTS), Regina, only a couple of miles from the ITS. As a civilian-operated flying school, it had complete control of our training, including messing, dormitory, discipline, ground school, and flying. Of the thirty-six airmen in our Portage group, by graduation time from ITS, three were grounded, four became air gunners because of poor marks, six were made air observers because of medical problems, and

nine of us went to No. 15 while the remainder went to an elementary school near Moose Jaw. Thirty-three of us formed the newest
class, and we were told at the very beginning that only twenty-
two would graduate, a warning probably meant to stimulate our
attention and concentration. This caution proved to be valid: at
the end of the seven-week course, fully one-third of our class failed
to graduate.

I remember how proud I was to be issued my first flying suit,
a helmet, goggles, warm flying gauntlets, and fleece-lined flying
boots. The lectures included information on aero-engines, air
frame mechanics, navigation, wireless telegraphy, airmanship,
the theory of flight, armament, parachute packing and parachute
jumping, how to properly swing a prop, and minor aircraft
repairs.

Our training airplane was the Tiger Moth, a light two-seat
biplane mounted on skis, an uncomplicated metal-framed, fabric-
covered machine which had been in service for many years. The
instructor sat in the front cockpit with the student seated behind
in a separate cockpit. The 105-horsepower Gypsy Major II engine
was as safe and dependable as a piece of machinery could be.
The airspeed indicator was a wind-pressure actuated gauge
mounted on a strut on the port side, quite external to the cockpit.
A nineteen-gallon fuel tank was located above the front cockpit
in the center of the upper wing, and a glance upward at the bubble
fuel gauge quickly confirmed the amount of fuel remaining at
any time. Wire rigging braced the struts holding the wings in place,
and it whistled and creaked when the Moth was put through
various flying stresses. I was later to learn that if a man could
fly a Moth well, he could fly any single-engined aircraft with ease.

My very first airplane ride was on December 12, 1940, and
lasted only thirty minutes. It was a simple familiarization trip,
probably to see if my first reaction to flying was satisfactory.
I felt at once that the thrill and challenge of flying were irresist-
ible, and I knew that I had to become a pilot, that nothing else
would do.

Frank Griblin, my instructor, was straight out of the textbook
on how to be a good teacher. A fine-looking man in his late twen-
ties he was very soft spoken, neither drank nor smoked, and had

the patience of a saint. He coached me carefully and thoroughly. I found that I had a heavy right foot, which did not hamper my actions in the air unduly, but played hell on the land as my heaviness caused the little Moth to lurch to the right. My coordination of foot and mind was astray, and as my hours accumulated, this one serious problem would not go away. The rules were that a would-be pilot had to solo by 12 hours dual or be washed out. At 11½ hours, the chief flying instructor, A.W. Ross, took me up and apparently gave Griblin authority to send me solo if my next dual flight seemed satisfactory. At 12 hours and 20 minutes Griblin parked the aircraft, got out, and patted my shoulder saying, "Okay, off you go!" Any apprehension of failure disappeared at that short note of endorsement.

My first solo lasted only ten minutes, but in that short space of time, I saw the light as head, hands, and feet performed perfectly, never to bother me again. My spirits soared even as I realized that I had come within just a few minutes of not making the grade as a pilot. My debt to Frank Griblin was heavy indeed and I was to mentally thank him many times over for his careful guidance and infinite patience.

Low flying, steep turns, forced landings, instrument flying, cross-country flights, and finally aerobatics rounded out our flying curriculum. My confidence quotient rose sharply as a result of the rapid improvement in my flying skill, and I was confident that I would become a qualified pilot even though the crucial twenty-hour test still awaited. We feared this test because it was the nemesis of many *ab initio* (beginner) pilots. But having triumphantly soloed we all became convinced of our success and advised friends and relatives that we were now pilots, a patent untruth, although it proved our optimism and hope. We planned our futures. Our hopes and dreams were high, sky-high.

I was scheduled for my critical twenty-hour test with Flying Officer Shaw, who had the reputation of a very demanding tester. At 10:30 one morning he yelled into the crew room "Olmsted, get into 4200 and start her up." This was it. I zipped up my flying suit, buckled on my parachute and with gloves, helmet, and goggles in hand, waddled out to the Moth. After walking around the machine, checking all the control surfaces for freedom of movement, I climbed into the rear cockpit and fastened my Sutton harness. A groundcrew member held each wing to prevent the Moth from lurching forward when the engine caught, because otherwise the chap who had to swing the propellor to start the engine might get struck by the spinning blade.

Switches off, throttle closed, everything was ready to start. The mechanic yelled "Contact." I shouted back "Contact." He swung the prop hard; I flicked the switches on as the engine caught. After warming up I ran the engine high enough to test the magnetos, one by one. All was fine as Flying Officer Shaw climbed into the front cockpit. As he did up his straps, I noticed that his heavy flying suit had a fur-lined collar which was turned up, almost totally blocking my forward vision. He looked so grim and serious I felt that mentioning this would not enhance my chances of passing the test. The air temperature was minus twenty degrees Fahrenheit and warm clothing, especially a fur-lined suit, was very practical protection.

In bright sunshine I taxied the aircraft to the take-off position, which was just a compacted section of the field outlined with small scrub evergreens sited in the snow. These provided something by which to judge our altitude during landing, as the large field would have been featureless otherwise. The test continued as I performed the various maneuvers that Flying Officer Shaw requested in a cold, impersonal tone. My fear of his reputation seemed to paralyze my arms and legs, although I was to later realize that his bark was much worse than his bite. Somehow my flying was just good enough to warrant his approval.

At the end of January, 1941, we remnants of the original class graduated. We split up into a number of groups to proceed to Service Flying Training Schools (SFTS) in various locations across the country, some to twin-engine units to eventually become bomber pilots with the balance entering single-engine schools. With fifty-four total hours, dual and solo, recorded in my logbook, I reported to No. 6 SFTS, Dunnville, Ontario, on February 9, 1941.

Ours was the first full class at the recently completed Dunnville station. We started flying with the North American Yale, a low-wing metal monoplane with a fixed undercart, powered by a Wright Whirlwind 440-horsepower engine. After fifty minutes dual, I soloed, revelling in the roar of the powerful engine and the speed and sleekness of the trainer. After a few hours I graduated to the North American Harvards, flying both Marks I and II. This was also an all-metal, low-wing monoplane powered by a Pratt and Whitney 550-horsepower radial engine and equipped with retractable landing gear. We flew day and night during this seven-week course, which also included extensive ground school classes. I was particularly fortunate in having Sergeant "Cap" Foster[3] as my flying instructor throughout the course since his teaching and dare-devil flying fashioned my style of flying.

Although Cap taught me everything the course required, he concentrated on aerobatics and low flying. The aerobatics prepared me to become as comfortable upside down or in other strange attitudes as I was flying straight and level. Cap knew I was absorbing his teaching, and because of this perhaps, I received more-than-average attention. On April 22, our course was finished. My flying time at Dunnville amounted to ninety-four hours with an "above average" rating as a pilot on my assessment certificate. Since we were now qualified as pilots, graduation was dignified with a Wings ceremony, attended by parents and friends. It was an impressive and emotional affair, not unlike a college graduation ceremony. Our faces showed our joy as the coveted wings were pinned on our tunics, and we all received a new rank — we became sergeants. I was now a qualified pilot, albeit inexperienced, but in the eyes of the RCAF, a bona-fide pilot. A note in my logbook dated November, 1941, only seven months after our class of thirty-four graudated shows that nine had been killed and one other would never walk again.

After spending two weeks' leave in Hamilton with my family, it was time to report to my new posting. I had just received my commission to Pilot Officer, No. J5125, which brought a substantial increase in pay as well as the expense of having to buy uniforms and all the trimmings expected of an officer. My uniform had to be the best Barathea cloth and it served me well until becoming lost at sea years later. My COTC training at

McMaster had apparently played some part in my promotion, thereby belying my rather poor opinion of that course.

On May 18 I reported to No. 1 Central Flying School, Trenton, a large permanent air force station on the shores of Lake Ontario's Bay of Quinte. This was extremely upsetting; Trenton meant that I was likely slated to become a flying instructor to help overcome the short supply of pilots as the Commonwealth Air Training Plan continued to open new flying training schools. While my efforts to have my posting changed to an operational assignment overseas were futile, I never came to like flying instructor responsibilities.

Our class numbered about forty, culled from the pilots who had obtained the best marks at the various flying schools across the country. Some had trained on twin-engined aircraft and others on singles, but all of us would be qualified to instruct on all types of aircraft, elementary, single, and twin engined, upon graduation.

Through June and July, I managed to accumulate eighty-one flying hours on Harvards, Tiger Moths, Fleet Finches, the twin-engined Avro Anson, and the Lockheed Electra or 10A. Our instructors were extremely capable pilots. Some had years of bush-flying to their credit and tried to pass on some of their skills to us. We often flew with others in our class, practicing instructional patter and instrument flying under the hood.

By the end of July, we had all passed whatever tests were required and were posted to various stations across Canada. I had flown six different types of aircraft, single and twin-engined, and left Trenton with a Category C certificate, my qualification to instruct in the air force. While this was the lowest possible rating, it indicated that I would improve as actual instructional experience was obtained. Any immediate hopes that I might have entertained of being sent to a challenging position were dashed when a number of us were posted to No. 31 Elementary Flying Training School in Calgary, Alberta.

The British Commonwealth Air Training Plan proved to be an imaginative and successful concept, which graduated over 130,000 pilots, navigators, bomb aimers, and air gunners by the end of the war. By agreement, Britain, Canada, Australia, and

New Zealand were to share proportionately in the cost of the plan, and the first facilities were scheduled to accept trainees by mid-1940. Prior to that Britain and the Commonwealth countries were actively training their own aircrew, and even after the plan commenced, those countries still carried on the elementary training of pilots, with the advanced flying training slated for Canada. For Canada, the logistical requirements of the plan were formidable, and yet the country eventually built and manned more than one hundred airdromes and training schools across the Dominion. The initial instructors were drawn from Canadian sources, and our large numbers of bush pilots provided a significant reservoir of experienced flyers. Large numbers of experienced American pilots also volunteered their services; some remained as civilians to instruct at private elementary schools, while others joined the RCAF to receive immediate officer rank. Initially there were very few British instructors, as every experienced RAF pilot was needed for the defense of Great Britain. Once the danger of invasion passed, however, Britain was able to send limited numbers of instructors to Canada to manage the few totally British stations operating within the plan. It was to this type of station that I was posted as an instructor.

Each instructor was given four to nine student pilots, none of whom had ever flown before. Training started with flight familiarization, gradually progressing through all the training curriculum until graduation day. Twenty- and fifty-hour tests were given by Squadron Leader A. Bailey, the chief flying instructor. Ground school was so coordinated with the flying schedule that our days were totally consumed, leaving little time for recreation.

My logbook shows that I flew 115 times in the month of August totaling eighty-four hours, averaging between four and five flying hours each day. Each student would get one instructional flight per day, health and weather permitting. Days off were few. As a result, we flew an enormous amount, rapidly gaining experience and honing our flying skills.

Not many of the Canadians enjoyed instructing, feeling that our talents were being wasted. We wanted to do something challenging, such as operational flying; at the very least, we wanted an airplane somewhat more challenging and sophisticated than the Tiger Moth. My constant dream was to fly Spitfires, a dream whetted by conversations with the occasional English Spitfire pilot visiting on a promotional tour. I would quiz them closely about fighter operations and what it was like to fly an advanced machine such as the Spitfire. These experienced pilots delighted me with their view that the Spitfire was a very easy aircraft to fly, unlike the Moth, which required constant attention when airborne. The Moth's controls were light and sensitive, the instruments few, with the needle and ball of the turn and bank indicator reacting immediately to even the lightest movement of the controls. The least skidding or slipping would move the ball off the center, a feeling quickly transmitted through our butts. We learned to fly literally by the seat of our pants, able to tell at any time just by the feel of the aircraft if we were flying correctly or not. What I gained in flying knowledge during this instructional period may not have been appreciated at the time, but it later allowed me to fly with never a glance at my cockpit instruments. Many more pilots would have survived had they gone through a similar learning process.

After several months instructing, my impatience was becoming unmanageable. My heart had always been set on flying fighter aircraft, and my present job placed me in a rut from which I might never escape. In desperation I penned a letter to my flight commander:

From: Pilot Officer W.A. Olmsted.
        No. 31 EFTS, DeWinton, Alta.
To: Officer Comanding "D" Flight,
        No. 31 EFTS, DeWinton, Alta.
Date: October 29, 1941.
Subject: Application for Posting

Sir:
I have the honour to request that I may be granted an interview with my Station Commander for the purpose of applying for Posting to Active Service with Fighter Command overseas.

I fully appreciate the fact that it is not for me to decide where my duties in the Air Force are to take me, and whilst serving in Training Command I have honestly tried to give my best to Flying Instruction, but I feel that I am not giving a fair chance to my pupils in that I feel my instructional abilities are of a very low standard.

> I have the honour to be, sir,
> Your obedient servant,
> W.A. Olmsted. P/O

Nothing happened for several months, but in mid-January, 1942, the Central Flying School Test Flight arrived for a periodic check of all the instructors. After flying with me and listening to my story, my instructing category was removed. What my future held was impossible for me to forecast, but I knew that I would not continue instructing. I left with 386 hours of instructional time added in my logbook. As a last act of defiance, when Squadron Leader Bailey, the chief flying instructor, interviewed me for the final time, he pointed out that he rated my ability as a pilot below average. In front of his horrified eyes I tore the instructor's certificate out of my logbook, destroyed it, and dropped the pieces on his desk. My instructional abilities were certainly low although my students usually stood at the top of the course of eighty pupils. My big problem was that I was just not temperamentally suited to be an instructor.

From Calgary I traveled eastward to a Conversion Training Squadron based at Rockcliffe in Ottawa. After stopping for a ten-day holiday with my family, I reported for duty on February 12, not having the faintest idea of what lay in store. I was soon set straight; I was to serve a penalty period[4] because of my unruly behavior, and was destined to fly bomb-aimers and air-gunners while they learned their trades. In short order my misgivings were replaced with enthusiasm because I was now getting an opportunity to fly more advanced aircraft.

The normal conversion course lasted a couple of months, but because of my experience, mine was a short eight-day event where I was the only pilot being converted. I spent twenty hours flying

Harvards, the twin-engined Bolingbroke or Blenheim bomber, and the Fairey Battle, the latter a remarkable aircraft which the engineers had not finished designing. An all-metal low wing monoplane of huge proportions, it was really an oversized, overweight, and underpowered Spitfire. Power was supplied by a Rolls-Royce Merlin engine developing 1150 horsepower, which was much too small for an aircraft that had been designed to handle an engine about three times as powerful. The Battle was rugged, fully aerobatic (for those willing to try), and a gentle, dependable aircraft in all flying attitudes. Perhaps my high regard for this obsolete machine was because of the Rolls-Royce Merlin engine which I hoped would soon power me through the skies of England in a more nimble type of aircraft.

On March 1, I reported to No. 1 Bombing and Gunnery School, Jarvis, on the shores of Lake Erie, where I was to spend five exciting and rewarding months accumulating a further 347 flying hours on eight different types of aircraft, by day and by night. My duties involved flying bomb-aimers over targets located in Lake Erie. I navigated as they instructed, and the accuracy of their twenty-pound smoke bombs was plotted by observer posts on shore. It was a challenge to fly correctly, since poor flying would show up in poor bombing results, and quickly became a topic of critical conversation. I made certain that I tried my very best for the students and I believe I succeeded.

The months passed with marvellous weather and flying conditions and we got all the flying time that one could possibly wish for. As a penalty period, I viewed Jarvis positively for many reasons, but particularly because of my exposure to the Merlin engine, which I came to know and trust, learning to detect by ear, instruments, and instinct any potential problem. During this time we also became inundated with twin-engined Blenheim bombers, which the RCAF called Bolingbrokes. We received three different marks or models, the short-nosed version and the two long-nosed versions, all powered with Bristol Mercury radial engines of 850 or 925 horsepower. We also had a newer model fitted with Pratt and Whitney Twin Row Wasps of 825 horsepower each. I found these aircraft, which were still flying on bombing missions into Europe, a positive delight to fly. Several of our machines had been shipped directly from operational squadrons in England and showed the marks of battle in patched bullet holes.

My greatest responsibility came when I was put in charge of the Bolingbroke aircraft forming a flight of some twenty-eight of these large machines. Being the only pilot on the station who once had held a license to instruct on twin-engined aircraft, even though the category had been removed, it became my job to teach others the ins and outs of twin-engined flying. The main problem for me was that none of the aircraft was fitted with dual controls. At altitude I would change seats with my pupil, talking him through every operation, but I made all the take-offs and landings. When the pilot was satisfied that he could handle the aircraft himself, I got out, leaving him on his own. All my students became proficient twin-engined pilots, with no mistakes and no accidents.

We had a very serious problem with the Bolies which revealed itself on hot, humid days when we were using the southwest runway. Frequently, just before we reached lift-off speed, one of the engines would cut out. Because it happened at such a critical time, it was nearly impossible to forestall a ground loop, which collapsed the undercart and smashed a wing and the engines. Had the Bolie achieved flying speed with some height, it could stay aloft briefly on a single engine, but fully loaded with pupils and bombs, the aircraft could not take off.

Everything was tried to remedy the engine failures. The plugs were changed after every flight. We used carburetor heat, thinking that perhaps some ice was forming in the carburetors as we taxied, and the heat would prevent this. We kept the engine cowls closed or open. We tried all the modifications and procedures suggested by RCAF Technical Service. Nothing worked and we kept conking out at a two-a-week rate. No one was ever seriously injured, but we did start to become nervous and twitchy, never knowing when we would be faced with an emergency.

I experienced two failures, and after the second, a Board of Inquiry was convened on July 17, 1942, under the leadership of Group Captain Lymburner, a skilled pilot and a very knowledgeable technical man. Since I was in charge of all Bolingbroke flying, an unfavorable decision by the board could perhaps show negligence on my part, which might even end my flying career.

As the hearing progressed, no solution to our continuing problem could be discovered. In desperation, while on the witness stand, I challenged the board. "Group Captain, there are twenty-one aircraft on the flight line now, ready to fly. The conditions today and the runway currently in use exactly duplicate the conditions under which we have experienced our engine failures. I think you can take any Mark IV aircraft, except a Mark IVW, and there is a good possibility you may have an engine failure." The IVWs with the Pratt and Whitneys had not given us any trouble; only the aircraft with the Bristol Mercury engines.

The group captain felt my suggestion was fair. He took off in a Bolingbroke, and just as he reached flying speed, his starboard engine cut completely. Being a superb pilot and not having the additional weight of two tons of bombs and students, he was able to bring the aircraft back safely. I had been vindicated. Within a few days we learned the solution to the engine failures. We used 87 octane fuel, which was the only grade on the station. This was inadequate for take-offs when full power was required, but was fine when we were cruising at a much lower throttle setting. As soon as we switched to 100 octane fuel, we never had another engine failure.

In the aftermath I heard that the group captain had recommended me for the Air Force Cross, but that idea was quashed by my commanding officer, Squadron Leader "Doc" Brooks. It was a fine tribute to even be considered for such an award and that thought has brought me as much satisfaction as if I had actually received the medal.

I returned to my regular routine until early in August, my long-awaited dream came true when I received my posting to England and overseas. Now I would have a chance to see if my twenty-three months of pent-up emotions would be relieved as I faced the future I had worked for, and I hoped in the aircraft that it had been my burning desire to fly — a Spitfire.

CHAPTER 2

ENGLAND AND BEYOND
September, 1942 — February, 1943

My short embarkation leave with my family involved stresses which made some of the final hours awkward and sad. I doubt that many men leaving for overseas do not have some misgivings about the future and whether they will ever see their homes and families again. I tried to conceal these feelings as I quietly made arrangements for belongings accumulated over a young lifetime to be sorted and stored. Packing for the unknown future presented special problems, particularly since I wished to take so many goodies which I thought were in short supply in England, such as cigarettes, soap, chocolates, chewing gum, and silk stockings. I made detailed arrangements with Mother on how our letters should be numbered, which would allow her to ask questions in one letter which I could answer in mine, referring to numbers not specifics, in language that a censor might not decipher.*

My father took me to the train since Mother was too heart-broken to leave the house. As he helped me onto the sleeping car, I saw tears in his eyes, only the second time I ever saw him weaken to show that sort of emotion. The first time was when his mother died. Choking a little, he admonished, "Bill, I release you from your promise not to drink. You are going away to do a man's job and men should be able to drink." With that, he turned and left, leaving me speechless — he knew perfectly well that I enjoyed a drink as much as the next person and rarely

---

*This scheme worked very well, in fact, and the material I sent Mother in more than two hundred letters, which she saved, provides some of the details for this book.

18

turned down an opportunity to quaff an ale or a rum and coke. In addition, I had never given such a promise.

The long train trip to Transient Officers' Mess, No. 1 Y Depot, Halifax, was a thoughtful and dreamy journey, and I imagined all sorts of situations as my thoughts flitted from fancy to fancy. I welcomed the transient officer's mess because the activity and final duties it required, coupled with meeting new and old friends, provided the stimulus I needed to bring me back to earth.

Two memories of Halifax remain. The first occurred when I took the decompression chamber test designed to see how we reacted to altitude and how high we could go without undue discomfort from the bends or disorientation. At 35,000 feet I got painful bends in my right knee and had to return rapidly to normal sea level atmospheric pressure. My records were inscribed with a note that I was to be relegated to low-level flying because of my reaction. I felt this was a decision favoring my career choice, for it seemed to assure me a place in a fighter squadron. As the future unfolded I was to fly many sorties over 33,000 feet with never a twinge. So much for pressure chambers!

The second impression related to the time when we would board ship. This was a great secret on the station, with never a whisper about a possible departure date. In town the story was different. We had to leave our laundry to be cleaned, or films to be processed, and were naturally concerned that we might have to leave suddenly before our items were ready for pick-up. We found that the merchants knew exactly when we were leaving and generally could tell us our ship. So much for secrecy!

At last we boarded the S.S. *Akaroa*, a small Shaw, Saville, and Albion Steamship Line combination refrigerator-freighter and passenger vessel. It normally hauled butter, mutton, and passengers between New Zealand and Australia but now found itself pressed into service on the critical North Atlantic run. Our ship was part of the second half of the largest convoy to date to leave Halifax for England, each section numbering more than fifty ships of all descriptions. It was called a "slow" convoy, which meant it travelled at a speed to accommodate the slowest vessels, and I believe we averaged about eight knots. Our skipper was the commodore and our ship the lead ship of the second section.

There were seventeen pilots on board, all of whom, like myself, had done a good deal of flying as instructors. My cabin mate was Flying Officer Arthur Bishop, the son of the World War I hero, Billy Bishop. Together, with the help of a few others, we succeeded in drinking the ship dry during our sixteen days at sea.

Our ship normally operated in the tropics and thus had curtains in place of doors, and these were completely useless in the cold of the North Atlantic. We were all willing to certify that we must be well within the Arctic Circle. It was so cold that we wore our greatcoats at all times, even to bed. I felt the tiny New Zealand vessel needed all the power it could develop to turn the propellors, with nothing left over to heat the lounge and other passenger areas. Making matters worse were the long hours we spent day and night on the outermost edge of the bridge searching the waves for signs of submarines and torpedoes. We seemed suitably impressed with the importance of our watches, yet I wondered about our effectiveness. Perhaps terror made us search harder than we otherwise might have.

With the arrival of dawn each day, we could see the ammunition ships far behind, slowed during the night by the anti-torpedo nets they extended into the sea as added protection against an unseen attacker. They spent the rest of the day trying to catch us while being careful not to make smoke, which would betray our position to submarines. None of us envied those poor lads on the ammunition ships, although they earned our very special respect. The occasional destroyer or corvette swept by now and again, flashing signals at our skipper, as radio silence was strictly maintained. The naval craft travelled swiftly, silently, guarding our flanks and frequently weaving in and out of our convoy lines. They were a reassuring sight, particularly when we would sail through the debris of a freighter from the part of the convoy ahead which had been doomed by torpedoes. Our portion of the convoy lost a ship or two on the way over, although no details were ever provided and our queries were turned aside.

The voyage passed slowly, and we whiled away the time playing bridge, with interruptions for spotter duties or meals. Actually we were treated to unaccustomed luxury, with steward and stewardess service and superb meals, including six-course breakfasts and lunches and eight- or more course dinners. Except for the penetrating and pervasive cold, running out of booze before the end of the journey, and the constant fear of being torpedoed and sunk, the trip was a time of rest.

The northern coast of Ireland appeared at last, impressive for all the amazing shades of green sparkling in tiny fields, beautiful and welcoming. We sailed through the Irish Sea to anchor very close to the masts of a sunken vessel which projected some dozen feet above the gray water. We gawked at the sights and watched as our convoy came to an orderly halt. I asked a nearby crewman what had happened to the sunken ship and he related a timely story. "Apparently," he said, "a tough, independent Norwegian skipper in that old tub of a freighter got tired of waiting in New York for a convoy out of New York harbor. One night he sneaked out all alone, and successfully sailed the Atlantic without a problem. Around Ireland and through the minefields he sailed, still alone, until he came to this position. Then he ordered the anchor dropped, and as it descended, it struck a mine, blowing up his ship, which then promptly sank beneath his feet." I could just visualize the tough mariner gloating as he stood on the bridge, jubilantly preening and beaming as he exulted over his success in making such a hazardous voyage without incident and then his face changing from glee to horror as he felt the explosion, realizing in a moment that his triumph was shattered.

The authorities decided that we would not disembark at Belfast from where we would be ferried to England. Instead we were to sail to Bristol on the west coast of Blighty. In single file we sailed slowly south in the Irish Sea behind several minesweepers carefully preparing a safe passage. Escorts of Spitfires and Hurricanes thrilled us as they patrolled ahead and on our flanks, indicating that there was always the possibility of an attack from the air, although we understood that this last portion of our trip was the most hazardous because of mines sown by both the enemy and our forces.

After disembarking at Bristol, we continued our slow southward journey by rail. Our path took us through Bath, where the bombed and demolished buildings brought us abruptly face to face with the ravages of war, something we had only read about. The reality was a sobering sight.

We eventually arrived at No. 3 Pilot Reception Centre,

Bournemouth, on the south coast of England to await further instructions. We were given comfortable quarters in one of the many hotels taken over by the RCAF for the duration of the war. New people and strange customs fascinated us, as did tea dances, English girls, and flat beer. Daily my admiration and liking for the English grew stronger, and I literally fell in love with the country, its different customs, and their quiet way of playing down shortages and difficulties.

A few days later some of us reported to RCAF Headquarters at 21 Lincoln's Inn Fields in London to meet Squadron Leader Hammond, our posting officer. Eleven of us sat in front of his large desk, not knowing what to expect.

"You pilots are going to get a break," he explained. "You've been taking the shit for a year or two and now I'm going to send you to whatever type of flying you want on the aircraft of your choice."

He turned to the first pilot on the right, Pilot Officer Chalmers "Smiley" Goodlin,[5] an American in a Canadian uniform. "What do you want?" he asked. Goodlin replied, "I'd like to fly Spitfires as a fighter pilot." Squadron Leader Hammond nodded, picked up a phone, and made a date for Goodlin to report to a Spitfire Operational Training Unit at Rednal in a few days. Smiley grinned from ear to ear, justifying his nickname.

I sat next to Goodlin and when Hammond asked me what I wanted, I replied, "Spitfire fighters." Another phone call and I was to report with Smiley to No. 61 OTU, Rednal, on October 6. After two long years my dream was at last coming true, and it took some time before I fully appreciated my good fortune.

The rest of the pilots also got their preferences, some going to nightfighting in Beaufighters, other to bombers. A couple even asked for more instructional experience! Smiley and I were the only ones signifying a preference for fighter operations.

A long, cold night train journey carried Smiley and me into the western Midlands, to our new station, Rednal, near the city of Shrewsbury. The first person to welcome me was a stocky, curly-headed, fresh-faced flight lieutenant, Geoffrey Richards, who was to be my new flight commander. He examined my logbook, noted my one thousand flying hours, and sighed as he returned the book, "Here, you take over the flight." He explained that he had been flying longer than me but only had 350 hours, which included a tour of operational flying. After completing the course I was to meet him again two years later by the side of a road in Holland. He had transferred from the RAF to the army and had just been rescued from the debacle of Arnhem, one of the lucky ones. He was thin, with long lines in his face and eyes glazed with fatigue, too tired to do more than mutter "Hello."

My greatest thrill came a day after arriving at Rednal. I had two short familiarization flights in a Miles Master before I was introduced to a Spitfire Mark I. Richards showed me the controls, explained all the instruments and dials, and told me how to operate the wheels and flaps and generally what to expect on my first flight. There was no dual instruction; the Spit was too small. You looked at it, studied it, got in and flew it.

My eyes took in every feature of this beautiful machine. Even on the ground, with legs extended, it looked as though it was eager to leap into the air. My attachment to the aircraft was instantaneous and total. I had never experienced this feeling toward any of the many different types of aircraft I had flown before, and I never felt it for any plane I ever flew afterward. Somehow I knew that this machine was the ultimate. Even the faded camouflaged coloring looked appropriate, making the body seem slimmer and the wings smaller, almost as though the aircraft was already in flight. Richards must have sensed what I felt. I was speechless, awed, but not the least afraid. My dream had come true, and I savored the moment completely.

With my parachute strapped to my back, I stepped onto the left-wing root, moved up one short pace, and entered the cockpit through the open hatch door. With some shifting I positioned myself in the metal bucket seat moulded to accept the parachute pack, which then acted as a comfortable cushion. The Sutton harness straps were positioned over my shoulders and hips to hold me securely in position. My body seemed to fill the cockpit space completely, putting the controls within easy reach. I looked at the throttle and pitch control quadrant mounted ahead of the hatch with the trim tabs and radiator regulators immediately below. The doughnut-shaped control column moved easily in every direction. I noted the gun button was in the OFF position. Directly in front of my eyes were the major flying control instruments, the air speed indicator, the artificial horizon, the rate of climb indicator, the altimeter, the directional gyro, and the turn and bank dial, all neatly centered, allowing the pilot to look forward at all times. Every instrument detailing the condition of the engine or the fuselage was easy to read and reach. About fifty different knobs, switches, dials, buttons, tabs, and controls were to be my constant guides in the future, and I was determined to understand them completely. It would not take me long to learn to use and interpret each function correctly.

I primed the engine and gave the thumbs up sign to the "erk" (mechanic) to give the engine power from his electrical cart. The Merlin caught immediately with a cough and a stutter, which quickly smoothed into a quiet, throbbing burble as I throttled back. The machine vibrated slightly, seeming to come alive suddenly in response to the engine's song of power, a very distinctive and easily identifiable sound. I hooked up the oxygen tube and plugged in the radio cord after closing the hatch door. At my signal the wheel chocks were removed, freeing the aircraft to move forward. Slowly moving ahead, I found there was no forward vision on the ground, the view being blanked out by the long nose and the broad engine cowling. By bursts of throttle and shoves on the rudder pedals and brakes, however, the nose could be swung from side to side, which allowed me to see enough to keep the aircraft on the taxi strip without "pranging" (hitting) some obstruction.

At the downwind end of the field, I ran the engine up to test the magnetos. No serious drop. I was ready to go. Dropping the seat to the lowest position, I asked for and received permission from flying control to take off. I made a last quick check of the brakes, trim, flaps, contacts, pressures, undercart, and radiator, ensuring that everything was in order to become airborne.

I opened the throttle smoothly. The engine responded with a deep-throated roar typical of the Rolls-Royce Merlin and the Spit accelerated rapidly. Christ, how it accelerated! I could not believe how quickly the machine gathered speed with the pressure forcing my whole body tight against the contoured seat. As more power was added there was a strong tendency for the aircraft to swing to the right, and I counteracted this by increasing pressure on the left rudder pedal. Faster and faster, the tail up now as the control surfaces gained effect with the increasing speed. After what seemed a short take-off run, the Spit freed itself from the ground at 100 mph. My speed built up rapidly as I moved the wheels-up lever and pumped with my right hand to bring the wheels up into their storage spaces in the wings. I could feel the nose rise and fall as I applied muscle to the pump handle, for this old model was not equipped with hydraulic gears. Within a minute the aircraft was clean, responding instantly to even the lightest touch on the controls.

The Spit climbed rapidly, trimmed easily, and could be flown "hands off" for short periods. Even though my shoulders touched each side of the narrow fuselage I could turn my head readily without striking the Plexiglas coupe top (canopy). What a workshop! It seemed from this very first flight that the Spitfire and I had reached an understanding.

I tried various maneuvers and aerobatics, marvelling at how easily and quickly the Spit responded to every command. This was an old, tired Mark I, yet its performance far exceeded anything I had known before. My spirits soared in tune with the machine and I hated to return to base and end this marvellous dream. Nevertheless, I brought the Spitfire in for a landing. Downwind at 150 mph, cross wind at 120 mph as I lowered the undercart, into the wind at 100 mph and then, drop flaps, cut throttle, and gently ease back on the control column as the ground rushes up. Nose high, view obscured, and it settles gently on the ground, tail wheel and undercart touching at the same time. A good landing!

The students at Rednal represented many countries, including Poland, Czechoslovakia, France, Belgium, China, Norway, America and many of the Commonwealth countries, although I was the only Canadian. During the next seven weeks, we practiced air-firing, formation flying, and some radio work while we learned to trust the controllers and their skill in bringing us home in bad weather, of which there was plenty, with low clouds and rain daily. Ground school lectures took much of our time as we tried to absorb all the information passed on by experienced instructors, most of whom were fighter pilots serving a rest period between tours. These experts had no difficulty in earning our total attention. This was the nitty-gritty of combat flying, and even a small, seemingly insignificant detail might save our lives at a later date.

We learned everything that was currently known about enemy aircraft. Aircraft identification, using scale models and silhouettes, was stressed as being most important, and we studied the models for hours on end. The importance of quick and accurate recognition at all distances and in all attitudes was critical. We learned how to abandon aircraft safely, how to map-read, and how to behave in occupied territory should we be shot down. We were taught the basics of airframes, aero engines, and how to care for and re-arm our guns. Escapers gave lectures on the do's and don'ts of evading or escaping, with the caution that much of what we were told must remain secret.

Kingo was an escape game we played in a very realistic way. At daybreak on a Kingo day enclosed trucks delivered us in pairs to drop off points fifty to seventy-five miles from base where we were to start our journey back without having the foggiest idea where we were dropped. The whole countryside, as well as the police and the Home Guard, was alerted, being warned that escaped enemy airmen were on the loose. We had to get back to the glass porch doors of the officers mess by teatime to win the game. We were not allowed to speak to any civilians unless we could do it in German, and each of us carried only one shilling in case we had eventually to phone the base for help. Other than that, we could make our own rules, exactly as if we were in an occupied country, with the only disappointing restriction that we had to observe being that we could not steal an aircraft from one of the many nearby airdromes. Our mess grounds were heavily patrolled by armed guards, and the last seventy-five yards to the mess were open grass, which made it virtually impossible to gain the mess within the time allotted. I got as far as the trees in front of the mess when a rifle was stuck in my back, signifying capture. None of us ever made it into the mess that I can recall, but we all were thrilled each time we played this stimulating game.

I thought then, and still do, that man's greatest challenge must be to escape or evade in enemy territory when the whole countryside may be hunting for you. Man hunting man! It must be a tremendous thrill and the ultimate accomplishment to escape. I applaud the many who had the courage, skill, ingenuity, and daring to do it successfully.

By December 1, we were moved in small groups to Montford Bridge, a satellite station, where we were to work and live as though we were a fighter squadron, doing patrols and practice "rhubarbs" (low-level flights searching for ground targets) and small sweeps. Our aircraft were Mark II Spitfires fitted with cannon and with wheels that retracted and lowered at the touch of a lever, eliminating the violent pump action required in the Mark I. Weather restricted our flying very considerably as the English winter set in: by the time our course finished on Christmas Eve, I had garnered exactly seventy-five hours on Spitfires.

One day at Montford Bridge, Geoffrey Richards and I were standing at the end of our runway debating the weather: was it suitable for flying? As we peered into the distance, we saw a strange-looking object flying toward us. We could not hazard a guess as to what it was, even as it got closer. Realizing that it was going to land, we ran to get out of the way as the object made a perfect wheels-up landing. We ran over in time to help six shaken American airmen evacuate safely. Each wing of their airplane was bent exactly in half, with the tips meeting high over the cabin. It seemed unbelievable that the machine could fly, let alone stay aloft long enough to land safely. What a story these men had to tell!

They had left California some days earlier, with their personal baggage, in this brand new DC-3, or Dakota, to use the military name, to fly across North America and the Atlantic Ocean to deliver the aircraft to an American transport unit based near London. They made it safely, in stages, to Prestwick, Scotland. There they refuelled and located their final destination. Being keen to end their long journey, they took off for the final leg down Britain's west coast after being well briefed on the poor weather conditions, the low clouds, and the dangers of the Welsh mountains.

Thinking that they had cleared the mountains, the pilot reduced his height, expecting to break out of cloud over the relatively flat English countryside. But he had misjudged slightly and let down a few minutes early. He struck a mountain peak with his left wing and engine nacelle, folding the wing tip up and inward, leaving him the use of only half that wing. A few moments later he struck another mountain top, with his right wing, in exactly the same manner as the first strike. It bent upward and inward, meeting the left wing over the center of the cabin. With his damaged engines and props racing flat out, they discarded all their baggage and anything else movable to lighten the aircraft. He broke cloud, flying straight ahead — he could not turn. Seeing our 'drome right in front, he made for it, gradually losing height since his engines could not maintain altitude in such a damaged condition. His landing was flawless.

The shaken Americans effusively thanked us for our help. We hadn't done a thing, of course, except to arrange transportation to their destination. If the pilot had waited another two minutes before starting his descent, he would have been free and clear of the round-topped Welsh hills. Very few pilots survive after hitting one mountain, but to hit two in the same flight and still land safely seemed unbelievable. This was a perfect example of great good luck, and the durability of the Dakota aircraft.

As our course was ending, we were all given an opportunity to select where we would prefer to operate — England or overseas. I had visited some friends with a Canadian fighter squadron, where I learned that they flew infrequently because so much depended on both the uncertain weather conditions and the volume of enemy activity. I thought I detected dissatisfaction, although the pilots were too proud to admit to it. Malta was hot news, and the recent landings in North Africa reported strong enemy resistance, forecasting a hard-fought campaign with plenty of flying and frequent opportunities to meet the enemy in the air. As a Canadian I had to volunteer for service outside of England and also apply for transfer to the RAF. It took only moments to decide, and I told the posting officials, "Send me to Africa."

At the same time we received our grading results for Course 21. I got an above-average rating in my flying, immediately behind the course leader, Jean Parisse, the famous Belgian aerobatic pilot, who was one of the most brilliant pilots I would ever see.

Our only casualty was little Bill Lee, the Chinese pilot, who, we discovered too late, blacked out easily when experiencing high g-forces during dog fights. One day near the completion of our course he blacked out in a mock combat and dove into the ground at over 500 mph.

I left Rednal for 402 RCAF Squadron at Kenley on the southern outskirts of London to receive a couple of familiarization flights on the very new Spitfire IX which I would be flying in Africa. The IX was far more powerful than our training Spits, capable of operating at the much higher altitudes where the enemy Me 109s roamed. Only a few of the IXs were operating in Africa at this time, but more were on the way.

Having received a cockpit check I taxied to the end of the runway preparatory to taking off. Then, just before receiving take-off permission from the tower, Squadron Leader Bud Malloy drove up in his jeep and ordered me not to fly. Bud was an experienced and capable squadron commander, and had earned an excellent reputation as a fighter pilot. His argument was that the station commander, Group Captain "Iron Bill" (Tin Willy) McBrien, felt that the field was too small for my first flight in a IX and I would likely have an accident! It was explained that when a frontline squadron lost enough aircraft through accidents, it was withdrawn and posted north onto Spit V's while another squadron replaced it, taking over the remaining IXs. No squadron wanted to be taken out of action, yet I felt it was a bloody poor excuse. I appreciated Bud trying to make it as easy as possible for me to accept although it rankled for a long time.

As I packed a few articles, some friends told me that in sixty sweeps they had only seen the enemy a couple of times and the only occasion they fired their guns in anger was during the ill-fated one-day raid on Dieppe. Some had tried for postings to Malta or Africa with no luck. I then knew they were envious of my opportunity to fly frequently and have many chances to meet the Hun in Africa.

I left by train for North Weald on the other side of London to fly with 332 Norwegian Squadron. They faced exactly the same restrictions and conditions as did the Canadians — aircraft damaged in nonoperational flying would not be replaced. They made no mention of this. The Norwegians could not have been kinder or more considerate to me, which was, I think, a spillover from their training days at Little Norway, their flying training center at the Toronto Island Airport. There they came to know Canada and Canadian girls — particularly the girls.

I made three flights doing everything to the aircraft that I could think of. The power of the 1650-horsepower engine was about fifty percent more than that in the Mark I, enabling the aircraft to perform magically. When the high-altitude blower kicked in at about 19,000 feet, it seemed as if another engine had been added. I climbed to 42,000 feet and could have gone higher except painful stomach gas pains forced my return to base. So ended my familiarization with the top Allied fighter of the time.

The Norwegians were a delight to be with — gay, handsome, always neatly dressed, and although they spoke their native tongue when together, when I was within earshot they switched to English, even though I might not be part of their group. I truly admired their politeness and consideration.

A slow train deposited me at No. 1 Personnel Dispersal Centre, West Kirby, New Glasgow, Scotland, where a small group of pilots gathered awaiting a ship to take us to Africa. I had spent some time in London arranging to ship my surplus baggage back to Canada since my carry-on luggage, including all personal effects and all flying gear, could weigh no more than sixty pounds. Going to a tropical climate and living in the field required new equipment. From stores I drew a camp kit, including canvas bed and bath, blankets, towels, eating utensils, tropical outfit, khaki battle dress, heavy boots, kit bag, and so on. My sixty-pound limit was easily exceeded.

We boarded the H.M.T. *Letitia* at Gouroch, outside of Glasgow. Our ship was a 16,000-ton vessel built before 1914 and sure showing its age. We had twelve hundred troops on board, including two hundred officers. Conditions were crowded, and I found that the non-commissioned men endured almost indescribable conditions, in particular, appalling crowding and terrible food. At twelve midnight we weighed anchor. At 12:02 we ran into another ship in the dark, tearing all our lifeboats off one side and seriously damaging their davits. This forced a delay of ten days while the ship was patched, enabling those interested, and who still had some money, to spend a few extra days in London.

Flying Officer Paddy Noble, an exhuberant Irish OTU graduate, and I pooled our dwindling financial resources and got a room at the Strand Palace Hotel in London's West End. Paddy knew London well and on foot was able to introduce me to many of the well-known sights which every visitor should see. He also showed me innumerable small pubs and bars which I'm sure most visitors would never find. Sleep came easily each night after all the walking and the consuming of huge quantities of English beer.

During our short London stay we experienced a number of small night-time air raids as the Germans renewed their bombing attacks in what were called "scalded cat" raids. The raiders nipped in, and dropped a few bombs before turning for home with throttles wide open. One night I was awakened from a sound beer-induced sleep to the strident sound of air-raid sirens with their insistent and sinister warning which seemed to say "Air raid, hurry, air raid, hurry, air raid, hurry," as the notes rose and fell. When the sirens faded away a terrific barrage of ack-ack guns took over, sounding so loud and so close I almost mistook them for bomb bursts. I drew back the blackout drapes and stuck my head out the open window to watch. I shivered and marvelled. It was a beautiful moonlit night with a thin haze layered between one hundred and one thousand feet. The night was made more brilliant by myriads of searchlights picking out the Jerry Junkers 88 bombers for the ack-ack gunners, whose bullets gave the sky a pinkish tinge. Some bombers became caught in the searchlights at what I judged to be about 10,000 feet, but others scooted about at less than 2,000 feet, too close and swift for the seachlights to catch. It was mesmerizing to watch hundreds of streams of bullets and tracers racing skyward before finally burning out. The noise was deafening, and I was later told that it was the most intense barrage that London ever put up. The noise from the huge batteries in Hyde Park a mile away sounded as though they were almost in our hotel room. The crump of exploding bombs added a sinister, deep note, and we could tell which ones fell close by and which ones fell farther away. Whenever there was a short lull in the gunfire, we could hear shrapnel bouncing off buildings, breaking windows, and ricochetting off roofs. The raid lasted for nearly an hour and apparently was the largest and most damaging raid since the original London Blitz.

On January 21, we reboarded the *Letitia*, dismayed to find another five hundred troops had been added to the passenger list including three Americans, an officer, a sergeant, and a private. As Americans were not allowed any alcoholic beverages while in transit, the simple ruse of having an American of each rank on board meant the ship was to be dry during the whole voyage. We were to sail 530 miles due west of Ireland, then south parallel to the coast of Europe, and when the Gibraltar latitude was reached, due east 530 miles into that safe harbor, hopefully. The escort for our convoy of fourteen troopships and freighters included a number of destroyers and the aircraft carrier *Argus*. Despite rumors of enemy submarines being on to us, we saw no action. As we reached the warmer, sunnier climes, we all took the opportunity to suntan. After days at sea, the lights of Spain and Morocco welcomed us as we entered the Straits of Gibraltar. We had arrived safely.

Because of congestion in the harbor, we waited until daybreak before attempting to berth. The early morning sunrise was spectacular while the lights of "Gib" shone brightly, mingling with the riding lights of the anchored ships. Destroyers, cruisers, corvettes, submarines, and cutters cluttered the harbor, providing a magnificent display of seapower and greatly complicating our docking procedure.

After all the troops had disembarked the RAF, as usual, was the last to leave. With two friends I determined to see the famous Barbary apes at once, for this, according to legend, meant that our stay would last only a few days. A Canadian Bren gun carrier was discovered with the driver putting in time watching us unload. The young man was delighted to help out and drove us to the appropriate location where we could view the strange animals. Quite satisfied we made our way to our new quarters at the Loretto Convent.

The convent had been badly damaged by French warships in retaliation for the British destruction of their warships at Oran.

Only part of the roof remained, and there were no doors, windors, or running water. I seemed to gravitate toward incomplete barracks. George Keith, a fine Canadian pilot who was later lost in Sicily after destroying six German aircraft, and Geoffrey Page[6] and I proceeded to console our spirits with beer and whiskey. Page was returning to operations after being shot down during the Battle of Britain and suffering terrible burns. For some strange reason only his knees were unscarred, and he delighted in wearing khaki shorts to prove the point. His scarred face and curled claws of fingers were most unsightly. It turned out that the hot African sun was too much for his burned and grafted skin, and he returned to England where he ended up as a Spitfire wing commander with a string of medals.

Our meals were something to remember forever. Breakfast was a piece of toast fried in fat topped with strips of limp bacon. Lunch consisted of the toast with a cheese cover and bacon. Dinner was exactly the same with the addition of a slice of fried tomato on top, probably for color. Naturally hunger was our constant companion, forcing remedial action. Because we had no duties other than wait for movement orders, our time was spent on Gibraltar's short main street, patronizing the several bars there. Whiskey cost threepence a shot, about six cents; beer was a shilling and threepence, or about thirty-six cents a glass. Intrinsic value meant little in Gibraltar, and since food and supplies all came by boat, value seemed to be based on size and volume, which permitted whiskey to underprice the normally cheaper beer. Small, dark Spaniards with large paniers filled with fresh shrimp roamed through the bars selling the delicious crustaceans for a penny apiece. We ate the small delicacies as often as we could, breaking off the heads and stripping the legs in one practiced movement before squeezing the juicy meat into our mouths. These delicious morsels banished our hunger, although by curfew time at 9:30 we were usually so full of booze that hunger was forgotten.

After three days of sightseeing and exploring this two-square-mile fortress with its 1,400-foot-high granite rock, nine of us were told to report to the airdrome at dawn. We all had frightful hangovers, not improved by our view of the 'drome. The

1,400-yard runway extended at either end into water; it was very narrow and was the only clear area on the field. The rest of the airdrome's surface was totally covered with aircraft of all descriptions, including three hundred Spitfires awaiting delivery to combat units. Only thirty of the Spits were Mark IXs. It occurred to me that a couple of well-placed bombs could write off hundreds of aircraft in one daring raid.

The briefing officer ordered me to lead eight other Spitfires, all fitted with ninety-gallon long-range slipper tanks, to Algiers. I was still feeling horrible with my hangover, but my request to be relieved of the responsibility to lead was completely ignored. As I loaded my skimpy baggage into nooks and crannies in my Spit, I had a feeling my aircraft looked different than the others. Sure enough, I had only a thirty-gallon long-range tank, which would not give me the range to reach Algiers. Two other aircraft were also fitted with the smaller tanks. The result was that I would have to lead these two pilots to Oran for refuelling from whence we would proceed to Algiers.

Off we went and my bloody radio didn't work! What to do? I foolishly decided to press on. We had been ordered to fly at 10,000 feet, which would have meant climbing through a solid blanket of thick cloud cover. The hell with it. I decided we would fly at five hundred feet or less, with the dense cloud just above us and the blue Mediterranean below. After carefully adjusting my compass and directional gyro for 165 degrees, I determined to fly the most accurate compass course possible. When I strayed off course, I compensated correctly for the proper time interlude to ensure that my course remained true. Without a hangover the problem would have been much simpler. My foggy brain realized that my course had to be bang on. After 250 miles, I hit my landmark, the seventy-five foot wide Salado River, dead on. What luck! Turning east we reached Oran to be met by boisterious Americans who plied us with Chesterfield cigarettes, gum, soap, and toothpaste, and also repaired my radio.

We finally freed ourselves from the friendly Yanks, and flew east to Algiers and my first landing on an all-metal runway strip. Approaching Algiers from the sea on a bright day provided another remarkable panorama. The blue Mediterranean lapping at the edge of the cyrstal-white city formed a brilliant contrast, with a background of brown and green fields and snow-capped mountains topped by a brilliant blue sky. The main airfield, Maison Blanche, was aptly named.

There were hundreds of Arabs working almost shoulder to shoulder on both sides of the runway, quite oblivious to the aircraft taking off and landing only a few feet in front of them. As I touched down a photo reconnaisance unit Spit took off behind me. Before reaching flying speed he blew a tire, and uncontrolled, he swerved off the runway. His propellor chewed into the bodies of the Arab workers, flinging the pieces in all directions, and before stopping, twelve Arabs had been killed. Within minutes the survivors were back at work as though nothing had happened. I wondered if the Arabs really regarded life as being so cheap. I also wondered at the flying control officer who took the poor pilot out to view the slaughter screaming, "See what you did!" As though the man had any alternative. I heard later that the pilot's flying career was ruined by that unfortunate accident.

After reporting in we found that the aircraft had to be delivered to Sétif, another two hundred miles to the east. Fuelling delays meant that we had to complete the journey the following day when the clouds were thick and ominous. They hid the upper part of the 7,000-foot-high mountains and Sétif itself, which was located on a large plateau at the 3,400-foot elevation. The Sétif controller brought us over the top of the 'drome and we waited for a hole to appear in the cloud cover. As soon as one appeared, we dove straight down coming out with 800 feet to spare. It was a little dicey and quite an introduction for us to such mountainous conditions.

We returned to Algiers, where we were placed in a pilot reinforcement pool at Hussein Dey to await a posting to a squadron. After 4:00 PM each day we could leave the pool to explore Algiers, to experience the sights, sounds, and food. It was surprising to see how dusty and dirty the city actually was when it appeared so sparkling white and clean from the air. We explored a small section of the Casbah, girl watched at the Aletti Hotel, and kept out of the way of the sheep and cattle which were herded down the main streets, playing absolute havoc with streetcars and road transport.

About 250 of us were in the pool awaiting posting orders. The ferry statistics made terrible news. Only about fifty percent of the Spitfires reached the supply depot and eight percent of the pilots were killed. Accidents, running out of fuel, becoming hopelessly lost, and mechanical failures accounted for these tragic figures. Considering that the aircraft were brand new and untested when they were assembled at Gib, that most of the pilots had relatively little flying experience, and that the country was so wild and strange, perhaps the losses were to be expected.

After a few days at the reinforcement pool, I received instructions to report immediately to 81 Squadron based at Bône, a small town with an excellent harbor snuggled in the Mediterranean shore. It was 260 miles due east of Algiers and reported to be the most forward Allied position. My posting disappointed some who had been waiting far longer, especially because I was about the only pilot with no operational flying experience. But my spirits were high indeed, because the future beckoned, and I knew that I was ready to accept the challenge.

CHAPTER 3

MY FIRST OPERATIONAL SQUADRON

February 1943

At 10 o'clock on February 15, three of us boarded a Dakota for the 2½ hour flight to 81 Squadron based at Tingley airfield near Bône. We stopped at Sétif to drop off some passengers, and were reassured to see that our escort of two long-range Hurricanes was to continue with us. Since I was able to convince our pilot that I had been a qualified instructor on twin-engined aircraft, he asked me to join him in the cockpit. We flew at an extremely low level over the beautiful, rugged Atlas Mountains while the pilot nattered away describing landmarks and points of interest. He also warned, "When we land, get the hell out fast. I'm not stopping the engines and I plan to take off immediately." I later found out why he was so twitchy about the airfield — we were to be attacked daily by surprise raids of enemy aircraft and a slow transport would provide an especially attractive target.

"We're here," he announced as he made a straight-in approach to a short narrow runway. Our wheels made contact with the metal runway tracking and the ensuing clatter indicated we were safely down. At the runway end, he turned the Dakota around yelling, "Goodbye, good luck." I shook his hand with a muttered "Thanks," picked up my flight bag, and with sergeants Tasto and Hulse, jumped to the ground. The cargo door banged shut, and down the runway raced the Dakota, raising a cloud of dust as the pilot took off in the opposite direction to our landing.

Within a few minutes two officers appeared, introducing themselves as members of our new squadron. We accompanied them to a semi-underground dispersal to meet our commanding officer and our new comrades. The CO, Squadron Leader Colin Gray, quizzed us on the extent of our flying experience and, appearing satisfied, introduced us to the squadron pilots on readiness.

My flight commander was to be Flight Lieutenant Jimmy Walker, a Canadian wearing the Distinguished Flying Cross (DFC) and Bar and soon to be awarded a second Bar to his gong. Jimmy said I was to spend a couple of days just standing around, listening to flight briefings, studying intelligence summaries, memorizing maps, asking innumerable questions and generally absorbing as much as possible about how an operational fighter squadron functions. While I was impatient to fly, I appreciated this practical introduction into a new experience, and I really cannot think of a better way to understand the larger picture of squadron life and duties as opposed to just flying a Spitfire.

Our 332 Wing contained four Spitfire Squadrons — 81, 154, 232, and 242 — and was one of three RAF wings based in the forward or frontline area. Because of the rugged terrain and the fluid nature of the ground fighting, our position varied from ten to twenty miles from the German lines. Our senior officer, Group Captain P.H. "Dutch" Hugo,[7] a twenty-five-year-old South African with a Distinguished Service Order (DSO), and a DFC and Bar, was one of the youngest group captains in the RAF. He had gained his experience as a fighter pilot in France before the Dunkirk evacuation and in the Battle of Britain. Later he led an England-based fighter wing. Hugo was a tall, handsome man, an impeccable dresser with a quiet manner and a mischievous glint in his blue eyes.

Our wing was fairly typical of the RAF command structure in the Middle East, although a wing could contain as few as two or as many as five squadrons. Normally, the group captain attended to the wing administrative duties, leaving control of the flying program to his subordinate, a wing commander. Hugo, however, loved to fly and fight with the result that he frequently led a squadron or the wing on important sorties. On other occasions the wing commander would lead one of our squadrons or take the whole wing. Each squadron was commanded by a squadron leader, responsible for about twenty-six pilots and eighteen aircraft. A squadron was divided into A and B flights with each flight commanded by a flight lieutenant who was responsible for the thirteen men and nine aircraft allotted to his flight. The pilots in a flight ranged from operationally green pilots, such as myself, to others who had extensive combat experience and were quite capable of leading a flight when the occasion arose.

Our squadron normally flew twelve aircraft on a sortie in three sections, or flights of four aircraft. The CO would lead the center or red section with a number 2 flying one hundred yards behind and to one side. The other two aircraft in the section would fly farther behind and to one side. Yellow section would fly a similar formation but five hundred yards to one side, either higher or lower than red section depending on the location of the sun. The third, or blue, section flew a comparable pattern on the other side of the CO. This was known as the "finger-four" formation, and had been developed as the war progressed as the best of the many types of flying formation tested.

The position of the sun was all important in dictating the relative positions of the squadron sections, since the Germans were extremely adept in using it to their advantage. The phrase "Beware of the Hun in the sun" was no idle expression, for more often than not he would use the extremely blinding brilliance of the sun behind him to mask his attacks. With the sections staggered in height, with the lowest flight being on the sun side and the highest flight on the up-sun side, we always had a cross-cover view that largely eliminated the possibility of surprise. Our very loose and wide-flung formation meant that twelve pairs of eyes were constantly searching the sky for the enemy while, at the same time, each man was able to see all of our aircraft clearly. A loose formation also meant we did not have to concentrate on keeping a close station to the aircraft ahead, but instead were free to continue the endless search of the sky for possible danger.

Our wing commander was an Englishman, Wing Commander Ronald "Razz" Berry,[8] DFC and Bar, who was soon to be awarded the DSO. He had been the previous CO of 81 Squadron, and had gained his combat experience as a very successful pilot during the Battle of Britain. Razz was a perfect foil for Hugo

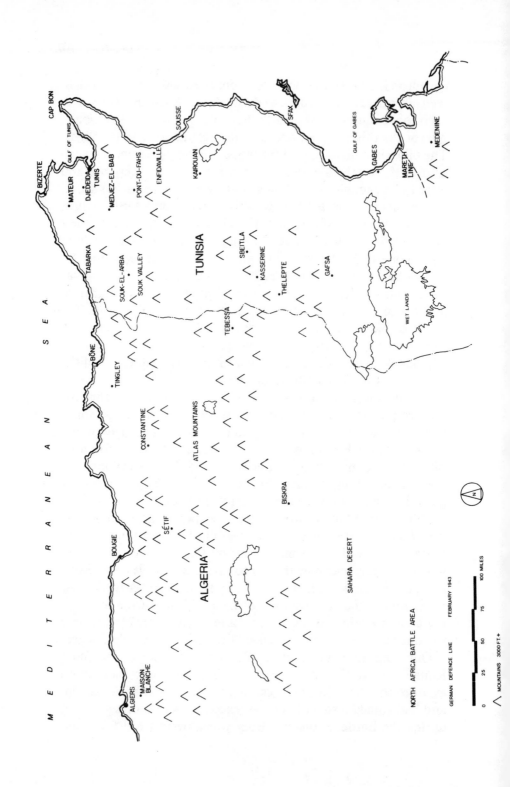

MEDITERRANEAN SEA

ALGIERS
• MAISON BLANCHE
BOUGIE
SÉTIF
CONSTANTINE
BÔNE
• TINGLEY
TABARKA
SOUK-EL-ARBA
SOUK VALLEY
BIZERTE
GULF OF TUNIS
• MATEUR
• DJEDEIDA
TUNIS
• MEDJEZ-EL-BAB
PONT-DU-FAHS
ENFIDAVILLE
SOUSSE
KAIROUAN
CAP BON
SFAX
GULF OF GABES
GABES
MARETH LINE
MÉDENINE

ATLAS MOUNTAINS
BISKRA
TEBESSA
THELEPTE
GAFSA
KASSERINE
SBEITLA
SBETLA

TUNISIA

ALGERIA

SAHARA DESERT

WET LANDS

NORTH AFRICA BATTLE AREA   FEBRUARY 1943

GERMAN DEFENCE LINE

0   25   50   75   100 MILES

∧ MOUNTAINS 3000 FT.+

N

since he was much shorter and wore an enormous, carefully groomed mustache which projected on either side of his oxygen mask when he was flying. A ruddy complexion emphasized his startling blue eyes, which twinkled most of the time, especially when he and Hugo were playing practical jokes on each other.

The carefree relationship between the two top officers of the wing, perfectly natural and unrestrained, transmitted a feeling of jauntiness and freedom to the squadrons which might have been difficult to develop in any other way. I have always thought that we were most fortunate in having two such experienced and understanding leaders. Everyone wanted to help in preparing the new pilots for what lay ahead.

Overall command of our wing was vested in the Eastern Air Command and the Twelfth United States Army Air Force, representing the British and American air forces respectively. The two separate commands were proving to be unwieldy and were about to be merged to form the North-West African Air Force with the main offensive operations being divided between a tactical air force, which was us, and a strategic air force. The tactical force flying fighters, fighter-bombers, light bombers and reconnaisance aircraft was to provide close support to the Allied armies deployed roughly on the border between Algeria and Tunisia. The strategic force included medium and heavy bombers and was assigned the task of attacking enemy bases, supply depots, harbors, and generally any target where heavy bombers could be effective. A unified command meant there was little wasted effort since the most efficient types of aircraft were sent on a given mission to do the job for which they were best suited.

My records contain an interesting comparison of the air force strengths for the Allies and the enemy at that time. The Germans were estimated to have 610 aircraft in Tunisia, Sicily, and Southern Italy made up of about 250 Ju 88 bombers and the balance of the remainder Me 109s and Fw 190s, both single-engined fighters. The Italians had about 600 aircraft, of which half were fighters and the remainder a mixture of bombers and transport aircraft. The Allied strength was known exactly. The RAF had 144 single-engined fighters, 22 light bombers, 41 medium bombers, 35 heavy bombers, and 23 transport aircraft.

The comparison, in total, meant that 524 Allied aircraft could face up to 1,200 enemy aircraft. The Allied numbers increased rapidly as the campaign progressed, although they only tilted heavily in our favor toward the end of the campaign as the enemy withdrew to Sicily to save their machines for a later fight. Because 81 Squadron was fortunate enough to be equipped with the new Spitfire IX, the equal of any German or Italian fighter, our role was to fly as top cover for bombers and to escort other Spits and fighter-bombers on sweeps, protecting them against attacks from above. I was told we would see the enemy on nearly every sortie and would probably engage them thirty percent of the time.

We received detailed briefings concerning army dispositions, the units involved, and the objectives sought within various time frames. I had a sketchy historical perception of the Western Desert side of the conflict with little appreciation of the appalling difficulties imposed by desert conditions. It was important that we keep accurate track of the Eighth Army's progress as it pushed the German Afrika Korps into Tunisia from the east and south while the Second U.S. Army Corps and the British First Army contained and attacked from the west.

I was fortunate to start my war at such an opportune time. Only six months earlier, the Germans held all of Europe and had reached the gates of Leningrad in Russia. They controlled Norway in the north and the Balkans in the south and were threatening to overrun Egypt, cutting off British access to the rich Arabian oil fields. German submarines roamed the oceans at will, wreaking havoc on Allied supply shipments. It was only in North Africa where the British were in continual contact with German land forces in a very unusual and often neglected war that the enemies met head on.

Britain had been present in Egypt for generations while the Italians had maintained a strong military presence in neighboring Libya. When Italy entered the war on June 10, 1940, the British attacked and severely trounced the Italians, taking 130,000 prisoners. Since Hitler did not want to see North Africa lost, he started in a small way to reinforce the remaining Italian forces. As the months passed, the Germans sent more men and equipment to bolster those meager forces, with the British pretty well doing the same thing. Then Hitler ordered General Erwin Rommel to take command and the renowned Afrika Korps was born. From then until the British appointed General Bernard Montgomery to command the Allied forces, the battles moved back and forth across the vast African landscape. Then came the battle of El Alamein on October 23, 1942, signalling the start of the ultimate German defeat.

The desert offered unique opportunities for innovative warfare as well as presenting brutal difficulties, since it embraced a relatively narrow band of land bordering the Mediterranean Sea but extending over 1,500 miles in length. There were few roads, few villages, few inhabitants, little water, and virtually no protection from ground growth and terrain variety. Everything was in the open, plain to see. As the British advanced, their supply lines became extended and their momentum eventually slowed because of a lack of reinforcements and adequate supplies. The reverse would happen to the retreating Germans. Their supply lines became shorter, and they were eventually able to halt the British advance. Then the Germans would advance and the supply problems would be reversed. During the whole period, Malta remained a thorn in the side of the German supply systems as their ships plied between Sicily and Italy to the Northern African shore. Malta sat astride the enemy shipping lanes, which allowed the RAF, operating from Maltese airfields, to wreak havoc on ships and transport aircraft.

On November 8, 1942, a joint Allied invasion, code named "Torch," had been launched against the western end of the North African coast. This started the final battle for Tunisia and control of the North African continent. As future events proved, I was to serve continuously with advancing, victorious Allied armies. I had missed our retreats and failures of earlier years. Many difficult situations lay ahead, but the knowledge that I was on a winning side must have given an added dimension to my enthusiasm and future actions. But I was to learn that even though the enemy was caught in a giant trap as his forces were compressed into the relatively small country of Tunisia, it was a brave, resourceful and dogged enemy who, like a rat caught in a trap, could be expected to fight valiantly without seeking or giving any quarter.

The importance of success in Africa cannot be exaggerated,

and the landings in November produced an immediate reaction — the Germans occupied Vichy France and rushed troops and equipment to reinforce Tunisia. An Allied victory would expose all of southern Europe, making it vulnerable to an Allied invasion at a number of possible locations. It meant that the Mediterranean would be secured, providing a direct sea route from America and Great Britain to the Indian Ocean which would eliminate the long voyage around the horn of Africa and immeasurably ease the transit of vital supplies to Russia and India. Russia had been demanding that the Allies open a second front in Europe to help ease their desperate plight, an operation which the Allies knew would be ill-advised at that time. Africa was an obvious and conservative alternative which would provide valuable lessons for future invasions. It also helped Russia immensely as Hitler rushed some of his best divisions and fighter squadrons from the Russian front to bolster his African defenses.

As I gained experience I learned to appreciate the depth and detail of our preflight briefings. We were always provided with information that was as precise as possible, locating our frontline troops, the most deadly anti-aircraft areas, and areas where enemy troops and equipment were concentrated. The information would be useful in the event that we were shot down and had an opportunity to evade and escape and also ensured that we did not attack and shoot up our own forces.

My squadron commander, Squadron Leader Colin Falkland Gray, DFC and Bar,[9] was a twenty-seven-year-old New Zealander who had joined the RAF before the war with his twin brother. During and after the Battle of Britain, he had run up a score of seventeen enemy aircraft destroyed plus innumerable probables and damages. Colin was a superb pilot as well as being a remarkable shot and he was blessed with remarkable eyesight. He was to be my mentor during my tour in Africa and to him I owe much. He taught by example and concise advice, usually couched in colorful language.

Gray was of medium height with a slim build, jet black hair, a gaunt face, and dark, piercing eyes. He smoked constantly, and never removed his cigarette from his mouth when he spoke. With a prominent nose and chin, I wondered if he ever burned himself as his cigarette bobbed up and down. Each new cigarette was lit from the butt of the previous one. From his example I learned that you could smoke in a Spitfire, which I was to do often in the future, using my gauntlet as an ashtray.

Colin loved to fly and went on nearly every trip that the squadron flew. I was his number 2 on most occasions, and was with him when he added another five destroyed to his tally. I would follow him on his initial attack on an enemy aircraft, but after that I was on my own. It would take extraordinary flying skill to follow his antics in the air, and he did not relish the responsibility for the safety of his wingman. His teaching stayed with me throughout my operational career, and I never had any reason to be skeptical of this individualistic and unusual approach to combat flying.

His unorthodox attitude probably explained his rather checkered career up to this point with moves from squadron to squadron in Britain. At considerable personal risk, he was known to have brought back his damaged aircraft time and again, and his passionate affection for the Spitfire prompted us to respect the aircraft and its capabilities almost as much as he did. Colin was a very gregarious person, and loved to be with his pilots from dawn until bedtime, participating in every squadron activity. He pitched in to dig slit trenches, build a dispersal, and take down and reerect tents. He did everything the rest of us did and performed better. I oftened wondered when he found time to deal with the necessary squadron paper work, but perhaps this indefatigable man did it when we were asleep.

Our squadron complement was limited to twenty-six pilots. Flight Lieutenant Walker, Pilot Officers Cal "Pep" Peppler and Harry "Babe" Fenwick, DFC, Flight Sergeant Doug Husband and Sergeants Rathwell, Olson, and Hamelin were fellow Canadians. Pilot Officer Maguire was a Rhodesian. The New Zealanders included Squadron Leader Gray, Pilot Officer Mongomery, and Sergeants Peart and Robinson. The English contingent included Flight Lieutenant Hagger, Flying Officers Goby, Barber, Booth, Rigby and Byford, Pilot Officers Doherty and Lehardy, and Sergeants Betterley, Calicott, Tasto and Hulse. I had trained Betterley at 31 EFTS, but here the tables were turned occasionally when I flew as his number 2.

We carried eighteen Spitfire IXs on strength with serviceability being very high, often one hundred percent. The pilots had to rotate flying duties, which gave us every third or fourth day off to rest. A normal flying day lasted from before dawn till after dark, with the result that our time off was put to good use resting, doing laundry, and writing letters. The CO and the flight commanders had their own personal aircraft, while the rest of us shared the remainder, usually two pilots alternating use of the same aircraft. This system meant that we became familiar with one aircraft and took considerable pride in its maintenance and appearance. They were our weapons of war, they allowed us to fight the enemy, and they were also our only means of survival.

The aero-engine mechanics looked after the engines and constantly quizzed the pilots on their running, smiling when they usually received glowing compliments. Similarly the airframe mechanics wanted to know did the machine handle well, did it trim well and did all the controls work properly? The poor armorers received the most criticism, for our 20 millimeter Hispano cannon frequently refused to operate. Sometimes it was dud ammunition or perhaps the feed belt became jammed; other times the pervasive sand and dust blocked the delicate mechanism; on occasion the guns froze at high altitude. When the cannons were fired the Spitfire slowed suddenly by about 10 mph. If only one cannon jammed the aircraft would suddenly veer to the side of the one firing cannon, thus destroying the pilot's aim. Cannon malfunction was a frequent and annoying problem, always seeming to come at the most critical times. I very rapidly came to appreciate the importance of a competent and interested groundcrew, and I daily helped to clean and polish my aircraft or watched as the ammunition was loaded into belts and thence into the guns. I also spent a good deal of time polishing the Plexiglas coupe top, ensuring that it was clean and free from scratches. I firmly believed that if I could see the enemy, he wouldn't get me. The enemy you don't see may well add you to his score.

Tingley airfield was a brand new airfield located some ten miles south of the earlier base at Bône, which had been nearly bombed and strafed out of existence and was still being attacked almost daily. High mountains bounded our north side, a marshy lake the west and flat plains the east and south. The airfield was named for Major Tingley of the Royal Engineers, who had realized that the wing needed a new location since Bône and its harbor were such prominent targets for enemy raiders. On his own initiative he had designed and built our airfield and installed a thousand-yard runway using pierced metal tracking supplied by the Americans. The runway was narrow, extremely slippery, and made a great racket when the wheels ran along the dimpled surface. Because of the narrow wheelbase of our Spits, it took considerable skill to keep the kites on the runway.

Major Tingley was a jolly, lovable character, short, roly-poly, and with a florid complexion, who spent his spare time with our squadron, Hugo and Berry were his particular delights, and he frequently joined them in their practical jokes and pranks. He regarded them as a father would admire his sons, although he loved us all, and we gave our affection to this brave and ingenious little officer.

At our camp I was allotted tent space with our intelligence officer or "spy" as he was invariably called, Flying Officer Arthur Pratt. After a hasty supper I settled down in his two-man tent and tried to make myself comfortable in very primitive conditions. My only baggage consisted of some flying gear, changes of shirts, underwear, and socks which, along with my shaving gear, were all I had room for in my small aircraft when I left Gibraltar. My bed, blankets, warm clothing, and the personal items that meant so much arrived three weeks later. Meanwhile I was able to scrounge a few blankets from others which had to serve for a bed, with the cold, wet tent floor as my mattress.

The spy was a short, dark stocky Englishman, very interested in his job and very precise. Over the next several nights, I was to learn the history of the squadron in great detail as told by an enthusiastic participant.

81 Squadron was formed in 1941 flying Hurricanes. It was soon shipped to Russia to instruct Russian pilots to fly the Hurricane and to advise them on fighter tactics. After several months there, the squadron returned to England to convert to Spitfires Vs to carry out operations, mainly sweeps, into France and the Low Countries. In November it moved to Gibraltar with Razz Berry

as its commanding officer to take part in the invasion of North Africa on November 8, 1942. It left Gibraltar with long-range fuel tanks which provided just enough fuel to reach Algiers and Maison Blanche airdrome. It was a one-way trip and the pilots could only hope that the invasion had been successful and that the airdrome had been captured and was in friendly hands. They landed, relieved to learn that the field had been captured only a few hours earlier.

For two days they patrolled the landing area and were successful in preventing many enemy bombers from reaching their objectives, while shooting down a good number. They continued to operate amidst total confusion, without food, sleeping in, on or under their aircraft until ordered to move to Bône. That small grass airfield had been secured only minutes earlier by British commandos, and as they landed, a high-flying reconnaisance Ju 88 apparently noted the arrival of the Spitfires, an early portent of the activity to follow.

The squadron was flying Spitfire VBs while the enemy was using the latest, superior models of the Me 109, Focke-Wulf 190 and the Italian Macchi 202. At first there was little fuel or ammunition and no servicing groundcrew. There was no air controller or early warning devices of any kind to provide an alert of approaching aircraft. The enemy would pop over the surrounding hills and be bombing and strafing before a defence could be mounted. A standing patrol of two aircraft was kept aloft to serve as guards over the 'drome, and usually these pilots could warn the ground that an attack was imminent and fighters could be hurled into the air to intercept the raiders.

Throughout November and December the pilots flew a gruelling schedule. Since Bône had an excellent harbor, which allowed freighters to unload supplies for the forward troops, it provided a tempting target for the enemy, who frequently raided both the harbor and the 'drome simultaneously with swarms of fifty to one hundred aircraft. Enemy bombers made nightly visits, further disturbing the exhausted pilots billeted in the small town. Frequently only two or three Spits would be serviceable to meet fifty or more raiders. The tension and strain were sustained and enormously exhausting. The squadron continued to fight until one night in early January the CO advised headquarters that his men were completely exhausted and he had only one serviceable aircraft left. He was gratified to leave the aircraft and withdraw all personnel to Constantine some eighty miles inland for a rest and refit.

After a few days rest at Constantine the pilots were sent to Gibraltar, to re-equip on Spitfire IXs. New pilots arrived, along with Colin Gray, who became the new commanding officer. Berry was promoted to wing commander, flying, and Hugo to group captain to command the wing. 81 was the first squadron to fly the Spit IXs in the African theater, and when I arrived, they had been operational for only a couple of weeks.

Other than Hugo, Berry, and the flight commanders, including Jimmy Walker, most of the pilots had been operationally inexperienced. While necessity quickly taught them survival habits, their effectiveness against a determined and skilled enemy was not notable, although their bravery and aggressiveness were outstanding. Seldom have Allied pilots been required to operate under such primitive and adverse conditions against such enormous odds.

Thus, when I became a member of 81 Squadron, we had the best British fighter aircraft of the time, an experienced commanding officer, two veteran flight commanders, a smattering of newly experienced fighter pilots, and a much larger number of totally inexperienced but eager "sprogs" (inexperienced pilots).

Because of the IX's superior performance, 81 Squadron was mainly used to provide top cover while protecting the other three squadrons in the wing, which were still flying the older Spit Vs. The result was that those pilots frequently encountered the enemy, while we remained higher to ensure that they were not bounced from above. We had our share of fights but nothing like the action which faced our colleagues. This situation changed slowly as the campaign advanced and the other squadrons started to re-equip with the IXs.

At last Walker decided to put me on a sweep. I had waited long enough and now would get my first chance at the enemy in the form of a free-lance sweep 130 miles behind enemy lines to Bizerte. Free-lance meant that we could fly as we pleased as long as we covered the Bizerte area.

I went to my aircraft, identified by an *M* on the side, and fumbled with my parachute straps and Sutton harness. The groundcrew was most helpful and I think they were as excited as I was. Somehow my nervous fingers got the engine started, and I followed the CO out to the take-off path as I was to be his number 2. Once in the air and on our way, I settled down and began to notice things. On my right were four Spitfires flying several hundred yards away in line astern and at staggered heights. This was yellow section, always on the right. Blue section of four aircraft was in the opposite position on my left. Ahead of me the CO's kite, red one, looked large and sleek as I maintained a position as red 2 about forty yards behind. Behind me were red 3 and 4.

We climbed steadily at 180 mph on the gauge. At 10,000 feet I turned on my oxygen and switched in my high-speed blower. At 21,000 feet the supercharger came in with a frightening bang. Finally in the cold, rarified air of 27,000 feet we levelled out. I swung my head from side to side, searching the sky in the prescribed manner. I saw Bizerte snuggled in its tiny bay, with the white buildings providing a sharp contrast to the deep blue of the Mediterranean, and the lakes, one blue and one a muddy brown, bordering the harbor on the south. This was enemy territory. The Huns would pick up the sound of our motors although we were too high to be readily seen with the naked eye. Would he send some fighters up to meet us? Maybe they were already climbing up. From Ferryville, the port village near Bizerte, a few rounds of flak welcomed us, quite inaccurate, not warranting evasive action or weaving. One of our pilots broke the R/T (radio telephone) silence with one word followed by the squadron call sign, "Flak, Tony squadron." We maintained complete R/T silence because the enemy radio direction finder sent a constant and nerve-jerking burr over our radios as they tried to block our radio transmissions. The irritating noise was to bother me a great deal in the future, and often I cursed the sound at the top of my lungs.

Enemy aircraft were reported several times, although try as I might, I could never locate them. I had not learned to focus my eyes on infinity, nor did I look in the right places. We did not engage the enemy and after circling Bizerte for about fifteen minutes, we headed for home. The country below appeared lush and green, although I knew from maps that it was rough and mountainous, and a very dangerous place in which to make a forced landing.

We dove for home in a long shallow sweep at over 350 mph. As we descended the air became noticeably warmer. I had not been aware of the cold over enemy territory because there were so many things requiring total concentration and attention. We landed quickly, and before I knew it, I was in one of the excited assemblies which always gathered after a show.

The CO asked Walker, "What did you see, Jimmy?" "Oh, nothing much," replied Walker. "A bit of transport and a few MTs running around Lake Bizerte. That French collier is still there in the same place."

And so on as each volunteered fresh "gen" (information) or confirmed the reports of other pilots. As I stood silently listening, I realized how much I had missed and what a lot I had to learn. No pilot can see everything, but Gray did not miss much!

The next day I scrambled with Squadron Leader Gray. We were on readiness together when the controller ordered us up to search for a bogey reported in our area. We climbed through rather dense clouds to 25,000 feet, heading north over the unseen Mediterranean. Although we followed the controller's instructions, we saw nothing. After a short search Gray headed for base in a gentle dive with my aircraft tucked beside his wing, deathly afraid to lose him since I did not have the foggiest notion of our location. As we broke through the clouds my confidence rose several degrees, because I now knew that I could handle my superb machine while following the maneuvers of a hot pilot without difficulty. Trust in my aircraft and belief in myself were to be important factors in preserving my skin in future.

February 25 was a full day for the squadron. In the early afternoon, together with seven other Spitfire squadrons, we escorted Flying Fortresses to bomb Bizerte. The Forts had their own close support of P-38 Lightnings while we had a roving commission, free to do what we liked as long as we stayed in the Bizerte area. The day was gorgeous, with a radiant sun shining full power so that even at our height of 27,000 feet it felt warm, giving me a sense of well-being. Below us, at 12,000 feet, was a thin layer of patchy cloud.

Then the Forts began their bombing run. Behind them at a safe distance hovered a cloud of thirty Me 109s. I could just picture those German pilots trying to make up their minds on exactly how to attack the prickly well-armed bombers. Other gaggles of 109s and Fw 190s flitted hither and yon. Aircraft were everywhere, forty Forts, over one hundred Germans, at least thirty-six Lightnings and ninety-six Spitfires. When the fight started, it looked as though it would be a real free-for-all.

I was flying number 2 to Gray when he suddenly announced, "Bouncing, chaps. 190s below. Tallyho."

I had all I could do to follow his sudden move. Some 8,000 feet below us I could see a large gaggle of Fw 190s quite unaware of our presence. At well over 400 mph, Gray closed in on the last 190. I saw smoke from his guns trail over his wings as he fired, but the 190 stooged along, unhit and unaware of what was happening behind him. The CO broke left, and I climbed up the back of the enemy, firing wildly with no strikes. I pulled away to the right, missing the German by only a few feet. I could look into his cockpit almost as if I were sitting beside him. He did not have a smile on his face, although he should have, considering he was still alive and unhurt. It was one of the few times I saw Gray miss when he fired in anger.

I pulled up vertically, since I had so much speed, feeling that altitude would be a good move. As I got to the top of my loop and started to roll out, I saw a great black cross and the stubby nose of a Messerschmitt 109 fewer than one hundred yards away directly in front. Again I fired a long burst before I pulled the stick back and dived vertically toward the ground. Missed again! As I dove I saw a 190 flying carelessly along on top of the cloud layer right below me. Again I lined up my sights when within range and fired, only to miss again. This was my first fight and the sweat was pouring off me. I figured it was time for a breather and dodged into the clouds with a sigh of relief.

I could hear the CO on the R/T telling the squadron to pull out and head for home. I knew the sky above was a mass of whirling aircraft, many short of ammunition and all anxious to head for base. I set course for Tingley and tried to figure out what had happened. Although the fight had lasted only a couple of minutes, as far as I was concerned, it seemed much longer, as though time had stood still. I had fired at three different enemy aircraft and missed them all. My first experience at firing my guns was an unfortunate prediction that I would miss again, many times. And although I could fly an airplane as well as most pilots, I had a hard time hitting another airplane, an enemy. This, from a fighter pilot's point of view, is a very serious shortcoming, since an aircraft is nothing but a gun platform. What is the sense of being able to maneuver the platform if you can't make good use of the ammunition? Twelve seconds firing time was our capability, but our two cannon and four machine guns could throw out an enormous quantity of lead in that short time.

One more thing was quite apparent. I must look around more and size up a situation more quickly. As I found out after landing, a Focke-Wulf had followed me down during my last dive, firing away. He might have shot me down had not one of our squadron pilots followed and shot him down. I didn't even know he or anyone else was behind me, chiefly because I was too intent on what was going on in front of me. I was no better than the pilot of the first 190 we had bounced and only good luck had seen me through, along with an assist from a squadron mate.

On the ground the spy tried to piece the action together as we yelled excitedly and gesticulated wildly to recreate each experience more graphically. We claimed several Huns destroyed and damaged for the loss of one of our aircraft. Even then, our pilot got back to base safely after bailing out of his Spit, which was hit so badly that the controls were shot away.

I talked to Gray to find what he thought I had done right or wrong. He did not reproach me for not staying with him. He emphasized that once a fight starts, it's every man for himself, a point I agree with, although normally it was considered a breach of flying discipline to leave your number 1. In this squadron everyone was on his own once a fight began.

"Billie," he said as he continued with his advice, "you're young, eager, and impetuous. You must learn to cool down, to look everywhere, but most of all, behind you. You've been here

ten days and that was your fifth ops [operational] trip. Under
the circumstances you did well, but you won't live long enough
to do better if you don't use your eyes. Learn to look around.
Get into that habit. A chap who sees all and is a poor pilot has
a one hundred percent better chance of living than a good pilot
who sees little.''

Shortly after four o'clock, while we were sipping tea, still
discussing the previous trip, a phone message came from our sector controller: "Scramble every available aircraft! A sixty-plus
raid is coming in."

We ran toward our aircraft barely taking time to do up our
straps before our engines burst into life. We took off, higgledy-
piggledy, forming up in a long line in the air as we climbed at
full power. Within a few minutes of jumping into my aircraft
I was at 21,000 feet.

Meantime we kept getting instructions from the controller.
"They are behind you now about six thousand feet above, in the
sun. Heads up! They've seen you!" I was always amazed at how
a man on the ground looking at instruments and tubes could have
such clear knowledge of what was happening so high above his
head. I learned to trust the controller's instructions, and in this
case we knew that the Hun was above us in force. But he did
not attack as we continued our frantic climb.

Then over the R/T came the controller's voice, "Fw190s dive-
bombing the harbor from east to west." Now we knew why the
enemy had not attacked us. They intended to divert us while their
bombers attacked Bône harbor without fear of interference from
our Spitfires. Down we dived, exposing our tails to the 109s above
us, and down they came.

We chased the dive bombers away, at the same time managing to protect our tails from the attacking 109s. In a few minutes
it was all over. Our success was Winco Berry shooting down a
109 when he had neither radio nor ringsight, a wizard job. Gray
destroyed another 109 as well.

To round out this active day we had a terrific flap during the
evening. A paratroop drop was expected on our 'drome with the
obvious intent of destroying our aircraft and killing as many personnel as possible. Each squadron sent one hundred men to stand

guard with some army and RAF Regiment reinforcements. We were well armed and carefully briefed to shoot anything that moved — no exceptions. This emergency lasted until dawn and proved very trying since we could not relieve ourselves, smoke, eat, or sleep. I was to experience this same type of scare a number of times later on, and although each occasion was a non-event, I never became adjusted to this frightening situation.

I completed the month flying sweeps or escorting Spitfire Vs, Fortresses, and Mitchells. We usually encountered fairly heavy and accurate flak, but few enemy fighters. Flying close escort to the Fortresses usually produced some excitement. Even though we tried to fly in a fairly constant guard position to best protect our big friends, they invariably fired at us because we got too close. This would occur when they wheeled to change direction, forcing us to make a crossover turn above them. We respected their very independent attitude, realizing that the Forts were heavily armed and quite capable of protecting themselves.

I lost my flight commander when Jimmy Walker was promoted to command 243 Squadron and replaced by Flight Lieutenant Ron Hagger. We were not too pleased with the new arrangement since we knew Hagger well and felt that he did not have the experience or qualifications to be our flight commander.

Our operations from Tingley airfield became more difficult as we were now about one hundred miles from the enemy ground positions because of the recent advances and victories of our armies. Most of our flying time was spent travelling to and from our targets. The time and fuel expended left little for combat or other activities, and we were often landing with only a few gallons of fuel left in our tanks.

Our battlefield was confined almost exclusively to the skies over Tunisia, a country roughly rectangular in shape and some 160 miles wide by about 260 miles from the north to the south at the Mareth Line, which was a chain of fortifications. On the north and east lay the Mediterranean Sea, while Algeria formed the western boundary. The interior was very rugged and mountainous with peaks and ridges soaring to 4,000 and more feet. To the south the ridges and trees gradually petered out into the Sahara Desert.

The Tunisians were essentially Arabs, with a pro-German bias. Both the Allies and the Germans offered rewards to the Arabs for the return of downed pilots, and we thought the Germans were indifferent as to whether captured pilots were delivered dead or alive. During our escape procedure briefings, we were told that the Arabs were cruel and inclined to torture captured airmen, with the Arab women being the most vicious. We were advised, if capture seemed unavoidable, to consider shooting ourselves. I knew that we were repelled by this sanguine advice, and I cannot remember its ever being followed. A great number of pilots were lost and never heard of again, however, and some may have resorted to self-destruction.

We learned that the Me 109 recently shot down by Berry had made a successful forced landing, with the German pilot being captured by the army. The airplane had been moved to Bône for shipment to England for examination and assessment by RAF experts, which gave some of us an opportunity to examine the fighter at close range. We also learned from military intelligence that the captured German pilot was a very talkative sergeant who claimed his CO was a truly experienced fighter pilot with 115 kills to his credit: 8 in the Battle of Britain, a further 106 on the Russian front, and another in Africa. He said his group insignia was the Ace of Spades and his leader had a large numeral "7" painted on the sides of his aircraft. He also said that Germany was sending her best aircraft and most experienced pilots to the African front, an indication that the Jerries meant to fight to the bitter end.

Of our examination of this late model Me 109 G4, the most surprising first impression to me was its very small size. Although the Spitfire was generally considered to be a small aircraft, I was impressed by how much bigger in size it seemed when compared to the Me 109. The 109 had been designed as a war machine with field servicing and ease of maintenance obviously a prime consideration. The engine panels were hinged and opened to provide easy access to whatever various parts might require servicing. Oil, fuel, glycol, and electrical lines were color-coded so that each was easily identifiable. It operated on 87 octane fuel, and the oxygen bottles could be recharged from nozzles without having to be removed. There was also a mechanism to cut off the cooling to one radiator, should it be shot up, and the engine could be operated safely on the remaining rad.

Concerning its airframe the Me 109 had other notable features. The small tailwheel retracted to improve streamlining. There was no rudder trim and the elevator control moved the whole tail which made these particular controls very stiff in high speed dives. The flaps were hand operated, and we felt the control surfaces were very small. The paint finish was impressive, much smoother and thinner than our Spitfire camouflaged finish. We all felt that if our aircraft were equally well finished our speed would be increased by between ten and twenty miles per hour.

The pilot's seat was nearly on the bottom spline of the aircraft, so that his legs were stretched almost straight out in front. In the Spit we had more of a chair-type seating arrangement which was a more comfortable flying position, although we could not withstand the g-forces as well as a German pilot. One feature I disliked was what I thought to be the limited visibility of the straight, metal-edged coupe top. Hinged on the starboard side, it was fared flush with the body streamlining, restricting vision to the rear. In the Spit we had a bulged plastic coupe top, which slid to the rear on a track. The bulge configuration gave us some rear vision and unrestricted viewing to the sides. One drawback with our hoods, however, was their susceptibility to marking and scratching. Sand was hard on the hoods and marring of the usually smooth surface could restrict our ability to see a distant enemy.

Like our aircraft, the Me 109 had a very narrow tracked landing gear, and the elongated nose would restrict forward visibility when on the ground. I felt that it would be touchy on taking-off, landing, and taxiing. I later found that the short, paddle-bladed prop exerted tremendous torque to one side on take-off, but gave much swifter acceleration than the Spit with its four-bladed laminated wood propellor.

The armament consisted of a 20-millimeter cannon firing through the propellor shaft with the breeching extending back to the space between the pilot's feet. It also had two machine guns of about .50 calibre mounted in the cowling on top of the engine. This provided great fire power with the guns aimed in a manner similar to the action one would use in aiming a rifle. Our sight was five feet higher than our guns, and several times when I was right behind a 109 with my bead aimed at the top of his rudder, my bullets would go underneath his slim machine. Sometimes I had enough time to move my aircraft's nose up and down slightly, thus getting a spraying effect from my guns to score strikes. Unfortunately, I missed all too often.

During the coming months I had many opportunities to examine these remarkable aircraft at close hand, and I even owned one for a week. My admiration increased as I came to understand the capabilities of the enemy aircraft better. Perhaps this knowledge would be helpful one day.

I eventually learned that the Me 109 had a superior performance when compared to Spit Vs since they could dive or climb away from our aircraft and were much faster on the straight and level. Further, the latest Me 109 model had 35,000 feet as its best fighting altitude, while ours was still 28,000. The Spit IX narrowed and surpassed some of the performance gap with a distinct edge going to our climbing ability. In turns the Spit enjoyed an unmistakable edge but in the hands of an experienced pilot the Me 109 could outperform the Spitfire in most categories.

I never had any desire to fly anything but a Spitfire, which I regarded as a gentle, reliable aircraft with a superb engine, the Rolls-Royce Merlin. On numerous occasions its ability to withstand abuse and neglect brought me back to safety. In a short dive or climb, the 109 would pull away quickly from a Spitfire and against a Spit V the enemy would generally escape. With the IX, however, in a prolonged dive or climb we could sometimes catch the enemy.

All of the 109s had been tropicalized or properly prepared to operate in desert conditions. This meant that their aircraft could be flown more confidently and constantly than the Allied Spitfires. Some of the Vs had been properly equipped with the Volkes filters fitted on the air intakes, but the bulk of our machines were shipped with no desert conditioning. Dust and sand quickly invaded the engines, demanding more frequent and thorough servicing. Our cannon would jam all too frequently, although the machine guns did not seem to be adversely affected by the grit.

We invented several devices to filter the air during take-off, the most critical operation. One was a metal filter, about a foot square, which was suspended by a hook arrangement in front of the air scoop. Just at the end of our take-off run, we would pull a wire in the cockpit releasing the filter, which fell to the ground to be recovered by the groundcrew for reuse. This home-made system was fine when it worked, but if the filter failed to dislodge, our only recourse was to return and land immediately. I detested the filter and after a couple of abortive attempts, gave it up as an exercise in futility. Since I was usually among the first two or three aircraft to take off, I did not have to go through as much dust as the aircraft following behind. During my tour, I always operated from dirt airdromes and our powerful engines constantly raised clouds of sand and debris that created problems which were never solved. On the ground I usually put my officer's cap over the air intake to prevent sand from collecting when the machine was not in use.

The dirt problem was significant, radically shortening an engine's life while increasing the daily servicing hours. Performance would deteriorate, much the same as the aging in a car, only much faster. Dirt also got into the cannons, plugging them so that during an attack they would jam.

CHAPTER 4

LEARNING THE ROPES
March 1943—April, 1943

Through March I started flying more frequently, averaging two trips or sorties a day. Gray officially made me a section leader, which I appreciated immensely as it proved I was getting the hang of operational flying after less than three weeks in battle. He also said that I would fly as his number 2 on important shows, or fly with the winco when he led the squadron. Our task was usually to fly as a high top cover to formations of a dozen Mitchell bombers who had a close escort of twelve Spit Vs, and whose targets were Mateur, Madjex el Bab, Djeida, Bizerte, or Tunis. We saw enemy fighters on every trip, although the enemy would only attack at odd times, particularly in the morning when they had the advantage of appearing out of the eastern sun; in the afternoon, we had the sun advantage as we approached from the west. Since our task was to protect the lower aircraft, we only left our covering position to meet aircraft attacking the lower formations. If we or the bombers were left alone, then we rarely saw action. It was rather frustrating to see the enemy on every mission but not be in a position to seek combat.

On March 3 we were flying high cover at 30,000 feet. On this trip I was leading a section and not in my usual position as number 2 to Gray. Suddenly a lone Fiat or CR42 appeared, diving very steeply. He was apparently trying to hit the CO, but he missed and hit Gray's number 2, whose kite exploded. The pilot, Sergeant Bellerby, one of my elementary flying school students, was killed instantly. Gray and the rest of us were so stunned by the suddenness and success of the attack that no one reacted quickly. In the space of a few seconds the attacker disappeared. I could imagine Gray's wrath building, even though he must have admired the courage and skill of the Italian pilot to attack, in an obsolete biplane, single-handed, a whole squadron of superior aircraft.

A few minutes later Gray reported, "Aircraft very low at four o'clock. Diving down now. Everyone follow. Tallyho."

And away we went, eleven Spitfires in line astern, charging down at well over 400 mph indicated, from 30,000 feet. I finally managed to see our target; a Fiesler Storch observation plane with a top speed of perhaps 130 mph hugging the treetops. The German positioned his machine at right angles to the direction of our attack, making himself an easy target while at the same time completely fooling us, since we had no idea whether he was flying at 40 mph or 130 mph and were therefore unable to allow the correct deflection to compensate for his speed. Gray fired and missed. I was second and I missed. So did the remaining nine members of our squadron. At our tremendous speeds we had only a second or so of firing time each, but that was no excuse for all of us missing such an easy target. The Fiesler Storch pilot must have had an remarkable tale to tell his fellow pilots when he returned to base.

Back at Tingley, Squadron Leader Gray was a very somber fellow. He knew the Italian pilot had been aiming for him and, with some luck or a better aim, would have been successful. It was humiliating not to have seen the attacker, but since we were so high, we never dreamed that a solitary attacker could be even higher. To be hit by only one attacker, who displayed rare courage and skill, was bad enough, but to compound this by allowing an undefended Storch to escape eleven attackers made the loss of Bellerby even more galling.

When 81 Squadron flew on free-lance sweeps we used the advantages inherent in our Spit IXs to fly at high altitudes, somewhere between 29,000 and 35,000 feet, with the final decision on height being whether or not we left vapor trails. These smoke-like condensation tracks betrayed our position to anti-aircraft gunners or to searching enemy aircraft. But high altitude presented additional problems and risks. Despite the ever-present brilliant sunshine, the air temperature remained a constant and frigid seventy degrees below zero Fahrenheit, which the thin metal fuselage could not prevent from penetrating the cockpit. There

was virtually no cockpit heating system worthy of the name, causing frantic efforts by a pilot to keep his hands and feet from freezing. No amount of additional clothing would keep the body from
becoming thoroughly chilled, although a dogfight or a chase
would send the blood racing through our bodies, and in my case
I found that I could perspire very quickly. I guess the prospect
of action where your life is literally in your own hands could produce the high degree of concentration and effort required to resist
the cold.

The rarefied air at high altitudes contained insufficient oxygen
to breathe, which meant that we depended on a constant and adequate supply of pure oxygen provided by a supply system feeding
into our face masks. Upon occasion a pilot would forget to turn
his supply on fully, or perhaps his system was not operating properly, and then strange flying antics would follow from this oxygen
deficiency. On March 9 I had a lousy engine, with the oil pressure
falling and the temperature rising. I also felt light-headed and
knew that I was having oxygen troubles. Suddenly, at 34,000 feet
over Bizerte my number 1, Pilot Officer Maguire, started spirall-
ing earthward. His aircraft dived, zoomed, and performed other
weird maneuvers which I tried to follow while yelling over the
R/T, "Wake up, Mac. For Chist's sake, turn on your oxygen.
Wake up, wake up." Finally at 10,000 feet he must have regained
consciousness because his aircraft started to fly more normally.
I called again, "Let's go home, Mac. We're right over Bizerte.
Stay awake and let's go." Back at base we discovered that our
supply systems were faulty, and I then determined that in the
future I would turn the system fully on as soon as I was strapped into my aircraft. Later, when I had the authority, I encouraged my pilots to follow the same procedure.

It always seemed to me that the German anti-aircraft batteries
were particularly accurate when firing 88 millimeter projectiles
at high-flying aircraft. I reasoned they could calculate our altitude
more accurately than at intermediate heights. The 88s were the
only guns which could reach us, and the huge black bursts tended
to explode much too close to be ignored. When a shell burst close
by, the explosion could be heard over the noise of the engine.
If the concussion knocked the aircraft about or flipped it on its

back, you could still escape unscathed, but a shell bursting within twenty-eight feet would usually puncture the machine. Much closer than that and the pilot and machine were not likely to survive.

On March 17, after several days of preparation we moved eighty miles eastward to Paddington airfield in the Souk el Khemis valley, which was within twenty miles of the front lines. We would be flying constantly over enemy-held territory, with prospects of even more action than before. The Bône-Tingley period saw our squadrons basically performing a defensive role, but with the move to Souk, we moved to the offense, with orders to be more aggressive, and to attack and eliminate the enemy at every opportunity.

Our new 'drome was one of seven located in a very confined area. Most were named after a London railway station and so we had Victoria, Euston, Marleybone, King's Cross, Waterloo, and Paddington, with Souk el Arba to give a topical flavor. The Souk valley is thirteen miles long by six miles wide and because of the number of squadrons and aircraft based on these fields, we often wondered whether we faced more danger from colliding with our own aircraft than we did from enemy action.

Paddington had one long Summerfelt matting runway, which we used without regard for wind direction. The metal fabric runway was easier to operate from than the pierced metal tracking we used at Tingley, although it was very hard on tires. It damaged easily if an aircraft crashed on the runway, but it could also be repaired very quickly. During the early days at Paddington, we had a great deal of rain and puddles formed on the runway that were so deep that flying was quite hazardous. We even refrained from using our flaps for landing under wet conditions since the water could dent and damage the flap when it was extended.

We normally took off from the end of the runway most convenient to our parked aircraft. This sometimes led to confusion during scrambles or in obeying hurried take-off orders because different squadrons might be taking off from either end of the runway at the same time. We lost a number of pilots whose aircraft, starting from opposite ends, collided in the middle of the runway with fatal and messy results. At times the dust would be extreme, and we would be forced to take off while part of the runway was obscured. There was little or no air traffic ground control, and when we obeyed instructions from our controller (code-named "Chuka"), we prayed for good luck.

I knew little about our controllers except that they were generally officers who had considerable flying experience but because of age or perhaps performance became controllers. Operating with minimum and marginal equipment, they would perform very well at times, controlling us onto enemy formations, while at other times they had us chasing ourselves. Their radar equipment had very limited range, probably about fifty miles, and their capability for assessing altitudes was usually deplorable. The controllers did have access to the "Y" service, a radio listening device which monitored the enemy radio transmissions, occasionally providing very useful information, and at times we would know within seconds when an enemy had sighted us. Then we would prepare to attack or defend ourselves, depending on the circumstances. Generally, however, our communications with the ground and the air controllers were appalling, and we tended to rely on our wits and the radio transmissions of other Allied aircraft. Despite occasional shortcomings, I learned to trust our controllers, for in the months ahead, they were to help save my life several times.

As our airfield could be attacked at anytime by marauding enemy fighters darting in from the cover of the surrounding mountains undetected by our controllers or patrolling aircraft, we determined to ensure our personal safety. Six of us, including Gray, found shovels and proceeded to dig an enormous hole in the sandy soil. This was to be our new dispersal, with comfort and safety being our prime consideration. Our aircraft were fuelled by hand from four-gallon disposable metal containers, and we stacked these, filled with sand, to build strong walls starting at the bottom of the hole. Tingley metal tracking made our roof, which we then covered with sand. The structure provided a safe, cool, and dry enclosure, reasonably safe from most enemy action except for a direct hit. Over top we stretched camouflage netting that was so effective that our dispersal was virtually invisible from the air and the ground. To mark our location we installed a sign post and weathervane near the entrance. The main sign read "Nein Pissen ont den Posten" and had arrows showing Bizerte: 80 miles, London: 1,900 miles, and Fouk el Duk (our dispersal): 10 feet. We managed to scrounge or build tables and chairs, and had electricity from a field generator, a radio, and cubicles for the personal belongings of each pilot. Scrounging in the wilderness of Algeria and Tunisia challenged our ingenuity and enterprise, and the desperately poor nomadic Arabs provided few articles which interested us. Our ability to devise substitutes never ceased to be a source of amazement and admiration. Our unique quarters became the envy of the other squadrons and the senior wing officers could usually be found in our midst sipping tea.

Outside we dug slit trenches, four feet deep by three feet wide, zigzagging in different directions. We used them frequently during the many enemy raids on our positions. Each morning the first men to arrive for duty from our camp checked the trenches for snakes which fell in during the night and were stuck there since they could not climb up the vertical trench walls. The snakes were extremely dangerous, intimidating even the bravest snake herpetologists. Our solution was simple. We just poured gasoline into the trench, lit a match, and watched the reptiles fry in a frenzy of lashing and twisting.

We all had American escape purses, which contained food tablets, morphine ampules and water purification pills, files, compasses, and maps of Europe and the East printed on silk or fine paper, all meant to aid in an escape. The purses also held about $250 in Tunisian and Algerian francs, four golden Louis and printed declarations in several languages and dialects offering rewards for the safe return of Allied pilots. Every time Paddington experienced a worthwhile bombing raid, many of us would claim that our escape purses had been destroyed, and they would be promptly replaced without much argument. We were thus able to save our pay and allowances while serving in Africa by using the liberated funds for our personal use. I never heard whether our misguided actions were discovered or criticized.

Despite the concentration of aircraft on our airfields, we were visited daily by our determined enemy, and every other night heavy bombers came over to say "Hello."

During daylight Fw 190s carrying bombs would pop out of the neighboring hills, attack, and be gone before our controllers could pick them up. Even with standing patrols, the enemy was usually able to attack successfully and with very few losses. Also, they were operating over their own territory for most of their flying time, and even if an aircraft became damaged from flak or fighter action, the German pilot had a better-than-even chance of making it safely to their lines.

The night bombing raids provided vicarious excitement although they did minimum damage. Our camp, located on high ground some two miles from the 'drome, provided a commanding view overlooking the airfields in the valley. Once we heard the sound of bombers approaching, we ran to get a ringside seat for the coming action while white and green chandelier flares were dropped by the enemy pathfinders. Our ack-ack guns criss-crossed the sky with seemingly slow-moving red hot balls of metal while fire from heavier guns lit the ground and bursting shells brightened the sky with winking flashes. Exploding bombs shook the ground with loud crumps as the ricochetting shrapnel and the harsh bark of the anti-aircraft artillery made a wild, horrid music.

Our location was on a south slope nestled in the green, rocky, and wild Tunisian hills, which glowed a gorgeous purple hue in early morning and early evening sunlight. The hillsides were brilliant with cowslips, daisies, asters, daffodils, poppies, and other plants flowering in every rainbow color. A herd of single-hump camels grazed serenely in the valley bottom while, on the upper slopes, Arab herders patiently tended enormous flocks of sheep and goats and, lower down, cattle. In the morning and evening we heard eerie music played by dirty, shaggy herders blowing wood flutes as they led the animals to and from the grazing grounds.

We lived entirely in tents: a large tent for messing purposes and small two-man tents for sleeping and privacy. Our ingenuity was taxed to make our primitive quarters comfortable, and we succeeded very well with scrounged carpets, homemade chairs, and a Valor stove in one end to work as a heater/barbecue facility. Sometimes we had electricity generated by our Chance light with something left over for a radio, if one was available. Then we might get the BBC news, but more often we listened to Algerian stations or a special forces program originated by the Germans. Axis Sally, broadcasting from Tunis, introduced the German station with a "Hello, suckers!" and spent her time trying to make us feel homesick with references to what our families and loved ones might be doing and asking why were we fighting in far-away Tunisia. Sally consistently tried to alienate the Brits and the Yanks since they were the major combatants, but none of the Allied nationalities escaped her barbs. Her theses and arguments were hilarious and had exactly the opposite effect from what she was trying to promote. But we enjoyed her musical selections, since she played the most recent recordings by the great American bands.

Batmen tended to our laundry needs and kept the tents clean and organized. Other than our days off-duty, a working fighter pilot had little time to attend to daily personal needs since we awoke at 4:00 AM, broke the ice in our wash buckets, quickly dressed appropriately, and departed by truck for the airfield. While cooks prepared breakfast over open-air stoves and fires, the pilots made their aircraft ready for an early takeoff. Often we flew before breakfast. By eight o'clock the heat would begin building up, making it extremely uncomfortable for those on instant readiness strapped in their cockpits and awaiting orders to scramble. We preferred a delayed readiness status of from five to thirty minutes, which gave us the latitude to do other things as long as we could be operational within the ordered time. By late evening we returned to camp for supper, a few drinks, and bed by midnight. Our working days were long, full of tension and excitement when we flew, and nearly as tension filled when we were not on a sortie, because we worried instead about our fellow pilots and were impatient to fly ourselves when our turn came on the next scramble or sortie.

On April 3 Gray called us together for a briefing. In his usual brisk manner he succinctly detailed our mission: "We're going on a diversionary sweep as top cover to 232 Squadron to patrol the Bizerte area while the heavies have another go at the Tunis dockyards. The brass hope that we will attract some of the attention away from the bombers, and I expect we will see some action. 232 will be at 10,000 feet, and we'll cover at 25,000. Keep your bloody eyes open. We're off at ten o'clock. The runway is good, so we'll take off quickly in pairs and form up over our friends. Any questions?''

It was a bright, warm morning as we taxied out ready to go. I was number 3 to Gray with Sergeant Tasto flying as my number 2. When Gray was halfway down the runway, I slowly opened my throttle while keeping the Spit over to the left hand edge of the matting to leave room for Tasto to stay close. Part way down the runway, with tail up and nearly enough flying speed to lift off, all hell suddenly broke loose. Focke-Wulf 190s flashed by a few feet above our heads with guns blazing and bombs dropping. One shot by me and was going so fast he found himself in front of Gray before the CO had his wheels retracted. Gray fired and the 190 banked away to crash in flames. What marvellous shooting! A bomb burst close to Tasto, riddling his machine with shrapnel and causing him to crash, unhurt. Aircraft were scooting all over the place with the Spits being fairly helpless, caught as they were off guard while flying at slow speeds. Gray radioed that he had engine trouble and was returning to land, while I kept my head twisting, trying to find something to shoot at as I made certain no enemy was using me for target practice. As I circled about I saw several Spit Vs climbing in formation and decided to join up with them, feeling there was additional safety in numbers. My plan failed, however, because they somehow thought I was a 190 and broke in all directions, leaving me and my good intentions all alone.

The situation was a confused shambles with Chuka controller finally advising that the airfield was being attacked by twenty Fw 190s, with other unfriendlies in the area. I decided to gain altitude to get a better picture of the action and perhaps become effective. At 25,000 feet I found Pilot Officer "Pep" Peppler, who agreed by radio to patrol with me. We listened to the exclamations, orders, and opinions coming from various pilots and the still-surprised controllers, who were now reporting additional enemy formations in strengths of thirty plus. After stooging around well inside German territory without seeing the enemy, we decided to return to base. Some activity was still being reported, but we gathered it was now well below us.

I was leading and started a gradual shallow dive to starboard, to be followed, although unseen by me, by seven Me 109s attacking from behind and below. My wing was banked up so that I could see neither the 109s nor Pep who was on my port side on the outside of the turn. Apparently he had seen them and yelled over the R/T for me to break, but I never got the message. Either he failed to push his transmitter switch fully on or his radio failed as he broke away, still out of my sight. Part way through my turn I decided to kick rudder to skid the tail around and give me a good view behind. My shock at seeing four Me 109s right behind with the closest less than fifty yards away and firing for all he was worth is still a vivid memory. The flashes from all his guns and the great white propellor spinner were fascinating!

Acting instantaneously and without conscious thought, I jammed on full right rudder, since that was the direction I was already turning, and pulled back on the control column with all my strength. I blacked out momentarily from the terrific g-forces as my plane did a flick roll up and over, but in a second was behind my attackers. They must have wondered what I had done to reverse the situation so quickly and decided to end the encounter abruptly. As I shot a two-second burst, the 109s half-rolled and dived straight down, pouring black smoke as their throttles were opened fully.

I tried to follow even as the 109s pulled swiftly away. How those 109s could dive! I knew that my bullets had fanned empty air space because I had not allowed sufficient deflection. This disappointment was offset, however, by the amazement that the enemy could have gotten so close without my seeing them, and I marvelled at my good fortune in escaping undamaged. Thus, early on I learned an important lesson — never, ever rely on the rear-vision mirror mounted on the top front of the windscreen. For the rest of my flying career I totally ignored the mirror, and when I had my own aircraft, I had the mirror removed. My future could depend on my turning and twisting my head and kicking the rudder regularly to permit full vision rearward. Because of this lesson learned so early, I was never bounced again without my full knowledge and was never hit by a bullet from an enemy aircraft. I realize that this was due in good measure to extraordinary luck, but it was also partly attributable to remembering this very important and vivid lesson.

As my aircraft was headed for home at 500 mph on the dial, I tried to contact Pep by radio. No response. We had lost each other during the attack, and I had no inkling of how he had fared. Five minutes after my landing he appeared, much to everyone's relief. As we unfolded our stories for the benefit of the spy, the final score was a 109 destroyed by Gray, another by Hagger, and a damaged for Warrant Officer Husband. Pep and I merely survived.

The next day I scrambled as number 2 to Gray and although we saw many Huns, because we were only four aircraft, greatly outnumbered by every formation we saw, we prudently declined to attack. In the afternoon I flew number 2 to the winco on a 29,000-foot-high sweep. Berry was feeling cautious, and even though our controllers vectored us beautifully onto several 109 squadrons, he also declined to attack. The enemy left us alone and therefore we were not provoked into combat.

I had learned much in the past weeks, lessons that were indelibly instilled in my being for all time to come. I came to understand the vast difference between a sprog fighter pilot and an experienced operational type and the still greater leap to our exceptional leaders. A fighter squadron is a unique fighting unit, entirely self-contained, which responds remarkably to the influence and character of the commanding officer. Our morale depended entirely on Gray, who demonstrated by extraordinary flying skill, outstanding desire, and courage and a happy, carefree attitude, that he was a consummate leader. Also, he was very lucky, having the remarkable knack of being in the right place at the right time to find and attack the enemy. That talent was something in the makeup of the man and could not be taught or passed on. Many other excellent leaders lacked that good fortune and so ended the war with a considerably lower number of "kills."

Hugo was another pilot with that uncanny ability to find the enemy with apparent ease and was probably the most modest and unselfish pilot that I would meet. One day I was on the ground when our squadron was scrambled hastily. As they were taking off with Hugo leading, a flock of Fw 190s scooted over our field, strafing and bombing. One got into Hugo's sights momentarily and was promptly shot down in flames. Back on the ground Hugo's number 2 claimed a destroyed aircraft before anyone could say a word. I knew Hugo should claim the credit and I said to him, "Sir, I saw you shoot down that 190. It was your kill." Putting a finger to his lips he said, "Never mind. Keep quiet. It will give him confidence and help him become a better fighter pilot. I've got all the score I want." In all my time in the air force, I don't think I ever met such a modest and magnanimous hero, and I have never heard of anyone else acting that way other than one Canadian, "Hap" Kennedy, who will be introduced later on.

CHAPTER 5

SUCCESS AT LAST
April, 1943

In early April the tenor of the African war seemed to change as abruptly as if a light had been switched on. It became obvious that the battle for the control of Tunisia was entering the final phase. In the south at the Mareth Line, General Montgomery and his Eighth Army had tried during the final week of March to pierce the German defences without success. The Mareth Line was actually a fortification system built before the war by the French to prevent the Italians from spilling over from Libya into Tunisia. It extended westward from the Mediterranean Sea straight inland for fifty miles with the western end anchored by a line of impassable salt lakes. When Rommel occupied the pillboxes and gun emplacements and rearmed them with German weaponry, he effectively blocked British entry to Tunisia from the south. Frontal attacks by the British against the fortifications failed, which prompted Montgomery to order the New Zealand division to trek far enough inland to circle around the natural barriers and launch an attack on the rear of the German positions. Once the New Zealanders were positioned, Montgomery attacked simultaneously on the fortified line, thus forcing the Germans to withdraw and avoid being caught in a trap. The plan worked, but slowly, and the Afrika Korps withdrew reluctantly from their strong defensive position. All of this took time, and during the several weeks' delay, the American and British armies on the western boundary of the Mareth Line consolidated their positions in preparation for the final push through extremely difficult, mountainous terrain against the well-prepared German defenses.

In preparation for the final onslaught, several significant changes had been made in the top commands of both the Allied and German forces. While General Eisenhower remained the supreme commander-in-chief of all Allied forces in North Africa, the British General Alexander became his deputy, bringing to his position great intelligence and experience. On the enemy side, General Erwin Rommel was recalled to Germany, relinquishing his command to General von Arnim with General Albert Kesselring retaining his position as supreme commander of Italy, Sicily, and North Africa. Of more significance to us was the appointment of Air Marshal Tedder to command all air forces, with Air Vice-Marshal Harry Broadhurst directing the operations of the Desert Air Force, which had operated for so long with the Eighth Army. Broadhurst, not yet forty years old, had won distinction during the Battle of Britain as a fighter pilot leading a squadron and later a wing, and he quickly became recognized as a courageous fighter and an innovator. He developed many of the techniques used by the air force when working in close cooperation with the army, bombing and strafing front-line enemy positions to help break down enemy defences. His tactics were constantly revised and improved to produce devastating results and reached their peak of efficiency later when I flew under his command in Europe.

Thus it was that on April 7 we were ordered to cover the Eighth Army's push through the last of the Mareth Line defences by providing additional air power to protect the ground forces from bombing and strafing by enemy aircraft. We set off in foul and rainy weather to Sbeitla No. 2 Airfield, some ninety miles to our south. It was a huge, stony, forbidding piece of desert and we landed in a 40 mph cross-wind and were soon covered in dust and sand, which got in our hair, our eyes, and our mouths, and more disastrously, into our aircraft. We stuck our Mae West life jackets in the air scoops to keep out the sand and my plane, sporting a serious oil leak, soon made my life preserver an oily mess. After attending to our kites we ran to a dispersal dug into a rock formation to find it filled with pilots who knew nothing about us or what we were to do.

Group Captain Hugo arrived eventually to brief us on our task — to provide escort to over forty P-40 Kittibombers. Overnight the Eighth Army had advanced a good distance, forcing the Germans into a disorderly retreat. Enemy transport was jammed for miles, hood to tail, in single and double file on the few roads as they desperately tried to avoid being surrounded and cut off. The Desert Air force deluged the roads and other escape routes with bombs and gunfire and our mission was to protect the P-40s, which would be bombing the crossroads at the northeast end of Lake Sebkret en Noual and then strafing the roads to the west. As usual, we were to provide top cover.

We took off according to schedule and stooged around for half an hour, wasting precious fuel waiting for the P-40s to appear over the 'drome. They finally arrived, surprising us as they scooted along at 1,000 feet at 280 mph. We had a difficult time keeping up with them, and we couldn't get any higher than 6,000 feet because of low, solid clouds. To make matters worse, we flew the famous flak alley in the Kasserine Pass, where the flak was heavy and extremely accurate, firing down from the hills at the low flying P-40s and up at us dashing along just level with the mountain tops. The bombers were weaving all over the place while we tried to follow through the four-mile-long gauntlet. Miraculously, no one was hit. We reached the crossroads and the bombers did their work with fair results. A number of fires were started, and I felt some sympathy for the soldiers below locked in almost-frozen positions on the narrow roads with no protection and no escape possible. There were some Me 109s about, which escaped from us by darting in and out of the clouds, but we did our job without losing a machine.

After the bombing we set course for Thelepte to refuel. It was a vast improvement over the dustbowl of Sbeitla and so large that the whole squadron could take off in line abreast in any direction. Arriving back at Souk we were all glad to be in familiar surroundings and to be done with operations in the desert. Our aircraft would not be the same again, however, because of the sand and we found that our automatic boost control units, which regulated the air/fuel mixture the engine got, had to be removed and cleaned before the machines could fly again. If only we had air filters! Despite that, the visit to the Eighth Army was rewarding in that it allowed us to appreciate more fully the problems of operating in the desert, and we were delighted to observe the destruction of hundreds of helpless German transports, confirming that the end of a great battle was almost in sight.

On April 11 three aircraft from 152 Squadron ran into each other on take-off when all had nearly reached flying speed. The runway was badly damaged and the broken-up Spits, along with pools of blood, bits of bodies, and a terrible stench, added to the chaos. This was a sickening sight, the result of pilot error and a needless waste of men and machines. Because our runway was out of commission we operated the next day from Souk el Arba. On the morning show I finally got airborne after four attempts to take off failed because my boost aneroid had stuck, preventing the engine from developing enough power to lift the machine off the runway. Finally it worked, but I had to scramble to catch up with the squadron.

We were escorting Fortresses to bomb Tunis harbor, and when near the target, Hagger, who was leading the squadron, saw several 190s. With his number 2, he dived after them, eventually destroying an Fw 190.

We did not see this action, nor did Hagger return to the squadron that day. After a few minutes as we maintained our protective station, I took over leading the squadron for the very first time. Some of the others did not appreciate a very green sprog leading them, and so we soon assumed a formation of five units of two aircraft, each flying line abreast, which was actually an extremely good offensive and defensive formation. We provided such good cover that the next morning we received a congratulatory telegram from the American headquarters saying, "We want to thank the Spitfire IXs for the excellent cover provided us — not one of the Fortresses was attacked."

As I write this I have to chuckle at the effort we expended to protect from twelve to twenty of our big friends. Only a year later I would look in awe at formations of nearly one thousand aircraft streaming across the English Channel to attack enemy positions in Europe. In many respects our African war was a sort of backwater affair provided with just enough men and equipment to defeat the enemy but with little surplus to help speed up the ultimate victory.

April 13 was another day of exciting action. In the morning

we were high cover to 154 Squadron on a sweep of the Enfidaville area where we were at 25,000 feet with fluffy broken cloud layering at 7,000 feet. The flak was heavy and accurate enough to cause us to worry about being hit. Over the target we saw five Me 109s slightly below and off to the side, tempting us to give chase. Twenty-four Spitfires started to dive on five terrifed Huns, who tried to escape under full power. With our height advantage they realized that they had no chance to escape by fleeing and so the two on the port side broke up and back, firing as we met head on. Paul Hagger and I turned to chase them while the remaining twenty-two Spits chased after the other three 109s.

Paul and I were just catching up to the two, he on the port and I on the starboard Hun when we had to break — three more 109s came diving out of nowhere, guns blazing. It was fascinating to watch them coming at us with their guns pouring fire. It was easy to shake them, however, and as they went past, we turned and dived behind them. They were tempting targets, but we had to break port again as another three 109s came diving at us, guns smoking. These stayed to fight and in the whirling about as each side struggled for an advantage, I found great satisfaction in somehow avoiding all the bullets. Eventually they gave up and dived away, with our machines in hot pursuit, but they were able to disappear in the lower cloud cover before we could catch them. As we ducked in and out of cloud, I thought of the Jerries diving at us time and again with guns firing and smoke streaking over the engine cowlings, and of their pure white propellor spinners and wing tips and particularly of the great black crosses on their sides. I always chewed gum while flying and discovered that, although my body was soaked in perspiration, my mouth was completely dry with the gum sticking to the roof of my mouth, my gums, and my teeth, quite difficult to remove. The struggle to stay alive during a dogfight demanded all of one's skill and concentration, sometimes producing unexpected physical reactions, such as, in my case, a bone-dry mouth. Once back at base we learned that Maguire and Rigby had each destroyed a 109.

During the early evening while our flight was sitting at the end of the runway at immediate readiness, Chuka controller ordered us off to search for twenty plus enemy bandits believed to be in our area. Our aircraft camouflaging was designed to blend in with the ground colors when viewed from above with the undersides colored a light blue intended to blend in with normal sky coloring. Both our aircraft and the Germans used the same coloring scheme, which was even more effective in the poor evening light than during the bright sunshine of the day. We had to be doubly alert to spot the enemy in order to attack or, if the tables were reversed, to escape. The hawkeye vision of Gray soon spotted a gaggle of Me 109s ahead and above and with a "Tallyho, buster!" he gave chase. As we followed, Hagger spotted three more 109s diving on us, and he and I turned to meet them head on. As the Germans streaked by, we wheeled about to get on their tails to give chase. After only a few seconds another group dived on us, and once again, we broke to meet them head on. Both sides fired but the terrific closing speeds allowed for only a second of firing time, and there were no apparent hits. Our targets went by us so fast that we knew there was no possibility of turning to catch them. Meanwhile Squadron Leader Gray was radioing for help as his four aircraft were scrapping with a dozen of the enemy. We hadn't the foggiest idea where he was and so could not be of assistance. Three more 109s whizzed by pursued by several Spit Vs, which had no chance to catch the much swifter enemy. It was time to head for safety and shortly after we made it back, Gray and his flight landed undamaged, all happy that darkness meant there would be no more flying. We could now proceed to our camp and supper.

Winco Berry normally led the wing flying his own Spitfire VB, but when he heard that some new IXs with the super Merlin 63 engine had arrived at Montesquieu, he asked that I go and pick him a machine for his own personal use, saying, "It had better be a good one!" For some reason I got railroaded a number of times on a similar mission, reflecting, I suppose, faith in my ability to distinguish good from bad performers. I found that new Spit to be such a pleasure to fly that I showed off its ability by beating up the airfield before turning it over to Berry with the comment "It's a really hot kite."

That afternoon we scrambled after fifty plus bandits, and it was one of the few times when my radio failed. We tangled with twenty Me 109s and after a short but fierce fight, I spotted several Huns below me just inviting an attack. Byford, my number 2, did not see them though, and without a radio, I declined to leave the safety of our squadron numbers. Another lost opportunity. Although we were obviously gaining better control of the fighting in the skies, the enemy was continuing to fight brilliantly and valiantly.

On April 17, fifty 109s and 190s bombed and strafed Paddington, with considerable success. Our ack-ack fellows got one, but our patrol fighters ended up with nothing.

Not all of our offensive actions were well planned or expertly executed. On the same day that we were attacked on the ground by strong German fighter formations, we received a panic signal as the last of them disappeared over the surrounding hills. Install ninety-gallon long-range fuel tanks! We in our IXs and 72 Squadron, which had recently received Spit IXs, were to be jumper aircraft with two squadrons of Spit Vs acting as our top cover. Our task was to patrol the Gulf of Tunis until we saw a large number of lumbering Ju 52 transports, then attack. To assist would be some seventy-five P-38 Lightnings patrolling north of us and a further one hundred fighters from the Eighth Army patrolling to the south.

We stooged around for one quick orbit, dropped our tanks, and headed for home flat out, each landing with over fifty gallons of fuel remaining. I could never understand why we retreated so rapidly when we could have remained in position for nearly an hour. It seemed to be a sad waste of fuel and effort, and I was to experience similar disappointments in the future.

My only answer, then and now, was that Winco Berry, our leader, was becoming operationally exhausted. Wonderful fellow that he was, he could see the end of the campaign and the fighting. He knew that at the conclusion of hostilities in Africa, he would be sent home to Blighty for a rest, a reward well deserved, and I believe that other pilots in comparative circumstances might well act in a similar vein. I would never question Berry's integrity, honor, or bravery. Certainly his performance was always exemplary and his ability as a pilot and a fighter is proven by the more than seventeen enemy aircraft destroyed he was credited with by the end of the Tunisian campaign. My thesis is that at times even the very best leaders must succumb to the pressures and responsibilities of combat flying and make decisions that, while rational, might not be in the best tradition of fighting airmen. My affection and admiration for Razz did not diminish. I was just confused and annoyed that we did not stick around longer when we appeared to have so much in our favor.

During the morning of April 18, seven of us with Gray leading were acting as top cover to a Squadron of Vs on a tac/r (tactical reconnaisance). My number 2 had failed to join up because of engine trouble, allowing me to form up on our leader as his number 3. We were forced to fly through intense and extremely accurate flak during the whole trip, which was both disconcerting and frightening, and five Me 109s had been shadowing us for some time when Gray decided to attend to them. When he turned to attack the 109s turned tail, and we took off in hot pursuit. Gray got one in his sight, firing all his guns with heavy strikes being seen in the cockpit area. I was chasing another, but when Gray broke off his attack, I unthinkingly broke off mine to follow him. I felt chagrined at my mistake, particularly since I was sure my target was unaware of my presence behind him and just out of range. We turned for home feeling we had had enough with thirty or forty other enemy fighters reported in our immediate vicinity.

Soon after landing a number of 109s dive-bombed our sister 'drome, Victoria, hitting a few kites on the ground and managing to escape unharmed. After the ground crews and pilots had emerged from the trenches, scattering about the field examining the damage and doing things that should be done after a bombing raid, another large gaggle of Fw 190s came in and really pasted the airfield. Twelve of our aircraft were destroyed and a number of airmen killed and wounded. None of the Jerries was hit by our flak guns, although two were shot down by our squadrons, which happened to be airborne at the time. At night the enemy returned with his bombers and caused another mess on the field. It had been a busy day!

The next day the CO, in his no-nonsense briefing, described the fighting situation: "We outnumber the Germans on the ground two to one and in the air five to one. We must clear the enemy out of Africa if there is to be a front in Europe this year. For the next three days we are to take part in a huge air offensive in an effort to knock every bloody Jerry fighter out of the sky. We are to concentrate on attacking airfields, supply depots, and motor transport vehicles. Our squadron will play an important role since we will be free-lancing inside the enemy lines. The brass thinks the Germans are going to hold Tunisia to the very last man in an effort to delay a European offensive. Therefore our business should pick up and undoubtedly the flak will increase in intensity. It should be an exciting and rewarding few days. That's all.''

The weather was warm and sunny, providing unlimited visibility. The countryside behind the enemy lines looked peaceful and attractive, bathed in a golden sunshine which contrasted sharply with the vivid blue of the Mediterranean. There were few enemy aircraft about, and we dared to fly in single squadron formations where only a few days earlier we required greater numbers. We felt quite competent to meet any challenge that the enemy could mount.

I will always remember the 23rd of April. In the morning Babe and Maquire each shot down a 109. Gray was on the tail of another, about 150 yards behind, when Jenkins, a new man on the squadron, popped up in Gray's sight just at the moment Gray pressed his gun button. One cannon shell hit the 109 and two hit Jenkins before Gray could release the firing button. Jenkins came home with a couple of huge holes in his wings, feeling very sheepish and ashamed. He had denied Gray another confirmed 109. Gray was livid. I could understand his frustration.

In the afternoon we did another free-lance sweep. I flew as yellow 3 with Sergeant Caldicott as my number 2. Just east of Mateur we sighted a gaggle of 109s some 10,000 feet below. Down we dived, but for some reason I wasn't going as fast as the others, so our Spits passed me quite easily. I saw a 109 just below heading in the opposite direction, and I was able to half-roll to get on his tail, losing Caldicott in the maneuver. I opened fire at 400 yards, rapidly closing to 150, without observing any strikes. Either he saw me or I hit him because he opened the throttle, emitting black smoke, and rolled onto his back. I followed, expecting him to dive away, but instead he rolled out and started a gentle climbing turn to port. I guess he thought he had lost me, but I fooled him as I followed his tactic, pressed the gun button to give him a three-second burst, and made a number of strikes in and about the cockpit. The 109 started to pour heavier black smoke as it rolled slowly onto its back. During this chase my head was constantly swivelling to make sure that no enemy was making me a target, and suddenly I saw a 109 diving toward my tail with guns smoking and tracers just missing my port wing. I yanked back hard on the control column, successfully losing both my target and my pursuer. I was certain that I had destroyed the enemy by killing the pilot; he could not have survived the cannon blows to the cockpit. But since I could not confirm anything more than what I had seen to that point, I was only granted a damaged Hun. Better luck next time! It was an indescribable thrill to actually believe I had an enemy in my sights who could not escape. My eagerness and excitement foiled me from shooting more accurately when in fact I should have blown my victim out of the sky.

Flying at high altitude increased our confidence in one respect: as we were always aware of the limits of German-held territory, we knew in the event of a forced landing exactly how far we'd have to travel to safety. Artillery fire from both sides clearly outlined the ground positions with gun flashes and exploding shells raising clouds of dust and smoke. We knew from our intelligence reports that the ground fighting was fierce and difficult, and it was strange to be able to fight in the air while watching a very different kind of battle going on far below.

In the early afternoon of April 26 we made a squadron sweep of the Medjez area with Berry leading and me flying yellow two behind Hagger. Just as we got to altitude at 20,000 feet, I spotted some 109s below, almost on the deck. I called the winco, who immediately ordered a "Tallyho," and we dived down to attack. The Huns, ten of them, split up and Hagger chose two who were heading east toward Tunis. He selected the one on the left, leaving me the remaining 109. We caught up to them rapidly because of the speed gained in our long dive, and just as we closed in,

Hagger's target broke away up and over my head while mine continued straight ahead. I opened fire at 250 yards, closing to 150 yards, with no strikes observed although black smoke started to pour from his engine. He turned ninety degrees to starboard while I continued to depress the gun button. He straightened up and started a gentle turn to port. I fired again closing to less than one hundred yards. Black smoke continued to pour out of his engine, and I observed a number of cannon strikes in the port wing root. He rolled slowly onto his back as I was forced to break away.

I left him below 2,000 feet but was unable to watch further as 109s, prepared to fight appeared from nowhere. Someone yelled, "Look out, Olmsted, 109 on your tail. Break, break, break." I twisted my head frantically from side to side, but couldn't see a thing. With a wide open throttle I climbed in tight circles to 11,000 feet. The sky was suddenly empty. Not an aircraft in sight! With great determination I headed for home, flat out and weaving like mad. Everyone went home separately after the fight and all landed safely. In the action, Hagger had got a probable, and the winco, Cronin, and I each had got a damaged. I felt certain my 109 had gone straight in, but not having seen that happen, I could only claim a damaged.

Life in a squadron of mixed nationalities was always stimulating and interesting, especially when we talked about our countries and discussed what we intended to do with our lives after the war. I don't recall there ever being a fight or a strong difference of opinion, although each man was fiercely loyal to his nation and proudly wore the shoulder flashes which denoted his country of origin. Tent living was invigorating, encouraging a great degree of cooperation and mutual assistance as we struggled to make the best of our primitive living conditions and the monotonous diet of canned foods.

We drank liquor in more than moderate quantities, usually in small groups meeting in someone's tent because the large mess tent became cold and uncomfortable after dark when a piercing cold supplanted the daytime warmth. Squadron Leader Gray seemed to be everywhere, never tiring, and we welcomed his ready wit and caustic remarks. He led by example with no formal lectures or instructions on how to improve our flying skills, shooting accuracy, or general squadron discipline in the air or on the ground. I believe we held him in such awe, for Gray was already a sort of legendary figure and acknowledged one of the deadliest shots in the Royal Air Force, that we failed to press him for answers to our questions and doubts.

This was a shame because most of us could have used some assistance. The prime requirement for a fighter pilot was to be a good enough pilot to master the aircraft at all times under every conceivable condition. This also meant that a pilot should be able to get close to his target, the closer the better, but unfortunately most of us pilots misjudged range or were unable to get in close enough to be effective. The next essential was to be a good shot, and here again most of us fell well short of the mark. I don't believe we fully understood the principles of air firing, such as range estimation, speed, and deflection, and we had no opportunity to practice air firing except in actual air combat. We frequently discussed markmanship, pondering how to be more effective, but without the opportunity to concentrate on practice firing, our level of achievement was low and only improved gradually as we became more experienced in combat.

When I was first learning to fly Spitfires at Rednal Operational Training Unit, I had practiced air firing on five separate occasions, which was probably typical for the training of a fighter pilot. It may have been adequate for a natural marksman, but for the vast bulk of us, more instruction and practice would have been extremely useful. It was one thing to fire at a passive drogue towed by a slow-moving aircraft flying straight and level and quite another to fire at a nimble fighter aircraft while keeping a sharp lookout to avoid being a target yourself. The firing time for our guns during an attack would be just a few seconds, during which time a pilot had to line up his target, assess the speed accurately, decide on the range, determine the amount of deflection to allow, ensure that his own aircraft was flying true with no slipping or skidding, and still keeping a lookout encompassing a large segment of the sky. Then the pilot could depress the gun button while keeping the ringsight properly aligned relative to the target. The amount of concentration required combined with great flying skill placed a demand on the pilots that only a few met, although we all tried our best. My personal marksmanship was poor, improving slowly as I gained operational experience, but it only became adequate months later when I was privileged to take a special gunnery course at the Central Gunnery School in England.

Eyesight was another important ingredient for success and here we all did very well because constant practice taught us very quickly what to look for and where to search for the enemy. We spent only split seconds looking in any one direction while our heads twisted from side to side scanning the skies. Often just a slight glint in the distant sky would betray an aircraft as the sun's rays bounced off a coupe top, yet the aircraft itself would be beyond our eyesight range. I always believed that good eyesight allowed a pilot to see the enemy, and then he could decide whether to attack or escape as the circumstances might dictate. We knew that the enemy who would shoot us down would be the one we did not see, for the Germans were experts at using surprise and cover from clouds or the sun to great advantage.

The German formations generally appeared to be disorganized — we termed them "gaggles" — as opposed to our more formalized and rigid fighting formations. When attacked the Germans held small formations together much longer than we did, and when they broke up into individual planes, their evasive action was often unimaginative, making them easier targets. On the other hand some of the enemy fighter pilots were superb, well able to take on any Allied pilot. A favorite enemy tactic was to fly two or three decoy aircraft, guarded by a much larger formation flying higher and behind, ready to pounce on our aircraft should they attack the decoys. On the whole I judged our pilots to be more aggressive, willing to stay and fight much more readily than the Jerries, and I found no reason to change this opinion even though the tactical situation at a given time might strongly favor the enemy. I never lost my respect for the German fighter pilot, but except for a few combats, I usually felt that I had a given engagement within my control.

CHAPTER 6

VICTORY

May, 1943

By the beginning of May we knew that the struggle for North Africa was nearly over. From the air we could see the total battlefield in one glance, from north to south and east to west, with its boundaries clearly marked by the smoke from artillery fire. We heard there was to be a lull in the fighting for about a week to wait for the Eighth Army to crack the German defenders along the Enfidaville Line. On the western front the Americans and the First Army were advancing slowly, suffering terrible losses in hand-to-hand fighting with no quarter asked for or given. Meanwhile the bombers were keeping an increased pressure on German strong points — supply depots, troop concentrations, and airfields. The air seemed to be filled with our aircraft, making it difficult to understand how the stubborn enemy could continue to resist.

With our squadron activity becoming rather routine and uneventful, we pilots sought new entertainment. One day Fenwick, Husband, and I were given two days off, allowing us enough time to visit Tabarka and Tubby Dresden's Rest Camp. Our trip by truck along mountainous roads was scenic, accompanied by the usual hazards and difficulties caused by steep, narrow twisting roads that have no guard rails to prevent careless drivers from plunging down deep gorges and sheer cliffs.

Tabarka, a small seaside village which had been nearly totally demolished by the retreating enemy, had a beach that was some fifteen miles long and extended several miles inland. It was pure golden sand with no trees or rocks to mar its symmetry. Tabarka was the site of a very large American hospital, and in double-quick time we all obtained dates with American nurses, who became our holiday companions. While we swam and frolicked, several thousand naked patients also played nearby. The enormous variety of nude men did not bother the nurses, but it was somewhat disconcerting to us three escorts. We dined with the nurses each evening in their mess tent and at 6:30 they left us — they were all on night duty. Nevertheless we felt this was one of the most refreshing and rewarding rests we had experienced since leaving Canada.

On returning to base we learned that the final push was to begin on the morrow, May 6. By 10:00 that morning the advancing armies were an hour ahead of schedule. Every objective had been taken, and the advance units had to slow down to allow the flanks to catch up. Fierce resistance was encountered everywhere, but the Germans could not withstand our overwhelming military superiority. The army boasted that they could not have been in Tunis that night, but it was not until ten o'clock the next morning that our troops were officially reported in Tunis, thus dividing the enemy forces in two. In the late afternoon Bizerte fell. The noose was drawing tighter. The Germans were doomed, and they knew it, but still they fought on like tigers. From then on it was push, push, push for our armies as they forced the enemy into the confines of the Cap Bon peninsula. In the La Sebala area they hung on for another few days only to be wiped out eventually. Finally the enemy in Cap Bon was all ours — few escaped. There were some remnants in the Enfidaville area, totally surrounded yet fighting on valiantly. Realizing the hopelessness of their positions, they surrendered, and it was here that General von Arnim was taken prisoner.

Our job during this period was to fly free-lance patrols. For the first two days we met the odd enemy fighter, but after that our only concern was flak, which was still heavy and accurate. We flew over Tunis and other places at 10,000 feet when a week ago we had flown over these same locations at 25,000 feet. How quickly positions can be reversed! We did some strafing and beating up of shipping, parked aircraft, and transports and troops, but this was soon stopped because our troops were moving forward so rapidly that it was difficult to determine the identity of a potential target accurately. Often we went out with the latest bomb lines marked on our maps and would return to find that the line had moved well beyond anything we thought possible, all in only one hour. To my knowledge we never made the mistake of attacking our own forces, but this was probably due as much to good luck as to good management.

On May 13, the day the African campaign officially ended, we moved to La Sebala airdrome, some seven miles north and west of Tunis. It was from here, only five days before, while flying at 15,000 feet I had watched twenty Me 109s take off to fight us. It was an excellent airdrome, wide and flat, completely grass-covered with no litter or useless material left lying around. Unlike the British, the Germans seemed to be tidy and orderly.

To observe the victory we decided to celebrate with a drinking party. A number of pilots were dispatched in various directions with four-gallon tins in hand and orders to return only when each container was filled with wine. Several hours later we assembled to drink and revel. The hours passed, and we drank and drank, but nothing happened. It was as though the date wine we'd found was water. Eventually, thoroughly disgusted, we retired to our canvas beds, quite sober. By morning we were all roaring drunk — the slow-acting wine finally revealed its potency — and drunk we stayed all day. Despite considerable tippling experience since that time, I have yet to find another drink as slow-acting yet as potent as that Tunisian date wine.

Some ten burned out Ju 52 transports lay broken and crippled at the edges of the field and several 109s stood intact and untouched in their bays hidden in the orange groves at the south edge of the 'drome. But we dared not touch any wire, tool, gun, or anything else which struck our fancy, since most were rigged with explosives set to go off at the slightest touch of an unwary scrounger. Often the most innocent-appearing object would be wired to explosives which successfully blasted an unsuspecting souvenir hunter to bits. The enemy could be extremely cunning and diabolical and proved his ingenuity in innumerable gruesome ways.

During the next three weeks we were to move to Utique airfield, then to Prottville, and finally to La Marsa. All had been well-established enemy operational fields, which minimized the amount of work we had to do to make them suitable for our own operations. This gave us sufficient free time to enjoy the after-math of victory, and individually and in groups we took off in every direction to explore, to enjoy, and in particular, to acquire souvenirs and mementos.

We found seventeen broken and battered 109s on one 'drome, full of bullet holes acquired in combat. We rejoiced to see the once-proud Ace of Spades crest laying shattered in the Tunisian dust. Later on I was to meet this top-scoring German fighter group again in France.

As we wandered about the country, we saw many strange sights, including German and Italian prisoners driving themselves in their own military trucks to our prison compounds. Sometimes a truckload would be guarded by one lonely Tommy sitting in the rear, rubbing shoulders with the prisoners in the overloaded vehicle. Generally, however, there were no guards. I watched Italian prisoners proceeding by truck or on foot to our hastily constructed prison camps. Their uniforms appeared to be neat and clean, and the Italians smiled pleasantly at us whenever we stared. They were a happy bunch! The German prisoners — the pride of the Afrika Korps — seemed to be young, tall, fair-haired and powerfully built. They laughed and joked amongst themselves, while with us they were arrogant or sullen. We were to understand that they regarded their defeat as only a passing misfortune and that they would somehow soon be rescued by Adolf to fight again. From a physical standpoint these men were marvelous specimens. Little wonder they were able to put up such a long, desperate struggle.

We roamed from Tunis to Bizerte and back again. On every hand lay devastated and hastily abandoned German equipment. We examined half-tracks, Tiger tanks, and the deadly 88 millimeter gun. We searched supply dumps, army stores, and discarded equipment. In a few days we were well stocked with souvenirs and trivial loot. The more fancied possessions included Mauser rifles, cap badges, flags, Luger pistols, and German manuscripts. A few managed to get hold of cars or motorcycles and particularly prized was the Volkeswagen, a superb little machine not unlike our Jeep. With wheels we were able to roam much further afield, far more quickly.

I visited Grombalia, formerly a supply and storage depot and a last center of German resistance, some thirty-five miles south of Tunis. The approach to the town was littered with the carcasses of horses and German soldiers, and surrounded by hordes of flies and in the intense heat, the stench of decaying flesh was overwhelming. The distinctive smell of German equipment, created by the paint or preservative used to color the various objects, added to the unpleasantness. By following this distinctive stink, however, we were able to locate souvenirs which we might otherwise have missed.

Tunis proved to be a lovely city, with wide streets and tree-lined boulevards. We shopped in quaint and well-stocked stores; we drank wine and champagne in the cabarets; we visited the docks and the harborfront which we had flown over so often, escorting bombers on dock- and ship-destroying missions. That our bombers had succeeded in destroying a lot of shipping was evident from the masts, funnels, and even keels protruding above the water. Yet, even though much of the harbor borders the city proper, very few bombs had gone astray. The city lay virtually untouched while the docks were obliterated, a vivid display of the effectiveness of precision bombing.

Our final Tunisian move to La Marsa allowed us to pitch our tents on an enormous expanse of sand some fifty yards from the Mediterranean. Each day we roamed the shore clad only in shorts and sneakers, which were discarded when the water, so warm that it ceased to be refreshing, beckoned. Bodies became tanned. Happiness, health, and laughter pervaded as we revelled in our freedom. The ancient Phoenician stronghold of Carthage was a mile away and we searched through the amphitheater, the temple of Apollo, and the forum. Little Arab boys followed our explorations eagerly, hawking coins and bits of pottery or mosaic work which they claimed to have discovered recently in the ruins.

The white buildings of La Marsa, glistening in the brilliant sunshine, the vivid coloring of the mountains, the brilliant blue of the sea and the sky, and the sense of being in the midst of ancient history filled our hearts and minds with peace. We almost forgot that a war was still being waged and that shortly our rest period would be terminated.

During March and April, 81 Squadron had operated with spectacular success. In those two months we had destroyed twenty-three enemy aircraft in the air, probably destroyed twelve, and damaged a further fifteen. This impressive tally was reached with the loss of four pilots and about a dozen aircraft. Our opponents were JG 53 or the Ace of Spades Jagdgeschwaders (a JG consisted of up to six squadrons) flying the latest marks of Mé 109s along with JG 51, flying yellow-nosed 109s, and JG 2 flying the deadly Fw 190s. These units were mainly based on the permanent all-weather airdromes around Tunis and Bizerte and the enemy pilots were among the most experienced and aggressive in the entire Luftwaffe. More than three dozen had scores of 50 to 150 victories apiece and many more had very creditable scores with the decorations to certify their success.

We had operated under much worse ground conditions than the Germans, frequently unable to fly because our airfields were under water, resembling lakes more than flying strips. Our living conditions were generally much worse, and certainly our communications and warning systems were far inferior. The Germans could also use the several main paved highways as additional or emergency landing strips while our roads would be so deep in mud that Jeeps and even huge Thorneycraft trucks would become mired and immobile. On wet days we could spend two hours fighting the mud to travel the two miles from our camp to the airfield.

We had tremendous respect and admiration for our comrades, both flying personnel and groundcrew. The airmen who kept our machines flying earned our special respect and, in turn, we won their admiration. To me, my aircraft mechanics were always remarkable men, whom I trusted implicitly, knowing that they would not certify my aircraft as airworthy unless they were absolutely convinced it was in top condition. They frequently worked around the clock, in the open air, under every conceivable weather condition. They endured bombing raids and ground strafing attacks, suffering casualties when caught in the open, unable to reach the safety of a slit trench. We had no hangars and frequent shortages of spare parts forced them to devise ingenious substitutes. They had little opportunity to rest or take a holiday break since our aircraft flew every day and had to be ready at all times for instant action. They were a happy lot, usually cocky, who loved to grouse about anything and everything although that never seemed to interfere with their dedication to quality work. Their commitment and efficiency under all conditions, and in all theaters of war where I was engaged, were complete and uniform. Without them we pilots would have been helpless.

Until early April, Jerry was the aggressor in the air with his fighters, and I thought we were largely on the defensive. Our major offensive action was escorting bombers of all descriptions to harass his vital points. Gradually the enemy became worn down, being denied adequate replacements and supplies, and bending to the relentless pressure of our constantly enlarging air forces. Then we became the aggressor, and as we did, the effectiveness of the enemy faded very quickly. His fighter pilots, however, were almost always audacious and certainly skilled and brave as they battled our ever-increasing numbers.

In the RAF and the Commonwealth air forces, it was customary to send a pilot to a rest period after he had finished an operation tour, with a tour consisting of approximatly two hundred hours' flying under combat or hazardous conditions. The rest periods lasted from a few to many months or, in some cases, for the balance of hostilities.

The Germans, on the other hand, remained operationally active for extremely long periods, sometimes years, with only short breaks for rest and relaxation or to allow battle wounds to heal. Many of our opponents had flown more or less constantly since the Battle of Britain — in Western Europe, on the Russian front, and even in the Western Desert. The result was that the average German fighter pilot had many more hours and sorties than his RAF counterpart. This additional flying time enabled a Jerry pilot to become an extremely efficient fighter, a good shot with many more opportunities to hone and practice his skills than our pilots. I know of many occasions when one of our extremely good pilots has been outfought by a German flying a supposedly inferior aircraft.

My constant wish throughout my Middle East tour was to fly

as often as possible, much more than I actually did. I knew that only through experience and frequent contact with the enemy would my skills as a fighter pilot, specifically my shooting eye, improve. I flew a lot, but not nearly as much as I would have preferred.

On reflection I realize that my experience with 81 Squadron and the lessons I learned so well from our leaders helped me immeasurably to survive my wartime adventures and without my flying background of over one thousand hours when I started with the squadron, the story might also have been very different.

While we rested and waited to be assigned to new operational duties, we reviewed the past and speculated on our move. We felt that nothing in the future could be as difficult as what we had experienced so far. (How wrong was that opinion!) The results of the victory were jubilantly recorded in the reams of reports, reviews, and assessments which arrived from various military sources, with rather revealing conclusions in many cases.

Our 322 Wing was the top-scoring wing during the North African campaign, which was understandable because of our outstanding leadership. In the later stages the character of the ground fighting changed significantly from night attacks to advances during daylight when our air force could clear a path through enemy positions by non-stop bombing and strafing sorties. Our bombing patterns would advance slowly, almost yard by yard, forcing the enemy survivors to huddle in head-down positions, only to be surprised and overwhelmed by our troops advancing behind the shelter of the bombing. It seems that a soldier largely ignores shellfire since nothing can be done about where the next shell will land. On the other hand they can see aircraft, judge where they are going to attack, and so take appropriate cover, which naturally reduces their battle effectiveness. There is no question that the effective use of our total air supremacy hastened the campaign's end, saving many Allied lives. The Germans would admit later that they could not fight against the tremendous concentrations of aircraft that we could bring to bear when and where needed, protecting our troops and permitting the army to exploit every situation to maximum effect. Our enormous superiority in air power can take much of the credit for the sudden collapse of the enemy in the Cap Bon peninsula.

Britain had its Dunkirk, but it appeared that the Germans were not prepared to attempt a wholesale evacuation of their trapped troops. This was a cold-blooded sacrifice of some of Germany's best and most experienced divisions, which could have been used to good effect later on, and of great mountains of equipment and supplies which fell into Allied hands. Of course, our side had near complete control of the air and sea routes, which may have deterred the enemy from making a major escape attempt. One group that did appear to have got away was the Luftwaffe. It appeared that they had escaped by air, using every machine capable of flying, regardless of condition, taking their precious groundcrew with them.

Originally, we felt that the Germans, declining evacuation, would fight desperately to the last man. Instead there was a total, swift, and confused collapse, even though the enemy still had excellent equipment and adequate supplies of food and ammunition. The final estimate of the German and Italian losses during the last few weeks of the campaign included the capture of twenty-six Axis generals and up to 290,000 troops. The amount of equipment and supplies captured were equally astounding and must have had some effect on the enemy's fighting ability later when the Allies landed in Italy and shortages of vital supplies hampered the Germans' ability to counterattack.

I can still clearly remember how the reputations of two men, Montgomery and Rommel, influenced our thinking and attitudes. As the war progressed I was to spend nearly all of my flying for or in support of Montgomery and whatever armies he was commanding at any given time. After Africa, Rommel became our opposing general in Europe until he was wounded by a strafing Spitfire on July 17, 1944.

Rommel was brilliant but unpredictable; he seemed to be able to sense and exploit our weak points with regularity and breathtaking speed. Thus, even when we were based miles from the front lines, we occasionally felt insecure wondering whether Rommel might suddenly appear. We actually regarded him with some awe, thoroughly respecting his genius and fighting ability, and his reputation has stood the test of time.

Montgomery was regarded more as a winner and savior. The Eighth Army victory at El Alamein, and the successful pursuit across the desert afterward, was really the first Allied ground victory against the Germans in the war. Montgomery seemed to overwhelm both his enemy and his superiors, insisting on his own requirements of men and equipment, operating under his plans, and brooking little outside interference. When he advanced, we felt that he would not retreat, that his plans and resources were so secure that he was assured of success. And so he established his own aura, which we and the Americans believed in implicitly and relied on. Our dependent attitude was particularly evident during the Salerno landings in Italy, when we anxiously awaited his arrival with the celebrated Eighth Army to relieve a desperate situation. Later I would alter my opinion of him as his inherent sense of caution and well-known streak of stubbornness seemed to influence his judgment and his ability to exploit an advantageous situation. I would blame him for allowing such huge numbers of Germans to escape at Falaise in France, and in partiuclar, condemn him for the ill-judged and disastrous Arnhem airborne operation, "Market-Garden," with its tragic losses. But in the next few months following the African victory, Montgomery was our star and as long as he was with us, he certainly inspired confidence and a winning attitude.

Our final African holiday came to an end as we became bored with our leisure and what small pleasures we had, such as reading, writing letters, swimming, and eating our monotonous fare of canned food. Everything we ate came from cans, although I give our cooks full credit for sometimes producing mysterious dishes neither easily identifiable nor always edible. We had no fresh meat or vegetables, and we only dared to eat thick-skinned fruit such as oranges or canteloupe which could be scoured before eating. Disease was all around us, and we were constantly lectured on the precautions required to avoid contamination. However, living and eating in the outdoors produced healthy appetites, which allowed our young bodies to remain active and vigorous, and we were incredibly healthy.

CHAPTER 7

ON TO FABLED MALTA
June, 1943—July, 1943

In the midst of our recess from combat flying, great changes were taking place within our squadron, our wing, and indeed, all of the other wings as well. Tour-expired pilots were posted for rest periods to return eventually to England with new pilots arriving as replacements from Cairo and Algiers. Wing Commander Berry returned to England and his position was filled by Gray, who was deservedly promoted to wing commander, flying. Much to our relief Group Captain Hugo remained as our senior officer.

For me came the excitement of promotion to the rank of flight lieutenant and a posting in charge of A Flight in 232 RAF Squadron. My best friend Peppler was also promoted and assigned to lead B Flight. Our new squadron commander was recently promoted Squadron Leader C.I.R. "Duke" Arthur,[10] a Canadian pilot with wide experience who had flown during the Battle of Britain and later served in 242 Squadron with the legendary, legless ace Douglas Bader and with Stan Turner, another distinguished Canadian pilot. Actually Pep and Duke had previously known each other while growing up in Winnipeg.

Duke was an extremely interesting Canadian who had left his homeland as a youngster in 1938 to join the RAF in England. A bit less than six feet tall, well built, and extremely good looking, he sported a typical full RAF style mustache. His dark eyes crinkled with laughter, which came easily, and gave one a clue as to his happy and carefree nature. He always appeared competent but with a quiet air which I soon learned to appreciate and which made me realize that I had once again "lucked in" with a very capable squadron commander.

For all his experience, he had faced the travails suffered by

95

so many very excellent fighter pilots in not having achieved a high score of enemy aircraft destroyed during his many operational flying hours. This did not detract from his fine leadership qualities nor did it lessen my enthusiasm in having such a highly regarded man as my new commanding officer. There were many fine fighter pilots with a great number of operational hours, but who, through bad luck, misfortune, or lack of opportunity, were unable to ring up respectable scores of enemy aircraft destroyed.

232 Squadron had been formed during the Battle of Britain, and was sent to the Far East in late 1941 to help with the defense of Singapore, flying Hurricanes. After losing nearly all its pilots and aircraft, the remnants escaped to Sumatra where they were absorbed in another squadron. 232 was disbanded only to be reformed again in mid-1942 to fly Spitfires over Europe. It then became one of the first squadrons to take part in the invasion of North Africa, flying Spitfires bearing the identification letters *EF*. When the squadron was reorganized once again after the fall of Tunis, we became a sort of half-breed outfit in the sense that we were to fly Spit Vs and IXs in equal numbers. I don't know of any other squadrons with this unusual mix of aircraft, and although it did make sense, it also indicated that there were not enough Spit IXs to service the needs of all the squadrons fighting in the Middle East. I had more than a suspicion that squadrons operating from England close to the manufacturing source would not be handicapped by such an unusual combination of different types of fighter aircraft.

When Pep and I reported to Duke for the first time, Duke looked me in the eye saying, "Olmsted, I'm going to lead the squadron flying with the Vs and you will lead the IXs, always acting as my top cover. You got that?" "Yes, sir," I replied.

Duke also indicated that while he would lead the squadron and attend to all the usual administrative details, he had a new and novel approach to the operation of the squadron. Pep, Duke, and I agreed that I would be responsible for all aspects of flying, flight details, and in general everything related to flying, whether training or operational. Pep was to be in charge of the total ground operation, including the welfare of all our ground-crew, the maintenance of aircraft, living and messing arrange-

My constant dream was to fly Spitfires. Here a Spitfire V taxies at Milazzo East — note dust created by propeller wash.

Harvard training aircraft.

Some of the Guard-duty gang at Portage La Prairie — October 1940.
Front row — Beaton, Wilbey, Stanley, MacRae, Olmsted, Houle, Price.
Back row — MacLean, Woodhill, Anderson, Washburn, Laubman, Barton,
*Rowe, **Ja**mieson, Pennock, Studen, Aquin, Chabut, Turner, Morin, Percival,*
Wakeling.

Crashed Bolingbroke typical of damage resulting from engine failure at
Jarvis — July, 1942.

Fairy Battle — Jarvis, 1942.

Bolingbroke Mk. IV — Jarvis, 1942.

Africa, March, 1943. Group Captain P.H. "Dutch" Hugo.

Tingley, Africa, February, 1943. Wing Commander Ronald "Razz" Berry.

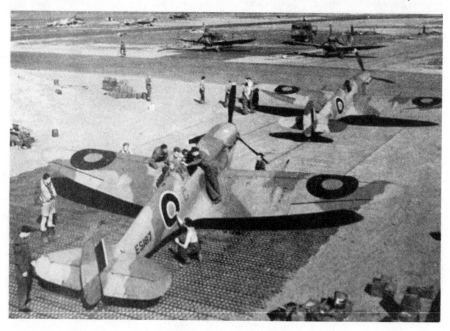

February, 1943. Some Spit V's on readiness at Tingley.

April, 1943. Paddington. Air Vice Marshal Curtis visits Canadians Olmsted and "Babe" Fenwick who has just shot down his sixth enemy.

Paddington Airfield, April, 1943. Gray describing how he just shot down his 21st kill. Olmsted, Hagger (back to camera), Gray, Tasto, and Young.

At Paddington, April, 1943.
Hagger, Gray, Olmsted,
Gobey, Young. Back row
— Tasto, and Pratt, our I.O.

View of Paddington Airfield, April, 1943. Note mesh tracking and surrounding
mountains.

Lunchtime in our Paddington dispersal. Gray, S/L Gus Carlson hamming it
up, and Hagger.

Fueling our aircraft by hand — Paddington — It was ever thus.

Paddington, April, 1943. Gray digging slit trench before breakfast. Urged on by other pilots on readiness.

Testing an aircraft engine with groundcrew holding tail down.

Our captured Me 109. Note distinctive spinner coloring and "Ace of Spades" insignia. Africa.

ments and in general the comfort of every man, officer, and pilot in the squadron.

This was an enormous job but one for which Pep was ideally suited. A big, six-foot, broad-shouldered, husky man with a shock of dark brown hair and a stringy mustache which never did respond to loving care, he was a twenty-three-year old physical-fitness addict. He drank little, unlike the rest of us, and smoked not at all. Pep had the unique ability to understand and appreciate the people he met immediately and to him everyone was basically good. Beyond that, he loved every living thing, great and small, and would fight for the weak.

I know that there were times when Pep has been on the tail of an enemy, ready to thumb the gunbutton, but he had become so mesmerized by the beauty of the scene, the blue sky, and the aircraft ahead, that his fighter pilot training would succumb to the more human feeling of "live and let live" for a brief second, just long enough for his intended victim to escape. Pep probably had more compassion than any other man I ever met. Even being a prisoner of war for a year and suffering several reverses later in civilian life did not change this outlook. Pep is today the same unusual and effusive man he was then.

We used the first few days of June to prepare the squadron for what we rightly assumed would be a move to Malta, that fabled island so rich in history and the creator of many fighter pilots' reputations. Despite Duke's promise to let me fly the Spit IXs he gave me a VC, labelled *E*, which I was to fly from then on. I had never flown a V before; it was a new experience and a disappointment — the plane was quite inferior in performance to the more powerful IX.

We were ordered to condense our baggage and belongings to what we could carry in our aircraft. The nooks and crannies in the Spitfire could store very little, so this required very careful sorting and selection on our part. Our spare belongings, including blue uniforms, greatcoat, and souvenirs, were packed for storage in a warehouse. I never expected to see my belongings again, and this premonition came true when all our baggage was sunk in Bari harbor many months later.

Our most-wanted baggage was loaded into the ammunition

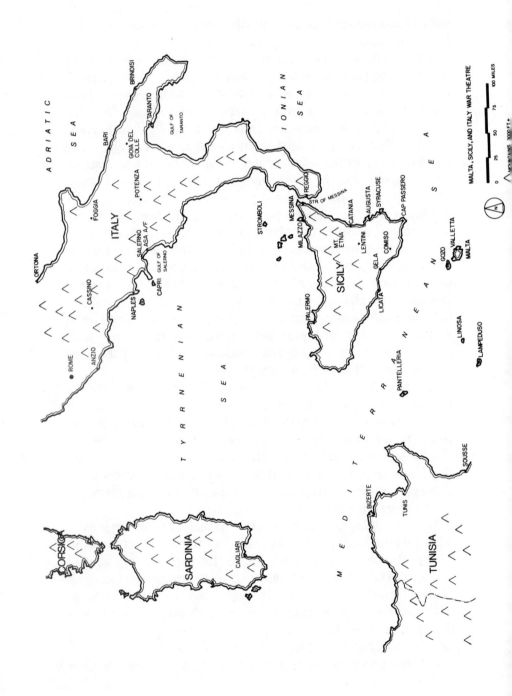

MALTA, SICILY, AND ITALY WAR THEATRE

bays in our wings and with a thirty-gallon jettison gas tank fitted to the belly of each aircraft, we took off for the 1½-hour trip to Malta. We flew on the deck, just skimming the top of the dead-calm sea, maintaining strict R/T silence. We intended to give the heavily fortified Italian island of Pantellaria a wide berth, because our Malta posting was to be kept a secret. Unfortunately Pilot Officer Cam developed a glycol leak followed by an oil leak. Cam struggled to gain altitude as Duke roared over the R/T, "Bail out, bail out, for Christ's sake, Cam. Bail out." Perhaps Cam was too occupied to reply, or perhaps his radio was duff and he never received Duke's orders, for he made no apparent effort to comply. Defying Duke's instructions, he crash-landed on Pantellaria with his aircraft smashing into a hundred pieces. We left him for dead, but later learned that, although badly wounded, he survived to be evacuated by submarine as a prisoner of war.

Since we had breached our supposed stealth instructions, we climbed to a reasonable altitude in the cloudless sky. My first view of the tiny island of Malta is still a vivid memory. Through the mid-morning haze, it looked like a small golden leaf floating on the sea. I thought it looked ridiculously small, measuring roughly seven miles by fourteen miles, and our new airdrome, Takali, stood out as obvious and exposed.

"Gonda control," called Duke, "Tampax squadron requesting landing instructions."

The reply came from Malta control: "Say again."

Duke returned, "Tampax leader requesting landing permission."

Gonda control again asked, "Say again, please. What call sign?"

Duke, now impatient, "Tampax leader."

"Please repeat call sign," intoned Gonda control.

By now Duke was obviously exasperated and certainly still seething over the loss of Cam. He roared into the radio, "Tampax leader. Tampax! Tampax! The stuff you shove up your snatch."

I could visualize the horror, the giggles, and the consternation that must have swept through the operations room. After another delay we finally received a polite and quiet reply instructing us to land at Takali airfield. We had arrived at our new home, landing on a broad, bumpy surface. Army groundcrews quickly assisted in getting us into the protection of large individual brick and stone dispersal pens.

From the airfield we were rushed to an underground intelligence center where Air Marshal Keith Park, who had been Dowding's second in command during the Battle of Britain, waited to welcome us. He briefed us on the past history of Malta, the courage of the defenders, and what the military expected of us.

We started the meeting with either of two emotions. Some of us must have been relieved not to have had to live through the hardships endured by the early defenders. Others, like myself, were envious that we had missed those desperate days when equipment, men, and supplies were so scarce, but there were daily opportunities to dice with the enemy, Italian and German. Air Marshal Park aroused a new emotion as he spoke, and we were delighted to realize that we were to be an important new chapter in Maltese history.

Malta consisted of five small islands with a total land area of just 120 square miles. Malta itself contained 95 square miles of rugged rolling gray rocky ground while Gozo, even rockier, was about 20 square miles. The remaining three outcropings were uninhabited. Being located in the geographic center of the Mediterranean basin, Malta had long been a trading and resting stage for vessels and people from the hugely diverse countries bordering the sea. Its symbols, the Maltese Cross, the Maltese Falcon, and more recently the George Cross were well-known to all of us, and we could only be impressed by the military importance of this tiny country.

The seige of Malta started on June 11, 1940, and continued to the end of 1942, when supply ships got through in sufficient numbers to turn Malta into an offensive weapon. After that, its aircraft patrolled the sea lanes in every direction, harassing or sinking ships intended for Rommel, Malta-based bombers destroyed enemy shipping in harbors as far away as Palermo, Naples, and Taranto, and its photo-reconnaissance planes spied on enemy positions no matter where they were located. From a beseiged fortress Malta changed into a dominant weapon in the Allies' Mediterranean arsenal, able to fill many varied roles. The pilot defenders had come from Britain and the Commonwealth, with fully twenty-five per cent being Canadian, many of whom established enviable reputations. Nearly 1,500 Maltese civilians out of a population of just under 300,000 were killed during the seige and the Royal Air Force lost about six hundred planes and hundreds of pilots killed or wounded. Malta had been down, short, even desperately short, of planes, fuel, ammunition, and food, but it was never out. Now Malta could exact revenge as it steadily increased its striking ability, and we were all proud to be part of whatever drama lay ahead.

I received a pleasant surprise when I walked into our Officers' Mess. After North Africa and the constant danger from snakes, scorpions, centipedes, and tarantula spiders, and our primitive tent living conditions, I could scarcely believe my eyes upon viewing the luxury of our new home in a huge mansion owned by Baron Chapelle. Located in the town of Rabat, it crowned the highest point of land in Malta, some four hundred feet above sea level. A huge balcony fronted the building, facing north toward Sicily some sixty miles away and also commanding a view of the whole island, including the principal cities of Valetta and Sliema. Our airfield lay exposed below with the protective dispersal pens melding with the thick stone walls enclosing the tiny farming fields.

The mess had many attractive features. There was a well-stocked bar, and an enormous and beautifully furnished dining room where pretty Maltese waitresses served our skimpy meals. We had a comfortable lounge complete with radio, magazines, and an always-crowded billiard room. Electric lights, running water, and sheets for our beds were added luxuries. Our only complaint was the scarcity of food, but this we augmented, reluctantly, by buying eggs from civilians at sixty cents each. We had shops, movies, and tailors who mended our clothes and supplied new summer outfits at modest expense. We met the people and marvelled at their language, an unintelligible mixture of Italian and Arabic, a purely Maltese tongue.

The island was riddled with huge tunnels and underground

caverns quarried from the soft gray rock, which were perfectly bombproof and in which the Maltese sheltered during raids. The army had offices in them and also stored ammunition, petrol, and equipment in these enormous rock enclosures, which undoubtedly saved an untold number of lives and permitted the defences to recover quickly after a large enemy air raid.

New squadrons were arriving regularly as the offensive capability of the island increased. Our sister airfields of Luqa, Halfar, Krendi, and Safi were becoming crowded with aircraft of all descriptions. We shared Takali with 81, 152, 154, and 242 RAF Squadrons, and our planes ringed the perimeter of the 'drome. Although Takali was large enough for our small fighters to take off in any direction, because of the hazard of sharp shrapnel pieces damaging our tires, we generally used the nearly mile-long, northwest runway. The army tried valiantly to keep the surface clear of the sharp metal pieces, but new debris appeared almost as rapidly as it was removed.

Everything about our 'drome gave mute testimony to the many fierce attacks of the past. Every building, wind sock, aerial mast, and fence was riddled with shrapnel and bullet holes. Our Nissen hut dispersal was well patched and emblazoned with a large painted caricature of a Spitfire with its cannons downing two Me's at the same time and Canadian George "Buzz" Beurling's head sticking out of the cockpit. This had been George Beurling's dispersal, and as a Canadian, I felt it quite appropriate that we should be operating from the same building. I found the bar stewards and the army and civilian types who dropped into our mess occasionally for a drink were only too eager to reminisce in glowing terms about the accomplishments of Beurling, Hesslyn, and McLeod, all early Battle of Malta heroes.

Our days passed quickly and pleasantly under glorious weather conditions. Winco Gray did very well in his new job, while refusing to allow the Malta defence organizers to tie him down with needless instructions and formalities. We cleaned our aircraft, tested our cannon, and checked the operation of our externally fitted long-range fuel tanks. Practice flying was mandatory since we were trying to familiarize our new pilots with our flying procedures, emphasizing exactly how we wanted them to act in the air under all conditions. We also severely tested the two Malta flying controls, Gonda and Petrie, to see how accurate they were in guiding us home. If you become lost or ran short of fuel, it was imperative you be directed back as quickly as possible to this fixed aircraft carrier. They were good, very good!

June 14th was my second operational sortie from Malta and was to be the first time I ended up leading my new squadron. Our task was to fly an evening flight at 22,000 feet as top cover to 154 Squadron seventy miles up the east coast of Sicily to Syracuse, then turn west for seventy miles, and then make a long, shallow dive over Biscari and Comiso airdromes on a sort of recce mission. We knew that there were at least 150 enemy fighters based on these two huge all-weather 'dromes.

Shortly after take-off Tampax red 3 had engine trouble and returned to Takali with his number 4. Not much later Duke developed engine problems and, after turning the squadron over to me, headed home with his number 2. That left me leading the squadron for the first time, with a total of eight aircraft. When we turned west at Syracuse into the setting sun, I lost sight of 154 Squadron. Their commanding officer, Tony Wenman, could not answer my calls for his position because his R/T had failed, and no one else in his outfit had enough sense to send me the information.

At the proper point I turned the squadron south and started a gradual dive to pick up speed as we crossed over Comiso headed for Malta and safety. I soon spied seven aircraft ahead which I took to be the bottom section of 154 Squadron and started to position my planes on their down-sun side, intending to let them cover us in our dive. They turned out to be Me 109s! In my calmest voice I called into my transmitter, "Tampax squadron, turning starboard to attack. Stay together. Go." As I climbed into firing position behind them, another eight Me 109s appeared at three o'clock and then another seven at nine o'clock with ten Macchi 202s coming out of nowhere to bring up the rear. We were truly boxed in. Outnumbered four to one, we were in a very difficult position — far away from Malta and deep into enemy territory.

While constantly reminding my chaps to stay together, I turned the squadron to meet every attack head on. Fortunately only one enemy squadron attacked at a time, giving me enough time in every case to position our aircraft properly to meet each attack. After each encounter I tried to head south and gained a few miles each time. I knew we could not last long since sooner or later we would start receiving hits, either from the fighters or from the heavy flak, or we would run out of fuel. While warding off each attack, I repeatedly called Gonda for help, knowing that Wing Commander Gray was supposed to be in the area on a free-lance sweep with 81 Squadron and their Spit IXs.

We kept dodging and turning for 10 minutes, firing whenever an enemy came within reasonable range. Our ammunition was running low. Once I glanced behind and saw my number 2 firing at a 109 just in front of me but out of his range, with me in the middle. Hastily I roared over the R/T, "Stop firing, you dumb clod, before you shoot me down."

Suddenly, down came 81 Squadron and every enemy aircraft rolled over, diving for the ground. Gray, with only one cannon working, got a Macchi, his 24½ kill confirmed. I chased a 109, without success, and deciding that we had enough excitement on my first time leading the squadron, we made tracks for Takali.

In the mess the drinks went down easily as we rehashed the flight. Gray put his arm around my shoulder, "Bill, you did a hell of a fine job. You did everything right, kept the boys together, and not one of your aircraft hit!" Of course we celebrated his victory. He displayed magnificent shooting skill in downing his quarry with only one cannon.

Duke was particularly brassed off. He hated the missed opportunity to score a victory. As he lifted a grog to strain through his mustache he said, "Billie boy, I'm going to continue flying the IX and you will lead in the Vs. There is no way you're going to get a DFC before I do." I understood his feelings exactly and took no offense. How could I?

Having my own aircraft, my *E* job, radical measures to improve its performance could be taken. I never cared for our machine guns, feeling that they were very ineffective weapons. Out they came, leaving only the cannons. I removed all of the armor plating, leaving only the light metal bucket seat to protect my backside and seat. I took off the rear view mirror. I junked the identification friend or foe box (IFF), a thirty-pound device located in the tail which emitted a constant special signal that allowed our radar to recognize instantly that the machine was friendly. I removed it since the thought of being mistaken for an enemy was not particularly frightening. I pulled the exhaust stacks and installed Spit IX exhaust stubs, six per side instead of three, to improve the engine's performance. Finally, with the enthusiastic help of my groundcrew, I scraped and polished the whole airplane to nearly bare metal.

The first time I test flew my modified aircraft, the damn thing shot upward like an elevator or helicopter, after just reaching flying speed. It was so light and unbalanced that it took some time to learn to fly and trim the kite properly. I knew no one else would be interested in flying my *E*, which had turned into something of a beast. But it was fast and maneuverable, so much so that I felt it was nearly the equal of the IXs below 10,000 feet. It certainly was a tricky bastard to fly properly, but I revelled in its improved performance.

During the rest of the month, we carried out eight additional sweeps over Sicily with the enemy seen, but not engaged. Then, on the 29th Duke allowed me to fly a IX as number 3 to Group Captain Hugo. We were to be top cover to 152 Squadron while they dive-bombed Comiso airdrome. Just as 152 started to dive over the target, Duke spotted five 109s behind him. The group captain immediately turned hard port, balls out, and since I was flying very wide line abreast of him, that quick turn left me far behind. Flying Officer "Mac" McMin, my number 2, followed as I tried to catch up.

From nowhere ten Me 109s came diving in on McMin and me, and we became involved in a life-and-death struggle. We twisted and turned to meet the attackers, who came from all directions, and became separated. In fact I was above him flying a clockwise pattern while he was below going in the other direction. This confused the enemy as much as it prevented us from joining up. There was no help to be expected from the rest of the squadron since they had their hands full with enemy fighters and in any case were now some miles away.

The leader came at me a number of times, surprising me because he had his wheels down. At first I thought he was a Ju 87, a Stuka, which would have suited me better. We made one head on attack after another, and when the aim appeared right, I would press my gun button. Tracer bullets appeared to be flying everywhere. As I met another head-on attack, I found myself ducking down in the cockpit so that if the coupe top were smashed, I might keep sharp splinters out of my eyes. There were so many enemy aircraft around I would have welcomed another set of eyes in the back of my head. I did a number of head-on attacks and fired on four of those with no observed strikes.

Finally, Mac and I became totally separated. I was over Comiso at 2,000 feet with heavy flak coming up from the defences below. Somehow all the ground fire missed me while at the same time it deterred the 109s from getting in too close. By now I was becoming extremely tired, my strength drained by the long fight and the constant rough handling of the flying controls. Gambling, I applied emergency boost by shoving the throttle through the restraining wires which normally stopped us from over-taxing the engine, and headed south for home and safety, still maintaining my altitude. Messerschmitts in groups of three and four passed over me, or roared by my side without attacking. Suddenly, a few miles from the coast of Sicily I saw three 109s in line astern immediately ahead and some five hundred feet higher.

I closed in on the rear 109 to seventy-five yards, opening fire with all my guns, and saw strikes over the body and wings of the enemy. The 109 pulled up sharply to starboard and from less than thirty yards I emptied the rest of my ammo into the cockpit and engine, seeing large pieces fall off the airframe accompanied by an explosion. The aircraft fell away to port and dived into the ground, although I could not see the final crash as the remaining two Me's were attacking. I did not stay to fight as I had no more ammunition. Malta was the place to be, and in diving toward the deck in the fading light, I was able to evade successfully.

Our excitement in the mess was heightened by copious quantities of beer, quickly quaffed. Duke and Flight Sergeant Patterson shared a destroyed 109, Group Captain Hugo had one destroyed, and I had my Me 109. We knew we had done well: battling over fifty enemy aircraft without a loss or even a bullet hole in any of our Spits. 152 got nothing and two of their machines were shot up, but all returned to Takali. Our victory party lasted for hours as we celebrated adding to Malta's impressive score of 1,200 aircraft destroyed, 500 probables, and some 2,000 damaged.

The lesson I had absorbed so early with Pep about always looking around and being wary, was the basic reason I was never hit by a bullet from an enemy aircraft. I do not discount good luck, for I have had more than my share, but I believe because I worked hard while flying that my tactics contributed materially to my survival. A fighter pilot has to be cool but reckless, daring but calculating, and courageous but humble in acknowledging that good fortune is as important a survival aid as is good piloting.

I never wore sunglasses or goggles in the air, since the available Raybans restricted my vision and the goggles pushed to the top of my helmet bothered me because they would keep hitting the coupe top as I moved my head from side to side to look behind. If my machine caught fire, however, and I was without goggles, the chances of suffering serious eye damage were very real. On the several ocasions later when I was badly hit, my aircraft defied all precedent and simply refused to burn. My goggle decision was foolish, I acknowledge, yet my luck was strong enough to overcome that and many other absurd risks that I created for myself.

During June we had a visit from King George VI and later Air Marshall Lord Trenchard, the reputed father of the modern Royal Air Force. These visits meant parades, requiring us unruly and scruffy pilots to spruce up our appearance. We resented this bother as it had been many months since most of us had been on a parade, and we joked about not being able to remember how to drill properly. A pilot's life when not flying was a very casual and unregulated existence.

During my time in Malta, strange events happened daily. One I particularly remember concerned the Americans, who wanted an airdrome to serve their shorter-range fighter aircraft. Malta had no space for another airfield and the RAF crowded the existing ones to capacity. The tiny island of Gozo, one-quarter the size of Malta and little more than a hilly, rocky peak of land, lay a mile to the west. The Americans asked if they could use the rugged piece of rock outcrop and were laughingly given permission. In came bulldozers and within a few days they had levelled an area large enough to serve as an airfield. What seemed an impossibility to the British was nothing to the imaginative and resourceful Yanks.

Another odd event occurred when one day I watched a 109 flying at 17,000 feet over Takali brought down by just five bursts of ack-ack fire — quite uncanny shooting. The pilot bailed out, landing fairly close to his crashed aircraft. He was immediately set upon by a good number of Maltese, and except for the timely arrival of soldiers, the young German pilot would have been torn apart and killed on the spot.

At another time during our noon meal in the mess, Group Captain Hugo collared me. "I'm having trouble getting my overload tank to operate properly. Take my aircraft, test it and let me have your opinion."

"Okay, Sir," I told him, "right after lunch."

I rushed down to the field, eager to fly a IX again. I examined his machine, *FL-P*, with its small, thirty-gallon slipper tank mounted between the plane's extended undercarriage. His ground-crew felt the tank should flow fuel properly and that the earlier troubles might have been because of an air lock or a bad seal.

I donned my parachute, fastening the four straps into the metal holding device located about my belt level. After crawling up the port wing and adjusting myself in the metal seat, the ground-crew pulled the Sutton harness straps tight, securing me firmly in the seat. I checked that the brakes were locked, and then, with a thumbs-up signal to the groundcrew, I started the engine.

I never tired of the feeling of strength and satisfaction one got as the engine of the Spit IX catches. I could feel the power throb through the seat as man and machine became one. The chocks were removed and I taxied out to the runway, doing the required cockpit check of trim, flaps, contacts, petrol, undercarriage, and radiator while swinging the long nose from side to side to get some forward vision. I stopped, pulled the brake lever hard, ran up the engine, and tested the two magneto switches. No unusual rev drop. I released the brakes, and slowly advanced the throttle, feeling the aircraft leap forward. The engine opened up into a reassuring smooth roar, and the controls became lighter as the Spit prepared to leave the runway in some four hundreds yards. Safely up, I climbed quickly to 20,000 feet.

The day was beautiful, with a blazing sun. The blue sea met the blue sky with scarcely any discernible horizon line. I switched on the slipper-tank fuel feed and practiced a few aerobatics to see if the fuel flow was adequate under strained or different aircraft attitudes. All seemed well, indicating that the test had been successful.

Suddenly I saw an aircraft diving at me from behind and out of the sun. Over Malta the enemy could be anywhere at any time. Anticipating the worst, I turned to meet the attacker. As he flashed by I could see that it was a sky-blue colored Spitfire, about a Mark V, although I could not be sure as to the exact mark. The pilot turned quickly and, in less time than it takes to write these words, was sitting on my tail. From twenty thousand feet to ground level, I twisted, turned, rolled, dived, lowered my flaps in turns, and dropped my slipper tank. No matter what I did or what maneuver I tried, that Spit was right behind me, with the correct deflection allowed to shoot me down. Nothing worked! Realizing that he would not fire and knowing how proud Hugo was of this particular machine, I did not try any further evasive tactic which might have damaged the airframe. At ground level, where I could go no lower, he flew alongside, gave a wave of his hand, and I heard "Ta ta, chum," over my R/T. He disappeared as quickly as he had appeared ten minutes earlier.

Had I been certain that he was an enemy, and if I had survived his first few attacks and my surprise, I could have done a few extra maneuvers, but I doubt they would have proven successful. It was the only time I can remember being so completely outflown by a pilot in a supposedly inferior aircraft. It was a chastening experience. All of my flying assessments throughout my air force career had rated my flying ability "above average," but I had just met, duelled with, and lost to a very exceptional pilot.

I related my experience, quite unabashed, to Hugo and others while sipping our before-dinner drinks. Hugo sympathized and said, "You must have met Adrian Warburton in his PRU Spit. I know he is a superb pilot, and the absence of markings would indicate it was a photo reconnaisance machine."

I was to meet Warburton later when we were both in hospital in Carthage, at which time he held the DSO and Bar, the DFC and two Bars and, so the story went, was up for the Victoria Cross. This incredible pilot had destroyed two Me 109s on a single trip in an unarmed aircraft, doing to them pretty much what he had done to me, but taking it all the way and forcing them to crash into the sea in a last ditch effort to escape him. He coolly took pictures to prove his claim of two enemy fighters destroyed since he rightly believed the intelligence blokes on Malta would have a difficult time believing his story despite some of his other, equally amazing accomplishments. I have been very fortunate in never meeting a German pilot with Warburton's talents, but they did exist. That flying lesson is as vivid now as it was educational at that time.

During the first week of July it became readily apparent that big plans were in the wind. Generals Eisenhower and Montgomery appeared on the island with headquarters in Valetta and there was a noticeable influx of soldiers from both British and American units. Air activity was stepped up, and we flew numerous diversionary fighter sweeps or escorted large formations of American bombers to attack the main Sicilian airfields. We usually saw enemy fighters without making contact, and we wondered if the Germans were also preparing for our next move. Ju 88s frequently attacked the massed shipping in Grand Harbour, achieving complete surprise because they cannily approached Malta at sea level from the direction of Crete or Cyprus to avoid detection by our radar. Our surprised ack-ack gunners had little success during these nuisance raids.

Our senior officers had been grounded for days, indicating that they were privy to very secret and important information which might be disclosed if one of them were shot down and captured. The rest of us flew regularly, and when not in the air, we spent hours shining and preparing our aircraft for whatever lay ahead. Because of the heat, we bought summer khaki drill dress with short pants, carefully sewing our wings and national identity tabs on the outer wear. No matter how scruffy and dishevelled we might appear, we seemed to have a compulsion to identify our nationality, and I always felt very proud of my *Canada* badges.

At eight o'clock on the morning of July 9, 1943, we senior pilots reported to the operations room for our first official briefing on the invasion of Sicily. There we were presented with a complete picture of what was expected to happen during the next few days. About thirty of us sat in silent admiration and even awe while Group Captain Hugo explained the size of the task and our immense responsibility as a covering force.

The invasion operation, code-named "Husky," had General George Patton commanding the American forces, whose task was to capture the western half of the island. The British and Canadian forces under General Montgomery were assigned the more difficult task of subduing the eastern half of Sicily, which included the major cities of Syracuse, Catania, and Messina and the dominating presence of 11,000-foot-high Mt. Etna. Neither army was expected to have an easy time in conquering the 10,000-square-mile island, but the rewards for success would be enormous.

In a calm voice Hugo described in detail why Sicily was to be our objective, a decision which had been made by the Allied planners only six months before in January. With the capture of the Italian islands of Lampedusa, Linosa, and Pantellaria, only Sicily blocked our complete command of the western Mediterranean Sea. Landings in Sardinia and Corsica would have presented an easier task because of much smaller defending forces and would be better located to invade France or the heartland of Italy. But Sicily, while judged to be a more difficult nut to crack, was thought to be a more conservative and predictable operation. And while our attack opened up the Mediterranean, we would also be putting pressure on the Germans to defend the Italian mainland, which would divert troops and equipment from the Russian front, thus aiding our Allies. There was also the hope that an approach so close to Italy might weaken the Italian resolve to continue with their war effort, but this was an unknown — an invasion could arouse the Italian's spirit of nationalism, and lead to a fierce defense of their homeland.

For an hour and a half Hugo briefed us fully, answering our

numerous questions. We were naturally most concerned with the air opposition, which was known to be operating from thirty island airfields. It was estimated the enemy could manage about 1,600 combat aircraft from all areas, including Italy and southern France. Our forces totalled nearly 3,700 planes based on landing strips from Algiers to Cairo, all under the command of Air Marshal Tedder of the RAF. Enemy ground forces were thought to number about 200,000 troops, largely Italian, but reinforced by two excellent German armored divisions, including the Herman Goering Division. Our invasion force, carried by 3,000 ships, would number 160,000 men — British, American, Canadian, and French troops — supported by an immense inventory of vehicles, some 600 tanks, and innumerable guns. Our reserves were enormous, and additional men and equipment were to be landed in the days following the initial attack as our invaders fanned out over the island.

This would be the most massive invasion attempted to date, and to us the detail and logistics, all planned months before, were mind-boggling. Throughout the balance of the day it would be our job to cover the invading flotillas of ships, which would unload their human cargoes on Sicilian soil at night. We were given mimeographed sheets detailing hour by hour every convoy, its makeup as to type and number of vessels, the applicable call and identification signs for it, and its magnetic bearing and distance from Malta. All we had to do was to take off at an appropriate time, refer to the sheet, and fly a course, say 177 degrees from sixty-eight miles, to pick up a particular convoy, say convoy "Collins," consisting of seventeen ships at twelve o'clock. It was a piece of cake, but very precise and demanding.

Airborne troops were to be landed at ten minutes past ten inland of the invasion beaches to capture and hold certain key positions and strategic points. The seaborne Eighth Army would land at Augusta and Syracuse, and south along the eastern beaches. The Canadians would land as a unit on the extreme southern tip of Sicily and would have their own beachhead. The Americans would land to the west of the Canadians on a very long stretch of beach extending to Gela. At the same time a seaborne force would make a feint attack in the Palermo region, but no landings were intended there. It was hoped the feint would fool the Hun, compelling him to retain his troops in that area rather than rushing them to the defense of the actual invasion beaches.

The atmosphere on Malta was tense and electric. Everyone, including the civilians, knew that something momentous was about to happen, for the shipping, massed in the harbors and rocky inlets, was plainly visible. This was the day Malta had been waiting for. Having survived the worst onslaughts that the enemy could mount, it could now share in a strike, a retaliatory blow, in the first Allied effort to make a landing in Europe.

We flew our first convoy patrol shortly after the briefing, skimming the sea at zero feet for nearly one hundred miles and then climbing to 3,000 feet when our convoy appeared. We maintained R/T silence and hoped that our fighter direction ship would have its convoy call letters clearly marked on either the bow or stern. When we made contact, we received the proper recognition signals, which we answered back by flicking our lights. We then commenced patrolling some distance away in huge circles. Everywhere I looked I could see other large convoys lying low on the horizon. By incredible timing and by adhering to the plans made months ago, all convoys arrived at their designated stations at the appointed minute. It was truly astonishing that so many ships of all different sizes and speeds could arrive from bases in England, Gibraltar, the United States, and Alexandria in the right place and at the right time.

As the day progressed the armada converged on Malta and then, toward late afternoon, fanned out west, north, and east. One minute I was admiring the mass of wakes and then suddenly every single vessel turned toward Sicily at the exact same moment, an amazing, memorable sight. From five o'clock on, only the best pilots were to fly and later only four of us, including the group captain and Gray, would fly after dark, leaving the fleet only thirty minutes before the first troops were to land. Our last flight was extremely dangerous since we were not to fly higher than mast height. What good we could do left me baffled. There was no horizon that night, for the beautiful day had turned into a devilish night with high winds and rough seas. We had no lights and our only reference was the phosphorescent wakes created by the bows of the ships passing through the heavy seas. I felt we were doing something very foolish, which possibly might do more harm than good. Hindsight has not changed my opinion.

We landed back at Takali guided by truck headlights shining down a suggested runway path. These lights, when combined with the blue flames blazing from our engine exhaust stubs, totally destroyed our night vision, and each landing was a prospective disaster. It was good luck as much as good piloting that enabled the four of us to return to the mess together.

We pilots had had a tiring day, flying a good number of hours under tense and demanding conditions. We speculated on what we might expect tomorrow from the enemy fighters, and we tried to imagine what it would be like to be one of the first soldiers landing on a hostile shore; none of us would have traded places with them. We felt the campaign would progress quickly once the Allies spread out from the southeastern landing beaches, although we also felt that due to the rugged nature of the Sicilan terrain, there would be much hard fighting for the ground forces, quite similar to that in North Africa.

After the Sicilian D-day we flew continous beach patrols, rejoicing in the success of the army while depressed that the enemy did not put in a more obvious effort in the air. Our responsibility, covering for the Americans, was a long patrol, over twenty miles from end to end. We flew up and down, rarely seeing anything to chase, and here the enemy once again showed his cunning and daring. The Germans could watch us patrol and just before we got to a turning point at one end of our run, a bomber would be sent in at the other end to attack a ship or ground target. The bombers appeared to have perfect coordination and we would sometimes be quite surprised after completing a turn to find a tanker or landing craft going up in smoke at the other end of our run. We then split our squadron into smaller sections to cover the beach more effectively. The Germans took advantage of this by sending out enough fighters to give the small sections a very desperate, often one-sided, fight.

Because of the limited airdrome space on Malta, enough aircraft could not operate to give total coverage of the beaches. We saw the enemy on every trip, but mostly it was a fleeting glimpse as a bandit would bomb and skip nimbly away, or else we would meet a large gaggle and have our hands very full. We saw evidence of intense ground fighting and the water's edge was marked with dense black smoke rising to 10,000 feet as a tanker burned or an ammunition ship glowed white hot for days. Day after day we flew long patrols, eagerly awaiting the time when we could establish an air base in Sicily and avoid the long flights over the water back to Malta.

For our July 17th sortie, I decided to remove my hood or coupe top to see if I could squeeze a little more speed out of my *E* job. None of our recent flights had been over 10,000 feet, and I reasoned that a few extra miles per hour coaxed from my Spit would be worth the cold and cockpit turbulence I expected from this untried action.

Immediately upon arriving at our patrol location we spotted seven Me 109s somewhat below us. Duke was leading half the squadron in the IXs and I was leading the other half in our Vs. He and I were quick off the mark after his "Tallyho, Tampax squadron," and we lined up on two of the enemy. They were flying side by side, and Duke and I were nearly doing the same thing behind them. The enemy dived north and levelled out two hundred feet above the water with Duke flying on the left and me on the right. Duke's machine was slightly faster than mine, and as he closed to an acceptable firing range, my target 109 throttled back slightly and made a pass at the CO, firing away. He must have been a good shot, or very lucky, for his wide deflection shooting nearly blew the whole tail off Duke's IX. I was still slightly out of range and could do nothing more than yell, "Watch out, leader."

After being hit Duke came back somewhat subdued, I thought. "Yellow 1, I think I'll return to base. The damage could be serious."

"Okay, Duke, I'll carry on and see if I can catch these buggers." Although ours were the fastest aircraft in the squadron, I felt certain some of our pilots would catch up to Duke to escort him back to Malta.

I carried on behind the two Me's, which dropped down to skim the top of the water as they streaked toward Catania. As we approached that very large airdrome, they seemed to slow down a little, enabling me to close the gap slightly. Perhaps they slowed down deliberately, because as I suddenly appeared at zero feet over Catania airdrome, there were guns blasting at me from every side. The 109s had obviously warned the field that they had a live sucker tailing them and the field should be ready for a kill. Without my coupe top to deaden some of the noise, I felt the guns were only inches away. The racket was overwhelming and terrifying. In mid-field I did a sharp ninety-degree turn to port with my wingtip just above the grass, nearly wiping myself out on a crashed Heinkel 111 bomber lying in the field with some white-faced groundcrew clustered around it. They didn't even wave, but then neither did I! As I straightened up I saw a stored pile of German long-range drop tanks dead ahead, and I sprayed them for a second or so before escaping the surprise party.

Upon landing at Takali a careful examination of my *E* did not reveal one single bullet hole! But neither had I hit the 109s. Duke was fine and Flight Sergeant Patterson had successfully destroyed one of the enemy.

I resolved never to fly without a coupe top again, and the sound of all those guns remained with me for a long time. Another lesson learned the hard way.

CHAPTER 8

CAMPAIGNING IN SICILY
July, 1943 — September, 1943

July 22 was the day we had been eagerly awaiting — our move to Sicily. We packed in haste with my groundcrew stuffing a parachute bag of belongings into the machine gun trays and somehow storing my bedroll behind the seat. After a hasty lunch we said goodbye to the staff in the mess, and took a last look at the comforts we had enjoyed for over two months, knowing that it would be a long time before we lived in such style again.

Our destination was Lentini East, a new field bulldozed out of a swamp bordering another swamp called Lake Lentini, the largest lake in Sicily. We were in the midst of the hot dry season when lakes and rivers dried up and the ground baked into a hard-pan surface heavily cracked with wide fissures. We were eight miles inland from the Gulf of Catania, some ten miles from the site of my Catania airdrome experience and five miles from the German front lines. It took us fifteen minutes of stooging around to locate our new base, a testimony to its primitive condition. I suppose a bulldozer had appeared one day, cleared a strip 1,000 yards long by seventy feet wide through the fields of vegetables with a few side swipes to make largely imaginary parking spots for aircraft. And then it was called an airdrome!

In effect we were operating from dried dirt and clay, surrounded by fields of fruit and vegetables. Clouds of dust and debris flew up when an aircraft engine was tested or when we taxied. Strict smoking controls were established because, since we were parked so close together, a carelessly started fire could wipe out our squadron quite easily. Worst of all there were no Allied troops between ourselves and the Germans — we were the front line! Behind us were bags of troops and tanks ready to rush to our rescue should we be attacked, but we were not particularly impressed with that arrangement.

When a squadron moved to a new location hacked out of the local terrain, the priorities were to first look after the aircraft and then to improvise a camp for living comfort. The camp should be a mile or so from the 'drome so that during night bombings and daytime attacks the personnel are relatively safe when resting. The spy and the adjutant had been in charge of our advance party, arriving three days before the aircraft flew in. They had B Flight groundcrew to help service all of our aircraft until A Flight crews arrived some days later. It was a sort of leap-frog process.

They had chosen a camp site on high ground a half mile north of the field, well dispersed in a grove of large olive trees. Below us was a huge irrigation ditch, carrying water to nurture the surrounding orange and lemon groves. The ditch had high banks and a couple of feet of moving water and became an instant hit as a giant bathtub. We had no tents — just canvas flysheets stretched between trees and poles, enclosed at the sides with completely pervious, useless, mosquito netting. It was all improvised on the spot and certainly not rainproof. Pep was my "tent" partner, however, and I knew he could dream up something if foul weather arrived.

Our mess was just a much larger version of our sleeping covers. But by clever and assiduous scrounging we were able to find chairs, good carpets to lay on the bare ground, tables, radios, gramophones, china, crystal, decanters, and other comforts, including a large variety of wines. It was completely open but for captured German drogue netting — in red, white, and blue themes, very patriotic — acting as walls. It also failed to keep out the ever-present mosquitoes. We enjoyed our outdoor living except that at night we could not smoke or display lights which might attract German artillery fire. Howard MacMinniman, a Canadian from Fredericton, was duly elected bar officer and Jim Woodhill, a Canadian from Halifax, was made messing officer. Obviously we Canadians had certain attributes or qualifications admired by the other nationalities.

It was weeks later when we complained about the lack of regular food supplies that we discovered we were supposed to exist on hardtack, cheese, and what we could obtain locally. Our invasion planners had made an important gamble in providing a bare subsistence level of rations, and we considered ourselves extremely fortunate to be surrounded by plentiful, and free, fresh fruit and vegetables. We had fields of tomatoes, ripening successively, with musk melons, watermelons, oranges, lemons, lettuce, onions, and other garden vegetables close at hand. Plentiful food, wine, and beautiful weather were great aids in promoting a sense of well-being among the pilots and groundcrews.

Part of our flying duties through July and August consisted of patrols over battle areas or free-lance sweeps which allowed us to seek out the enemy on our terms. The bulk of our flying, however, was providing escort cover to Kittibombers, Baltimores, Bostons, and Marauders bombing troop concentrations, crossroads, the town and port of Messina, and supply depots in southern Italy. Duke allowed me to lead the squadron on numerous occasions, and several impressions of that time stay with me.

We saw very few enemy fighters. The German high command likely felt that an attempt to hold Sicily was a lost cause and was conserving its strength for the assault on mainland Italy which would inevitably happen once Sicily was subdued. But the rugged Sicilian country was ideal for the delaying-action warfare waged by the Germans even though our overwhelming air superiority caused them heavy losses in men and material.

Sometimes we had to penetrate quite thick layers of cumulostratus clouds to attain bombing height. I always drew the squadron in close to me as we entered clouds, having complete confidence in my instrument flying ability, and we would pop out of the cloud top in perfect formation. On the other hand, the bombers we were escorting would emerge in ones and twos, well scattered, heading in all different directions, which indicated that some of the bomber pilots certainly needed instrument flying practice.

It was also the custom of the bombers to fly beyond the target, make a 180-degree turn, place their machines in a slight dive to pick up speed, and drop their bombs on the way home, generally with excellent bombing results. Then they would open the throttles fully wide and head for safety. The P-40s, the A-20A Bostons, and the Marauders easily left us behind while we could just stay with the Baltimores. As far as I know, none of the fleeing bombers was ever attacked after leaving our protective cover, which seemed to justify the tactic.

My final impression was the vast amount of intense, accurate flak which the enemy was able to put up around the Messina Straits. There was some 88 millimeter anti-aircraft fire, but the bulk of it was smaller calibre and so heavy that the bursts would virtually create a cloud cover over the defended area. The pilots' expression, "the flak was so heavy you could walk on it," was truer here than I was ever to see it elsewhere. Later, when I was dive-bombing in the Ruhr, the flak was extremely heavy and accurate, but it was still not as intense as we experienced at Messina. Flak hit me a number of times with some 88 bursts so close that my aircraft would be tossed onto its back or blown into a steep dive. One pilot remarked that our constant attacks in the Messina area would eventually tire out the ack-ack gunners. Another pilot remarked, "Bullroar. It just gives them more opportunities to practice and get better." I subscribed to the latter theory.

When flying escort duty, we could see the German Seibel ferries and small E and F boats, German patrol craft, plying the two-mile escape route between Messina and the mainland, but the intense flak prevented us from strafing them when they would have been most vulnerable in the open water. Our losses would have been prohibitive. The enemy escape was assisted by rather poor thinking on the part of the Allied supreme command, who seemed more interested in attacking strategic targets in mainland Italy than in concentrating on destroying the enemy backed into a tight position in the northeast corner of Sicily. This situation, similar to the Falaise gap failure in France a year later, allowed all of the German troops and the majority of the Italians, along with thousands of tons of equipment and supplies, to escape.

Not all operational trips went quite as planned. On July 25 I led the squadron in the morning with no enemy seen except for heavy, accurate flak. Half an hour after landing, we were off again to intercept Ju 52 transports which we heard would be off the Milazzo coast at a certain hour. We left after our patrol period was up to be replaced by 81, 152, and 242 Squadrons. Fifteen minutes later they ran into a gaggle of transports accompanied by a strong fighter cover. Our side shot down twenty-five Ju 52s, Me 109s, and Macchi 202s, for no loses. This is a vivid example of the luck involved for a fighter pilot in being in the right place at the right time. Because of timing and a shortage of fuel, our squadron missed the party by only a few minutes, much to our chagrin.

Later, after lunch, Group Captain Hugo led us on another Ju 52 hunt on the deck. We saw no aircraft but a German hospital ship was seen with an escort of flak ships. Hugo had made a name for himself in England as a fearless ship attacker. I was aware of that reputation and knew that ship attacks were extremely hazardous, partly because the target is small and partly because the very skilful gunners know you are coming. As we attacked, the shore batteries opened up to assist the flak ships. I heard a terrific bang and knew I had been hit. After more attacks we climbed over the mountains heading for home. On the ground I found a huge hole, eighteen inches wide, behind the cockpit at waist level. Two feet farther forward and the shell would probably have cut me in half. My luck was holding!

One hour later we took off once more to look for Ju 52s. Since my *E* Spit was being repaired, I had a new VC replacement Spit labelled *H*. Our squadron was on the deck while 81 Squadron was free-lance above us at 15,000 feet with 154 Squadron providing closer top cover for us. Lucky 81 ran into twenty Me 109s, quickly shooting down four before the enemy dove away to safety. Returning home our top cover was right in among us when my number 4 reported two Me's behind. As I turned I saw the 109s shoot down two Spits of 154 Squadron before diving away. This was a bad show on the part of our top cover and should not have happened. Their leader did not even know he had lost any aircraft until he was being interrogated back at base by the spy. One Spit eventually made it back badly shot up while the other pilot bailed out. It had been a very long day.

During the evening I kept pressing Hugo to discover how he had received the advance warning that the transports could be expected. He smiled shyly and explained that we had spies on the mainland who were able to pass vital information from time to time. That explanation did not satisfy me at the time, and I now surmise that he was privy to some pertinent information obtained by the Allies' use of the German ULTRA cipher, to decode high-level enemy communications.

We restored a captured Macchi 202, which a few of the more experienced pilots test flew. I made two trips in it, finding that it handled extremely well, was very fast on take-off, in level flight, and in diving, and had excellent maneuverability. I could visualize the 109 as being even better, but the Spit, with its dependable Merlin engine, was still my favorite aircraft.

A new amphibious vehicle, the DUKW or "Duck" had been used for the first time during the invasion with great success. It was a huge machine, rather like a landing craft on wheels, which travelled high off the ground, and proved to be highly maneuverable on land. One day as some of us were trudging from the 'drome to our camp, one such "Duck" stopped beside us, and General Montgomery, an easily recognizable figure, gave us a short pep talk, emphasizing the Allied success and encouraging us to "keep up the good fight." We were duly impressed and it illustrates the degree and extent of close contact Monty preferred to have with those under his command. He was a dynamic leader, and one who certainly enjoyed being in the limelight.

One operation I particularly credit to Montgomery was his decision to have the army and the air force cooperate to better understand each other's operating procedures and difficulties. To do this we were to send two pilots to a front-line regiment for a few days, where the pilots would live and operate as front-line soldiers under battle-field conditions. They went on patrols, sheltered in slit trenches, and endured shell fire. They returned to us very shaken and chastened men, glad to be well out of soldiering, and spent hours describing their adventures.

For our part we hosted two army officers. They stayed at the airfield from four in the morning to ten at night, as did we, and they attended our briefings, listened on the R/T hookup in the dispersal to our chatter and action in the air, and generally participated in all our activities except the flying. Back at camp they had drinks, dinner, and more drinks, finally bedding down at midnight. Then, up again at 4:00 AM to face another day. They hated our routine and were unable to endure our long hours and too little sleep because they lacked the excitement and tension of flying, which buoyed the pilots and allowed them to keep performing efficiently. There was no way the army officers would have traded places with us, either. This worthwhile program lasted only a couple of exchanges, and I never heard of it being tried again, which was a pity.

The South African Air Force or SAAF had their 'drome several miles east of us, under the leadership of Lieutenant Colonel L.A. Wilmot. Two miles to our west was another RAF wing under the command of Wing Commander Stan Turner, the very distinguished Canadian pilot. Our three forward airfields held fifteen fighter squadrons, or nearly 300 Spitfires. This attractive target received sporadic day and night time attention from the enemy with little damage resulting from any given raid. On the night of August 11 that changed, and we suffered the most serious damage from an air raid that I was to experience during the whole war.

At ten o'clock in the evening I was sitting, beer in hand, with the sergeants, making plans for suitable recreation on the following day since our squadron was to be stood down for twenty-four hours. The mosquitoes were lively and kept us busy flailing our arms around. Up above a full moon shone bright and clear, light enough to read by.

As we chatted we noticed about twenty flares suddenly appear in the sky approximately over where the SAAF 'drome was located. Bombs started to burst, ack-ack guns began to bark, and we had a sad sort of ringside seat. The bombing appeared to be heavy and accurate with the roar of the Ju 88s' engines sounding loud and clear.

Then we saw a green indicator or target flare over the center of our 'drome, dropped from a Ju 88 at 4,000 feet. Very quickly more than thirty white chandelier flares appeared, brightly lighting our whole field and some of the surrounding terrain, including our neighboring airfield, Lentini West. Our ack-ack started firing, but with no observed results. Ju 88s began dive-bombing, dropping hundreds of incendiaries, 25-pound anti-personnel bombs, and the dreaded butterfly bombs, as well as some heavy bombs weighing up to 1,250 pounds.

While the bombs rained down, we ran for our tin helmets and then dived into slit trenches, trying to cower out of sight. The 'drome rapidly became a blazing inferno as ammunition dumps exploded and fuel supplies burned fiercely. The grass started to burn, aircraft caught on fire, and our few ack-ack gunners were obliterated. The fires, the moon, and the flares made the scene incredibly brilliant with every potential target clearly exposed. The rising smoke hovered like a low cloud in the sky, reflecting a weird reddish glow from the fires below.

I scrambled for a slit trench only to discover it was filled to capacity. I finally eased myself under a truck, but when a couple of bombs landed nearby, I retreated to find temporary safety under the wireless trailer with Duke.

We could hear and see the Ju 88 bombers circling awaiting their turn to dive and bomb. Then an aircraft would start to dive. We would hear the noise increase and the whine of the engines become a shrill scream as the bomber gained speed and came closer. They came so low before pulling out of their dives that the bombs made no screaming noise before they hit. We were helpless. We never knew where the bombs were hitting until we felt the concussion of the explosions. The Germans obviously intended to demolish our airfield and campsite, for once our planes were burning, they dropped bombs by the irrigation ditch and in the surrounding groves of trees.

We were serviced by an American Negro regiment, and these magnificent men performed heroic service throughout the raid. They were on the 'drome during the raid, working in the firelight with bombs dropping all around, and with the gunners in the bombers strafing them. Our fuel was stored in haystacks scattered all around the field and as one pile was hit, the blazing gasoline ran through and along the fissures in the hard ground, igniting everything in the fire's path. The soldiers were filling in the cracks to stop the spread of the fire from one pile to another, totally ignoring the bombers, the bullets, the light, and the enormous heat. It was a most heroic exhibition of devotion to duty, far beyond anything I had ever witnessed.

At last, the 88s flew away, having kept us pinned down for an hour. It was now time to sort ourselves out and attempt to restore order. Our first job was to run down the hill to see how the men who had taken to the ditch had fared. We feared the worst because several sticks of bombs had fallen in the waterway. Soon everyone was yelling for stretchers. There were many killed and wounded, and the ditch was filled with dead bodies. Other victims had been blown to bits and their bodies would never be found.

I found one airman lying on his back with a boulder pillowing his head. I asked him what his injuries were and if there was anything I could do. Very quietly, although obviously in great pain he said, "They got my left leg, left arm, and shoulder." He was covered from head to foot in blood, and I felt his injuries were much worse than he had diagnosed. I gave him a cigarette as we placed him on a stretcher. He died six hours later.

Another pilot, Flight Sergeant King,[11] had no obvious wounds but could not move any part of his body. He talked coherently as Pep and I saw him off in an ambulance, but after that, he was never heard of again. A few days later his well-deserved promotion to warrant officer came through.

The stretcher cases were hurried away. Walking casualties were guided to the field hospital, and the scene was cleaned up as much as possible, although long after it was over, we were still looking for missing bodies.

In the meantime our 'drome was blazing. Ammunition dumps were exploding with loud popping noises and the slugs were whistling over our heads. Petrol dumps were flaming high, incendiaries glowing, and a pall of smoke rising thickly. Duke and I made a hasty inspection, and found only two aircraft that had not been damaged, mine being one of them. Despite the chaos the runway was being restored by army engineers, who were filling in the bomb holes to make the 'drome usable. A couple of aircraft were not too heavily damaged, and these were being repaired amidst the confusion and destruction.

At 3:00 AM we returned exhausted to our beds and tried to get some rest before dawn broke. At six o'clock I went down the hill to have a bath. I examined a few of the bodies, finding that some were unrecognizable. Others were badly battered, missing the top or bottom half of the body. Some lay in holes looking very gray from a cover of dust and here and there was an arm, a leg, or a head. The bath helped, but I still felt nauseated and ill.

Our three hundred aircraft were almost totally wiped out. From the fifteen squadrons we raised about twenty flyable aircraft to put up as a front to fool the enemy about the extent of the damage. Only twenty-five percent of the aircraft could be repaired, and some of the repairs would be major and time-consuming. The Germans knew they had hit us hard, although I doubt they knew the real extent of the destruction and misery they had left behind.

One of my pilots was a young English sergeant by the name of Syd Lucy. As it was related to me, when he was flying with 232 Squadron in Africa before I joined the squadron, he was shot down at 18,000 feet by an Fw 190. His Spitfire started to spin toward the ground. His flying controls were useless and the coupe top was jammed shut by the cannon fire. When his frenzied efforts to either control the aircraft, or to escape it, failed, he huddled down in his seat and closed his eyes, prepared to die.

As he sat hunched in his seat, a stronger force took command of his Spitfire, causing the steep spin to flatten out as it neared the mountainous ground. It finally hit the trees in such a manner that the machine shot forward in a straight line, through a small flat field, performing a remarkably good forced landing. When the motion ceased he shook himself as if from a dream. Having been prepared to die in a hideous and hopeless manner, he could not believe his good fortune in being alive and unhurt.

He was soon released from the aircraft by friendly Arabs and returned to the squadron, where he was sent on rest for three weeks.

Then I joined the squadron and could watch him as he started to fly operationally again. His hair slowly streaked with gray, his skin became pale and scaly. In every other respect he seemed unchanged and unaffected by his hellish experience.

During the night of our disastrous bombing raid, he was standing in the irrigation ditch between his two best friends. Flying Officer St. John, on his right was riddled with shrapnel and died instantly. The man on the left was blown to smithereens. Lucy was not even touched!

A few weeks later we were having a dice with some Fw 190s when I saw one on Lucy's tail. I yelled at him "Break, break, break, Lucy." He obliged with a nice smooth rate-one turn. Somehow he was not hit by the enemy, and I sent him home to England immediately, tour expired. He was not a fighter pilot, even if the spirit was willing, and I felt that he had done his full share. The poor guy deserved to live.

At 4:40 AM on September 3, 1943, the Canadians and the Fifth Division crossed the Messina Straits to invade the Italian mainland at Reggio and San Giovanni. The terribly difficult battle for Sicily had taken exactly thirty-eight days to complete and win. The invasion of continental Europe was about to begin. We continued our duties, escorting bombers attacking enemy troop concentrations in Italy and patrolling battle areas to ensure that attackers from the air could not harrass our troops.

On September 6 we moved to Milazzo East, a new airdrome, to begin some of the most hazardous flying yet demanded of us fighter pilots. Our new field was located on the north coast of Sicily, with the Tyrrhenian Sea at one end of our short, dirty clay runway and the lower slopes of Mount Etna at the other end. The sea end was sixty feet lower than the south or mountain end, but since the prevailing winds, when there was a wind, came from the Mt. Etna direction, we were always taking off and landing uphill. Bulldozers had again carved our narrow strip out of fields of fruit and vegetables, with very few cutouts to provide parking places for our aircraft.

Group Captain Hugo ordered us to fit ninety-gallon long-range fuel tanks to all of our aircraft since our fighter operations would require extended-range capability. We thought Naples might be our new target, and we needed no further prompting to ensure that each aircraft was as well prepared as brains and sweat could make it. Meanwhile, we lived on hardtack, cheese, and tea, augmented by local grapes, hazel nuts, tomatoes, eggs, figs, and prickly pears.

The next day, September 7, Group Captain Hugo called us to a briefing warning us that it was now D-day minus two, that is, the next invasion was just two days away, and that no one would fly until the big "do." The invasion, code named "Avalanche," was to be launched on the 9th, between Salerno and Agripoli, just south of Naples and Mount Vesuvius. We would be completely under American control until further notice. The Americans were to land in the northern half of the beachhead while the First Army would land in the southern section at beaches named "Peaches" and "Pears." The army was landing six divisions with German resistance estimated at sixteen divisions. The Jerries had 110 plus Me 109s, 45 Fw 190s, and an appreciable number of Dorniers, Ju 88s, and Stukas. We asked Hugo repeatedly, "What about the Italians?" His only reply was to tell us to ignore the Italian factor — no further explanation! This was not that reassuring, for we knew that the Italians had formidable forces available, which, in defense of their homeland, might put up a pretty good show.

The navy was to shell the inland defense positions and act as ack-ack batteries. Included in the very strong naval forces were three British battleships, *Nelson, Rodney,* and *King George V*, plus a number of "Woolworth" aircraft carriers with Sea Fires, the naval version of the Spitfire.

Our job was to act as high cover to all air support forces, maintaining an altitude of 16,000 to 20,000 feet. We were to stay on station for twenty-five minutes until relieved by another Spitfire squadron. Below us, at 14,000 feet, sixteen Lightnings would always be on patrol while at 6,000 feet we could expect eight Mustangs. At any given time there would always be thirty-six fighter aircraft providing a defensive aerial umbrella. The Sea Fires would be buzzing about doing their thing, but it was expected they would be mainly used for defence of the ships. Our wing along with Stan Turner's 324 Wing were to be the only RAF units involved.

We would be operating at extreme range, greater than Allied fighter aircraft had been forced to do in the European theater to date. Our trips would be at least 2½ hours in length, entirely over the Tyrrhenian Sea, and two hundred miles from base, and we would be encumbered by the heavy, ninety-gallon overload tanks. It was an unprecedented action, and we were given the further disheartening news that the air-sea rescue provisions were so primitive as to be nearly nonexistent.

The normal range of a Spitfire without extra fuel tanks and

allowing a few minutes for a possible dogfight when fuel consumption is raised, is about 115 miles one way. The endurance in time is from 1¼ to 1½ hours. Some aircraft were more fuel efficient than others but a leader always had to stay within the safe range of his poorest machine. With ninety-gallon jettison tanks, the range and endurance of our aircraft were exactly doubled — if the extra tank worked properly!

A dramatic moment happened on the evening before the invasion when Group Captain Hugo called all of the pilots to the intelligence tent for 7:00 PM. He had a large old radio sitting on a table and he fiddled with the dial trying to get a particular station. His brow creased with frustration until finally he was able to tune in a German announcer. Hugo translated perfectly the news of the unconditional surrender of the Italian government and all Italian armed forces, effective immediately. Now we could understand Hugo's earlier remarks about ignoring the Italian defenses. We were tremendously relieved at this exciting news, although many difficult conditions still lay ahead.

Our Milazzo airfield was a disaster as an operational field. All of our trained groundcrew had left by ship on D-day to head for Italy to welcome us later, and their place was taken by the servicing commandos, who knew little more than how to gas up and re-arm our kites. The pilots did their own daily inspections and made any obvious minor repairs. It was also a dust-bowl which created problems in getting airborne. We allowed two aircraft to take off in formation because the wind was so slight that it took ages for the dust to clear sufficiently before the next pair could move into a start position.

But by far the worst aspect of the Milazzo airfield was the fact that the runway ran uphill toward Mount Etna. A number of pilots did not gain the power to achieve flying speed before reaching the end of the runway. Weighed down with nine hundred pounds of extra fuel, they crashed helplessly into the trees. A pilot would not know he couldn't take off until he was totally committed, and then all he could do was crash and meet a quick, fiery death through no fault of his own. To worsen matters, everyone on the ground or waiting in line to take off would have to watch each fiery disaster. Most of the crashes involved our Spit Vs which had four hundred less horse power than the IXs, while still carrying the same overweight. Fortunately my *E* performed well, due as much to good luck as to good management.

I had two pilots who simply refused to take off or fly. I immediately placed them LMF (lack of moral fiber) and they were promptly shipped off the base. It would have been disastrous to still carry a pilot who refused to obey orders, even under difficult or impossible conditions. The ripple effect could have been devastating. I felt what I did was necessary, and have never regretted the decision.

Although the dirt runway was the cause of most of our accidents, we suffered from other problems, too. The heat of the sun caused some tires to blow out when airplanes were taking off. The blown wheel would then dig into the ground, often hurling the aircraft onto its back when it was travelling at high speed. The aircraft usually caught fire the moment it turned turtle, killing the pilot before he could be rescued.

One terrible accident in particular stays with me. After my second long trip of the day I was staggering from my Spitfire, trying to light a cigarette, when behind me I heard a curious popping noise. I turned in time to watch a Spit V do a perfect nose over tail cartwheel and land right side up, fifty feet from me, totally enveloped in fierce flames fired by the 100 octane fuel. The pilot, a young decorated Czech flight lieutenant, could not be seen because of the flames, but his left arm, hanging immobile out of the cockpit, had a long, deep cut which did not bleed. I ran to within a few yards, but it was obvious the pilot was already dead. Nothing could be done to help.

Others gathered around while the heat and flames rapidly consumed the aircraft and exploding ammunition whistled through the air. In less than five minutes all that remained was a small part of the tail plane and the engine. Everything else, including the pilot, had been reduced to charcoal or globs of melted aluminum.

His unusual accident was caused by his left wingtip striking the pointed spinner on a parked aircraft just before reaching take-off speed in such a manner, and with exactly the right angle and force, to cause his aircraft to somersault completely. At the top of the somersault, the highly volatile fuel spilled onto hot engine parts. There was an explosion and fire, and the force of his landing broke the undercarriage and smashed what remained of the belly tank. He must have died with his first breath, never realizing what had happened and certainly unable to control his destiny.

Although we had many thrilling moments in the air over the beaches, our losses due to enemy action were negligible when compared to the casualties we suffered at Milazzo East airfield. We flew at least two patrols every day, getting extremely sore backsides from the pressure of our bodies on our seat dinghies and the poorly positioned air bottles which would inflate the dinghies in an emergency. It was interesting flying over the bridgehead, but we saw only the occasional enemy fighter. In maintaining our cover position we afforded high protection, but had to miss the very limited action. It was humorous, however, to watch four or five Seafires (the navy version of the Spitfire) chasing a Ju 88 with no hope of catching such a fleet bomber. Single-engined bombers would dart in and about the shipping occasionally, but with no accurate bombing results. I never saw one of our ships struck or burning, very different from the Sicilian invasion beaches, and a tribute to the intense anti-aircraft fire the ships hurled at any aircraft, allied or enemy, which came within range.

CHAPTER 9

THE SALERNO LANDING AND OUR ITALIAN "ALLIES"

September, 1943 — October, 1943

The brilliant sunshine was dazzling, emphasizing the sparkling blue color of the Tyrrhenian Sea, which I hoped we were crossing for the last time. In less than an hour Mount Vesuvius with its wispy smoke plume appeared to beckon with an innocent charm. The beauty and apparent calm of the rugged landscape belied the dreadful life and death struggle taking place on the ground. I turned the squadron toward Naples and from a height of 25,000 feet I called to the pilots, "OK, Tampax squadron, switch to main tanks. Now drop overload tanks." A dozen partially filled slipper tanks fluttered toward the city below, tumbling like falling leaves. They would take a few minutes to reach the ground. Our aircraft became lighter and more streamlined, hence more responsive to our engine power and the controls. They gained a sort of released feeling, appreciated by all pilots.

Later I again called over the R/T, telling the squadron we were heading for our new home. With that I started a long gentle dive toward our new base located on the very shores of the invasion beaches.

My first impression of Asa airfield was of its extremely small size, barely eight hundred yards in length with a huge ditch at the west or seaward end and a raised roadway at the other end. I landed first and radioed advice to the rest of the squadron, warning them to land carefully at a very slow speed in order to stop short of the menacing ditch. No sooner had I switched off my engine than thirty Fw 190s began to strafe and dive-bomb the front-line troops just beyond the edge of the airfield. Artillery fire, ack-ack guns, and smaller calibre firearms thundered and cracked on every side. My pilots were unaware of the extent of the problem as they hovered in the circuit at slow speed, trying to land, quite befuddled by all the artillery fire and wondering where in hell all the 190s had come from. Amazingly, they all landed safely.

During the past three months we had operated from very primitive airfields, hard on both the aircraft and the pilots. Asa, if anything, was even more difficult. The ditch at the beach end was huge and soon became filled with aircraft which did not stop in time, their backs broken and propellors snapped, graphic proof of the need to land carefully. The ditch was three hundred yards from the invasion beach, which was lined with scores of landing craft and protected by barrage balloons intended to discourage enemy dive bombers. On take-off we would weave between the balloon cables since we had to take off and land from east to west, always coming in over the enemy lines and taking off over the shipping. Immediately north of us, the rugged Sorrento Peninsula rose up, a barrier hiding Mount Vesuvius and the Neapolitan plains beyond. To our east the mountainous spine of Italy hemmed in the beachhead, harboring well-concealed German artillery and troops. To the south the flat plain of the beach landing area extended for about twenty-five miles before being cut off by a mountainous wall at Agropoli. In an effort to prevent the roads in the beachhead from becoming blocked, all traffic heading south used one road while northbound traffic used a road close to the front lines. The one-way traffic pattern was strictly enforced. Our camp lay one mile north of the airfield, but to reach it we had to travel twenty miles on crowded dusty roads, first south, then north.

Our airfield was ringed with Allied artillery and ack-ack guns, and the artillery fired day and night, lobbing shells into the German positions a mile away. I grew to dislike Asa with a passion because its location presented much more danger than we would experience from German aircraft. When we came in to land with our last turn made almost over the enemy troops, we would naturally be flying at a greatly reduced speed with wheels and flaps down. The concussion of the field artillery firing so close would cause the aircraft to rock and buck with the real danger that one would lose flying speed. Loss of control at such a low altitude made a fatal crash inevitable.

Operation "Avalanche" had started on a very optimistic note with the commanding American general, General Mark Clark, stating that he would be in Naples in three days. It seems, however, that our planners had underestimated the inherent difficulties in preparing to attack southern Italy. The ground is generally mountainous, much like Sicily, with the Apennine mountain system running down the center of the country like a backbone or spine. Roads and railroads were sparse and primitive, basically confined to the coastal areas, and rather easily defended by the enemy. These factors played a major role in slowing our planned progress. A further complicating factor was that the Germans had guessed that Salerno was the likely spot for an invasion and dug in beforehand. Two days before we landed the German tanks advanced in one major sector to the edge of the beach with a confident prediction of victory, another Dunkirk. The Allies rallied, even arming cooks, clerks, and mechanics to repulse the enemy pressure. With help from navy shelling, air force bombing, and stout resistance from the ground troops, the Germans advance was halted and then slowly pushed back. Of all the invasions I covered, Salerno came the closest to being a disaster.

Despite these problems it must be appreciated that the decision to invade Italy was made about the middle of June, leaving only 2½ months to plan, organize, and launch the first Allied invasion of the European mainland.

As a squadron and a wing we were to find it extremely difficult and dangerous to continue operating in the middle of a battlefield. The incessant noise from the artillery was nerve-wracking as the guns belched and roared on all sides of our field. Incoming enemy shells destroyed a number of our aircraft, although few men were hit because they spent so much time in handy slit trenches. In the bay the navy would put up a smokescreen to hide the vessels from attacking aircraft, and when the wind blew toward shore, we were enveloped in smoke for long periods of time.

Between our field and the water's edge was a huge, wire-enclosed stockade restraining hundreds of bedraggled and forlorn-looking American GIs. Our speculations about them were never really satisfied with the explanation that they had come from various landing craft which had capsized or had been sunk during the landings, forcing the men to let their heavy weapons and equipment go as they swam to safety.

It was generally accepted that pilots were well-informed on the current military situation, that is, where the enemy was entrenched and in what strength. During the next few days as we travelled the single lane roads at a snail's pace, we would be accosted by officers, many of senior rank, asking, "Where's Monty? Where's Monty?" It seemed to us that the army was uncertain of its ability to hold the beachhead and was looking for reinforcement from General Mongomery and his Eighth Army, which was pushing up from the south. Montgomery had nearly 250 air miles to overcome from Reggio Calabria, his landing beach on September 3, through extremely difficult terrain, facing an enemy experienced in fighting a defensive action. Just the knowledge that such a legendary commander and his tough and experienced Eighth Army were rushing to relieve the invasion forces was an incalculable psychological lift to the beleaguered troops.

Our camp was located in a grove of trees not far from the 'drome, but even closer to the enemy lines. We were instructed to sleep with our pistols at hand to ward off intruders or paratroopers as the enemy apparently was successfully penetrating our positions at will. Sleep was impossible, however, because we occupied slit trenches at night, hoping that the bombers and shells would miss us. The mosquitoes did not miss, however; they were everywhere, a large fierce variety impervious to all our meager repellants. The arduous operating and living conditions sapped our strength and within a few weeks over half of our total manpower had contracted malaria. In between bombs bursting, shells exploding, and artillery firing, we could hear the rumble of tanks, the shouts of men in the front-line area, the clatter of machine guns, and the sharp bark of rifles. We were literally in the middle of a battlefield, day and night.

Arriving at the airfield each morning was an adventure, first in getting there and next in examining our aircraft to assess the damage suffered during the night. Shellfire damaged or destroyed ten percent of the Spitfires each night. Then another few would be damaged by great white oxen which roamed the field at night, gratefully scratching their hides on our wings and frequently breaking the all-important pitot head extensions, which were externally mounted tubes that measured airspeed. The field guards fired their Sten guns at the huge beasts, but they ignored the shots because the bullets seemed to bounce harmlessly off their thick hides. Despite the airfield and the difficulties associated with our surroundings, we flew regular patrols and missions, meeting or seeing enemy aircraft on nearly every flight.

Duke was showing the effects of sleep loss, which left me to lead the squadron on nearly every sortie. But he never lost his sense of humor or any of his inherent good judgment. His soft-spoken instructions and air of relaxed competence provided the leadership we needed to keep us flying and to spur the erks to service the aircraft as efficiently as ever. We continued our role as high-altitude cover to other aircraft, and the enemy still attacked occasionally with audacity and surprise. On one trip, just as we had become airborne and were climbing at 160 mph above the massed shipping, thirty Fw 190s dive-bombed the ships, going by us at more than 450 mph. These hit and run raids did little damage, although by the same token, the navy gunners rarely hit anything, and we were never able to catch the speedy attackers. We had to brave the heavy flak, for the armed escort vessels did not bother to distinguish between friend or foe but fired at anything that came within range of their guns. Despite all the practice we gave the gunners, they never hit any of us.

On our September 20 flight, for once I had the advantage of height. We were perched at 23,000 feet when I saw a group of Fw 190s at a very low altitude that appeared to be just stooging around. Putting the squadron in a steep curving dive, I was able to crawl up the back of a still unsuspecting Focke-Wulf. When less than four hundred yards away and just ready to fire, my front armored windscreen clouded over completely, the result of leaving a very cold altitude for much warmer air in a very short time. This strange and disquieting occurrence was to happen to me several times in Italy, although I never experienced it elsewhere. The enemy escaped, much to my chagrin.

On September 21 flying my Spit V as top cover to Duke in his IXs, we ran into eight Fw 190s. We dropped our thirty-gallon jettison tanks and bounced them properly. I locked onto one who broke up and away from me, and as I turned into him, I fired my cannon, striking him in the starboard wing root. He half-rolled, and I followed, heading straight for Mount Vesuvius, throttle wide open, and clocking well over 500 mph. As my quarry pulled out, I was still close enough to fire and hit him in the tail area. A piece flew off his machine while clouds of black and white smoke poured from his engine, obscuring the body of his aircraft. At that moment my windscreen again clouded over completely, obliterating my view of the target. I broke off the attack and headed for the beach. Suddenly, out of nowhere, twelve Me 109s bounced me. Again I was all alone, and for a few minutes, I worked hard twisting and turning to avoid their fire. Fortunately the 109s were not aggressive and soon broke off their attacks. Back at base I was able to claim one Fw 190 damaged. My aircraft was a write-off since the speed of my dive and the force of my pullout had bent the wings and rippled the skin. I still think it was a fair exchange, for I was certain the 190 crashed, although without evidence all I could claim was a damaged.

Montgomery and his Eighth Army linked up with our forces on September 23 and from then on the enemy was pushed slowly but steadily back, and our territory became more secure. On September 24 we moved the wing to Serretelle airfield, a permanent 'drome located four miles south of Asa, which had a 1,500-yard-long paved runway with superb dispersal and parking facilities. We found a large farmhouse nearby which we quickly converted into living quarters for the officers while our men were comfortably bivouacked in the surrounding orchards. Our meals got better, and our happiness with our improved operating and living conditions was quickly reflected in a cheerful, effective squadron.

Then a series of events took place which could have foretold the future had we been clever enough at divining. While each episode by itself was of no major importance, taken cumulatively they spelt the end of our wing as an extremely successful fighting unit. To begin with, Group Captain Hugo, in the only poor decision I thought he ever made, decided that we should have a wing mess and that all the squadrons should live together under the same roof. Until now each squadron had acted in an autonomous manner, responsible for its accommodation, always in tents, and messing, done in improvised open cook stoves. We lived as a unit, frequently miles from the other squadrons, developing our own routine within the flying requirements assigned to us. This style of living and fighting promoted a strong sense of unit identity, fostering pride and efficiency as we subconsciously competed with the other squadrons in our wing. We strove to have better living conditions, better kept aircraft and greater accomplishments in the air.

But Group Captain Hugo lost sight of the past in selecting an enormous tobacco factory, large enough to house a dozen wings, as our new camp. It was full of tobacco and for days we cleaned out tobacco loons, a difficult, dirty, and strenuous task. Thousands of pounds of tobacco were carried out of the building and made into stinking and rotting piles. To worsen matters, the squadron and flight commanders were to room separately from the rest of our officers and pilots, dividing our forces and damaging our morale. The communal mess was also a disaster and the quality of meals reached a new low. This was the first time I became really aware of the value of high morale and of how quickly discontent and inefficiency can erupt from lack of that important ingredient.

We continued to operate under the Americans, who provided among other things fuel and rations. The fuel was supplied in forty-five gallon drums and hand-pumped into our aircraft tanks. One day as I was screaming down the runway, my engine coughed and poured out black smoke, thick and oily. I was able to complete the circuit to land safely, quite perplexed by the engine problem. Examination of the fuel showed that it was ninety octane compared to the 100 octane our engines required, and each and every barrel of fuel had been spiked with paraffin. Apparently this sabotage had taken place in America before the fuel was shipped across the Atlantic. Our engines had to be stripped down and cleaned, which would take several days. Naples was about to fall to our forces, and as we couldn't fly, I decided to take a few days off with some of my pilots to sightsee in the famous city.

I loaded cases of food and five pilots into my three-ton Chevrolet truck and headed sixty miles north toward Naples, passing through totally destroyed Battapaglia, heavily damaged Salerno, and numerous hill towns. Massed supply convoys crowded the road, and slowed our progress enough to allow us to absorb the sights and sounds of a battered countryside. Refugees of all ages and description lined the road, trudging in both directions, some probably to return to their homes, others seeking new homes and safety. Some carried a few belongings while others pushed wobbly carts laden with salvaged possessions. The dust raised by the passing trucks covered them with a gray film, but they totally ignored that discomfort. This was the first time I had witnessed huge masses of people on the move. Their helplessness and pitiable condition etched a picture I cannot forget.

We passed through the edge of Pompeii, nestled at the foot of Mount Vesuvius, and while the ruins beckoned, the vast amount of material and the hordes of soldiers encamped in the historic remains dissuaded us. Our highway to Naples now ran straight and smooth, and once through the city's southern entrance, we entered a new world as we experienced for the first time the reactions of a defeated enemy city. The Germans had been forced to leave a few days earlier, and by now, October 2, the Allies held a strong position extending from just north of the city straight across the Italian peninsula to just south of Termoli on the shores of the Adriatic Sea.

The streets were so crowded with Neapolitans begging for food and cigarettes that we had great difficulty in moving around. Eventually we were able to make a cursory examination of the city, travelling from the dock and harbor area to Posillipo Hill, to the top of the renowned Certosa of San Martino and along the Via Caricciolo. Like Tunis, the city had suffered little from stray bombs while the docks had been totally demolished with ships sunken alongside every pier. I felt that our forces would have to perform a major restoration job to use the shipping facilities again.

The most serious damage done by the Germans was as they were withdrawing from the unhappy city. With diabolical cruelty they had cut the sewers, allowing them to run into the water mains and contaminate them. The city was literally without water except for a few scattered wells, about which clustered long lines of women and children waiting all day for a few quarts of the precious fluid. Here we saw faces filled with misery and hate, and I had some doubt as to whether the hate was for us or for the Germans.

Despite the crowds and the wandering vendors hawking fruit, ices, and wines, the city seemed more dead than liberated, stinking with filth and rot. The shops appeared to be well stocked with perfumes, silks, and art objects, available at sky-high prices and sold by listless and uninterested salespeople. The city was also infested with booby traps and time bombs, and planted with prostitutes ridden with disease, all of which would eventually take a heavy toll of both Italians and Allies.

We had to spend the night in Naples and that meant finding a safe place to park our truck. In the Piazza Garibaldi, where only the previous day General Mark Clark had arranged a small parade to acknowledge receiving the official surrender of the city, we noticed a building with enormous double wood doors which we felt might lead to shelter. Once inside the courtyard, which measured about eighty feet square, we found a safe refuge. A three-storied brick building totally enclosed the yard, which amplified our shouts of pleasure as we started to unload and make camp for the night. Within minutes we were surrounded by some twenty fairly young girls — redheads, brunettes, and blondes, in all sorts of clothes — asking for food, chocolates, and cigarettes.

By clever questioning we discovered that we had berthed our truck in the midst of a state-authorized brothel! The eager girls declared that they would prepare our food and provide free service for as long as we cared to stay with them. I remember the food, our supplies, of course, as being well prepared, but the rest of the night is a hazy memory. With so many of them and so few of us, we were kept busy the whole night jumping from room to room, from blonde, to redhead, to brunette and back again. In mid-morning they left en bloc to attend their weekly medical examination, which was required by law. We were confident we had not been exposed to disease and from all reports, none was contracted. It would be hard for the rest of our comrades to believe that we had spent such an enervating and exciting evening at no expense to ourselves. Although they spoke little or no English and we certainly spoke no Italian, this theoretical barrier proved to be no obstacle at all. I know we all carried warm memories of that night for years to come.

Arriving back at Serretelle we learned that we had to pack up and prepare to move to Capadichino, the main Naples airdrome. Our advance ground party left while we continued to do our operational flying, basically patrolling the Naples area. Enemy fighters were seen occasionally, but our larger problem was extremely heavy and accurate flak. Most of our work was now at 35,000 feet, but the flak still pursued us. I would get the impression of black pencils flitting by vertically in front of my eyes and exploding. At this altitude the 88 shells were reaching their maximum vertical range, and as their velocity slowed, it was possible to get the impression of something going by your plane. Even at this height it was still eerie to be virtually helpless. Many of us were hit by the very accurate German gunners, and during this short period we lost pilots to flak and a couple to fighter action.

On October 13th we took off for a new station with the move to Naples being scrapped. Our new base, Gioia del Colle, was located on the extreme east coast of Italy, close to the port city of Bari and some thirty miles north of Taranto. Our advance party vainly waited to receive us in Naples, and then made the trip overland and joined up with us a few days later.

Since its formation less than a year earlier, the wing had operated continuously over active war fronts. Its aircraft had covered three invasions and campaigns, during which three hundred enemy aircraft were destroyed and hundreds more probably destroyed or damaged. The pilots and groundcrew were in urgent need of a long rest when those orders to move across Italy came through, and the letdown was traumatic.

The eastern coast of Italy, unlike the western side, had been evacuated and left virtually undamaged by a swiftly retreating German army. It was here, in the towns of Bari, Brindisi, and Lecce that I discovered a new and perhaps truer side of the Italian character.

Gioia del Colle airdrome was an enormous, all-weather grass plot, 2,000 yards in diameter. It was so big that our entire squadron could take off at one time, in almost any direction. It had been a training base for Italian bomber pilots and their training continued on Savoias and Cants while we shared the 'drome. They were not very good pilots, and they crashed their planes regularly.

The base commander, an Italian colonel, thought he saw an opportunity to extend his authority when our wing of four Spitfire squadrons started sharing his facilities. Within a day of our arrival, he issued instructions that we were to stand at attention and salute when the Italian flag was raised and lowered at dusk, that all RAF non-commissioned ranks were to salute all Italian officers, and that Allied officers were to salute the Italian senior ranks. Within hours of the issuance of these ridiculous orders, Group Captain Hugo had them rescinded and reversed.

The Italian winter was fast approaching, heralded by frequent rainy days and bitterly cold, damp nights. We pilots and ground-crew were only prepared for warm weather operations, our main dress being summer khaki. Our blue uniforms and warm clothing had been packed and left in Africa and were supposed to follow when we settled in one spot long enough for our baggage to catch up.

Our ground personnel were billeted far from the 'drome in a cold, damp, and poorly constructed barracks, with no beds and only two blankets per man. We urgently required beds, stoves, additional blankets, and warm clothing. On the other hand, the Italian ground personnel were billeted in warm, modern barracks, furnished with beds and ample blankets.

We had been campaigning for nearly a year with our shabby, mismatched clothes being positive proof of the dirt and hard living we had experienced. The Italians were neatly, even smartly, dressed, and they seemed to relish the contrast between them and us, not acknowledging that we portrayed victory while they stood for something quite different.

Our men began to wonder if we had won or lost the war to the Italians. We met this superior attitude in cities and rural areas, but it was particularly noticeable in the streets — the natives rarely gave us any room when we passed on foot. They ignored us completely. Prices in stores were immediately raised when we entered. And, although not openly hostile, the locals refused to assist us in any way, which was exactly opposite to the cooperation we had found on the west coast.

This eastern half of the country had little contact with the Germans throughout the war and suffered little or no damage as the enemy had hastily retreated, allowing the Eighth Army to advance with minimum opposition. Indeed there was little resistance until our troops neared Foggia and the thirteen important airfields in the area which formed the principal German air force maintenance base in Italy. Perhaps the strange and hostile attitude of these Italians resulted from being sheltered from much of the war's destruction, and this stimulated resentment at being overrun again, this time by us, even though we were now supposed to be "Allies."

The pilots lived in a modern farmhouse that Cam and I had commandeered, located a mile down the road from our crews. The house was stone, very large, and equipped with all normal conveniences. A magnificent stone and wood barn was located almost beside the house, and our practiced eyes told us it would convert easily into a superb mess and lounge. Further away was a large two-storey stone building divided into separate dwellings to house the farm families. We found that we were on a large farm owned by an absentee landlord who lived in Bari. We had blundered into the fuedal system at work, for the tenant farmers were little more than serfs, owning nothing and working hard for just a small share of the crops harvested.

The farmers and their large families treated us in a friendly and generous manner, quite unassuming and yet helpful in many respects, pointing out ripe vegetables or small lambs ready for slaughter or chickens which could be spared. We watched as they washed their gnarled feet to stamp grapes piled in huge vats, and we delighted in the sweet nectar released from a bunghole at the bottom. We returned their friendship with generous donations of canned M and V, Spam, plum pudding, cigarettes, and chocolate. The owner would have been apoplectic had he suspected that his tenants were gleefully sabotaging him behind his back.

When we first found the farmhouse, Cam and I had stood guard while Duke used his van to round up the rest of the pilots. Possession was our strong point, and we did not want anyone else, Allied or Italian, to take it away from us. Before our reinforcements arrived, however, the owner drove up with two fully armed carabiniari, obviously intent on forcing us to vacate his property. We drew our pistols, looking as menacing and determined as possible; we both had had enough of being pushed around by our "Allies." The would-be evictors sensed this and after much shouting and gesturing they left, promising to return.

As it happened the owner did return daily, bringing us food, chickens, and farm produce while he inspected the buildings. We pretended that he was being helpful and generous, not just trying to protect his property.

We built a huge bar in the barn, stocking it with champagne, whiskey, gin, and a variety of wines and liquers. The straw originally stored in the barn had been thrown out and the barn interior had been thoroughly scrubbed, leaving little barn or animal odor. A tiny forty-four-year-old Italian pianist named Vincenzo de Lisio had fastened himself to us a few weeks earlier, and in return for food, attention, and security, he provided us with innumerable hours of delight. Before the war he had played at Grosvenor House in London, a high point in his musical career. Once hostilities started he entertained Italian and German troops on all fronts until meeting up with us. We scrounged an old piano so that Vince could entertain us with renditions of Bach, Beethoven, or Chopin or contemporary Italian and German music. Our relaxing evenings in a warm barn under soft lights dispelled our thoughts of war and our frustration over our work's being made even more difficult by horrid weather. We drank to excess, sang until our voices became hoarse, and felt a peace and happiness we had not known for many months. To his musical talents Vince added the skills of a gourmet cook and an expert scrounger. This little skinny man, barely five feet tall, repaid us many times over for being allowed to live with us. Sadly, his end was brutal, for in December he was accidentally run over by a truck in the blackout, dying instantly.

On October 23 Jim Woodhill, while on a Bari-Brindisi patrol, came across an Me 210, which he chased and damaged before his cannon packed up. We were delighted to think that we might encounter the odd enemy aircraft to relieve the boredom of uneventful patrols.

That afternoon I was doing a similar patrol at 22,000 feet with Bowring as my number 2. For a change I was flying a Spit IX, fitted with a thirty-gallon long-range tank. After about thirty minutes' stooging around, our ground control interceptor "Blackbeer" called, "Tampax leader, I have two bogies for you. To converge steer zero-three-zero degrees and climb." "Roger, Blackbeer," I replied as I opened my throttle wide and started to climb.

At 27,000 feet I suddenly saw them coming from the east. At our altitude and on our course we would have met or converged at some point ahead. They were Me 109G6s with long-range tanks suspended under their bellies.

We saw each other almost simultaneously. The 109s immediately turned hard starboard as they dropped their long-range fuel tanks, and we dropped our tanks as we dove after the fleeing enemy. I got in one short burst of cannon fire before the Me's drew out of range. They maintained a steady dive to 14,000 feet, still staying ahead of us, but the gap was small enough to leave us some hope of combat. We were screaming across the Adriatic Sea toward Albania, which is less than one hundred miles from the Italian mainland.

As their dive become shallower, I kept my dive a little steeper, so that I pulled abreast of them, but at a considerably lower altitude. Then I pulled up the nose of my Spit to climb to their altitude. The Me's, seeing my intention, also started to climb, with the port machine lagging a bit behind the other. "Yellow 2," I called, "hold your fire. We'll catch these guys as soon as our blowers kick in."

Sure enough, at 19,500 feet my supercharger engaged with a roar and a jolt, causing my aircraft to leap ahead. Within seconds I had closed the gap to one hundred yards and opened fire with all my guns. As my bullets struck, my target jinked slightly to port, running into my massed fire and taking numerous strikes on his port wing root, engine, and cockpit. There was a small explosion, pieces flew off the 109, and a reddish brown smoke poured out, which enveloped both his aircraft and mine. He slowly rolled onto his back and headed straight down, with more pieces flying off the machine. I then turned my attention to the starboard 109. After a short burst my cannon jammed. I called to Bowring, who was now very close, to go in and finish him off. Bowring did just that and with a smart bit of accurate shooting hit the 109 so hard that it exploded in front of our eyes.

It had been a long chase and the coast of Albania was appearing below us. It was time to retreat before fuel or enemy fighters became a problem.

Blackbeer congratulated us, and I thanked him for his excellent controlling, which brought about our interception. He phoned our success to the wing, and everyone there was on the field waiting to greet us. For the only time in my operational career, I made a high speed dive over the 'drome and did a victory roll on the deck.

Group Captain Hugo was particularly pleased, for ours were the victories which officially raised the wing count of aircraft destroyed to over three hundred. It also marked the closing chapter in my flying in this theater, for after another half dozen trips, I was finished.

To acknowledge and publicize the wing's achievement, RAF Public Relations bulletin No. H-378 issued October 28, 1943, detailed at great length the history of the wing beginning with the African landings.

The exodus from our squadron and wing because of illness accelerated. Before we were finished, malaria took more than a sixty percent toll on our men, aircrew and groundcrew, all ranks affected. My heart was broken when Pep, for so long my best friend, was shipped out with jaundice and malaria. I had a severe case of worms and checked my stools daily searching for improvement. No luck. We all had fleas, impossible to avoid or clear up, acquired in the early days of the Sicilian campaign. I actually missed the blighters when I was cleaned up in hospital later on for although they tickled day and night, they never travelled below my beltline and rarely bit me. Many of the other fellows were not so fortunate and suffered considerable discomfort.

The wing was being torn apart by rumors, postings, and disease. 81 and 152 Squadrons were posted to Burma to leave on November 3rd. The remaining squadrons were flying with ninety-gallon overload tanks with rumors of sweeps to come over Yugoslavia and Albania. New men arrived and old friends kept leaving. Our farewell parties were almost continuous. With most days being socked in with rain and low clouds, we knew well in advance whether or not we might be required to fly. Our parties became more frantic as we substituted Pol Roger champagne, acquired in vast quantities at about a dollar a bottle, for food at lunchtime. It was terribly disheartening to see our hard won *esprit de corps* vanish within a few short weeks, displaced by lassitude and uncertainty.

Like the rest of us, Duke was showing some strain from the unsettling situation, but his calm and steady good sense prevailed, preventing a total collapse of squadron morale. He was an RAF trained and dedicated professional whose sense of humor would rally us frequently to hope that our future prospects might improve.

It is hard to emphasise how important activity is to pilots. Fighter pilots are a special breed of airmen, with an average age of only twenty-one or less, trained to fight alone, to think rapidly and intelligently, and to be capable of making split-second decisions while retaining a sense that the squadron and its survival are more important than the individual.

We were used to living under enormous tension since a pilot's survival depended almost entirely on his flying ability, the performance of his machine, and tremendous good luck. Almost all of our flying was over enemy territory, but the hazards of flying extended even to simple take-offs and landings so that a pilot was constantly exposed to life-threatening dangers during all of his flying hours. We were tense and keyed up, ready to deal with any problem which arose. There was also a great deal of physical effort expended in flying, particularly in a dogfight. With speed, the flying controls stiffened appreciably, requiring considerable strength to handle. Despite freezing temperatures in the cockpit, a pilot in a strenuous dogfight would work up enough sweat that his body and clothes became soaked. Dogfighting was machine against machine, man against man, a very individual and particular sort of battle, where you knew your survival depended solely on your own skills. The relief at surviving a dangerous trip left a pilot tired but exhilarated with a high which lasted for hours. Many of us drank too much, slept too little, and spent a good deal of time playing pranks on other squadron members. We laughed a lot and I cannot remember a single fight or serious disagreement among any of our pilots. When we lost a pilot, we did not grieve. A few moments would be spent in thoughtful reflection, but since we rarely had a funeral because most men lost were never recovered, we rebounded very quickly after a loss.

Thus, with little flying to key us up, long dreary days of dismal weather, poor health, and a large influx of replacement pilots, our energy and enthusiasm sagged. Our parties and drinking were efforts to regain what we had lost, but it was not to be. We tried hard to maintain our morale and we failed. It was sad.

I became sick and had to put myself in the care of our medical officer, Flight Lieutenant Pugh, who ordered me to bed for a few days. On November 6th he diagnosed my illness as malignant or recurring malaria and ordered my immediate evacuation to Number 30 Mobile Field Hospital just outside Bari. Realizing that I was now definitely tour-expired, I asked Group Captain Hugo to recommend that I be repatriated to England and to use his influence to have me placed on the Central Gunnery School course. I have blessed him ever since because he was able to do just that.

My sad farewells were made from the back of the ambulance. With a temperature of over 103 degrees, I seriously needed expert medical care. Every bump and jolt of the ambulance took me further from the life I had loved so much.

I had met many fine men over the past year and known a particular companionship that exists amongst men who fight and die together. Someone would provide a laugh in our most difficult moments to ease tensions, and I was to find that our good times together usually made up the bulk of our conversations when we would meet again in later years.

I had seen many pilots come and go in the squadron, and I had watched them change. From boys to men the change was rapid and noticeable although the outward appearance remained happy and carefree. The big change was inside, in heart and mind, quickly giving them a maturity far beyond their years.

Squadron life as an active fighter pilot was the only kind of existence I longed for. Completing a tour including over two hundred missions for a total of over three hundred operational hours and having to leave the squadron were the bitterest disappointments I had yet known. But, I was a fatalist and believed that everything that happened, happened for the best. That thought would bolster my spirit and spur my ambition in the months ahead.

CHAPTER 10

BETWEEN CAMPAIGNS
November, 1943 — July, 1944

Shortly after I was bedded down in a crowded ward, Doctor Atkinson, otherwise known as "stethoscope Pete," carried out a thorough examination of me and ruefully explained that I had yellow jaundice as well as malaria. The cure for malaria was to take regular swallows of captured German liquid quinine. Down it went and up it came. Nothing would stay in my stomach, not even dry bread. For eight days this process continued as my strength faded and I seemed to lose interest in living. Because of incoming army casualties, a number of us were to be shipped to a more distant hospital. After a twenty-four-hour wait in a cold, drafty hangar we painfully boarded a Dakota bound for Number 25 Military Field Hospital, Catania.

The Catania hospital was a large building, centrally located, seemingly all windows and terrazzo floors. I have no idea of what use the building served before being converted to hospital service. Here some thirty of us, all in much the same condition, occupied an enormous sunlit room. A doctor stood in the doorway with his arm around the waist of a pretty nurse interviewing each of us in turn, prescribing for all of us a strict no-fat diet. He never came closer than the doorway although nurses and orderlies tended us in a careful and competent manner. The no-fat food was almost inedible, but fortunately Sicilian vendors marched through the ward daily, selling oranges and other fruits, nuts, and chickens which had been cooked in olive oil. I cared little about the no-fat instructions; I felt that I had to regain some of my lost strength and renew my interest in living. By consuming a whole chicken daily, I could feel my strength gradually return, although I was not certain about any improvement in my health problems.

After two weeks I was once again shipped out. It took three tries: on one we survived a blown tire on take-off and on the next we had to turn back because of bad weather. On the third attempt I reached the First General RAF Hospital at Carthage, Tunisia. The treatment for jaundice in this hospital was eat anything you wish, including fatty foods. At night we were each served one bottle of Whitbread beer, also prescribed in our cure. Many of the other patients were still too ill to drink their daily beer rations, so I courageously offered to help them out. Naturally my nocturnal trips to the washroom increased dramatically.

On one of these trips a duty nurse asked if I might assist in identifying a casualty who had just been brought in. She pulled back a blanket to expose a uniformed body lying on a stretcher. Rows of ribbons, a thin face, and blond hair — it could only be Wing Commander Adrian Warburton, DSO and Bar, DFC and two Bars. Apparently he had been driving his open jeep home from a party, quite intoxicated, when he failed to negotiate a sharp curve in the highway. His jeep went one way and he flew out the other side, breaking his hip on contact with the ground. Whether unconscious from drink, drugs, or pain, he didn't move, but the nurse assured me he was very much alive. Within a day this remarkable pilot had taken over the ward, securing VIP treatment and driving the nurses to distraction with his constant and frequently irrational demands for attention.

Warburton had flown Spitfires as a fighter pilot during the Battle of Britain, acquitting himself extremely well while destroying a number of enemy aircraft. It was in Malta, however, where he performed so brilliantly that he became a legend in his own time.

He commanded 683 Photo Reconnaisance Squadron there, and I remember hearing his name frequently broadcast over the station Tannoy loudspeaker system when I was at OTU. It seemed that every time Beurling achieved success and was awarded yet another immediate decoration, Warburton would be awarded one as well. It was as though the two were competitors although performing very different roles, Beurling as a fighter pilot and Warburton as a photo recce pilot.

Warburton was acknowledged to be an extremely skilful pilot, equally at home in single or twin-engined aircraft, and I could attest personally to his single-engine ability after he trounced me so thoroughly months earlier.

One day he could be flying a Beaufighter, taking low-level oblique shots from three hundred feet in Taranto harbor which showed the admiral's laundry flying from a clothesline on the deck, daring the heavy flak to touch him. The next day he might be flying a Spitfire with one of the fighter squadrons. On another day he could be flying a long-range Spitfire over northern Italy, photographing important views of potential targets for Bomber Command. But it was the role of a reconnaisance pilot involving solo trips over great distances into enemy territory that appealed to him most.

There were so many stories of the accomplishments of this fearless and daring pilot that it was nearly impossible to believe that all were true.

Soon after the North African landing, for instance, our military brass wanted to know if Bizerte airdrome was in our hands. Apparently our communications had broken down completely but the information was considered vital. From Malta Warburton took a twin-engined bomber and started a landing with wheels and flaps down. He successfully escaped the heavy ground fire which greeted him, returning to Malta to declare that the airdrome was not yet secure. This story was confirmed by British Commandos who were in a position to observe the attempted landing, but were not strong enough to capture the facility and, in fact, were soon driven back over fifty miles.

Then there was the story of how Warburton's senior officer felt that he was too valuable to lose in the role of fighter pilot and so to discourage his attempts to harass the enemy on his reconnaisance flights had all his machine guns except one removed. His score of enemy aircraft contined to climb even with only one gun. The last gun was finally removed and on his very next sortie he claimed two ME 109s destroyed, without guns, and had the pictures to prove his claim. He had frightened them in exactly the same manner as he had outfought me except the enemy, in panic, had misjudged and crashed into the sea.

On another occasion when he had been shot down, he made

his way to Gibraltar where he demanded an aircraft to fly back to Malta. He was asked "Who the hell do you think you are?" To which he replied, "I'm Warburton." "And who in hell is Warburton?" Adrian replied quietly, "I am *the* Adrian Warburton." But his fame had not spread to the busy Rock yet. In any case, after establishing his identity he was permitted to take a Spitfire to fly the impossible distance to Malta. On the way he shot down one Junkers 88 and damaged another. His exploits were miracles of courage and skill and so daring as to be scarcely creditable. Alas, fate caught up with him after he arrived in England upon his release from Carthage hospital. One story I heard was that he had been mysteriously lost while acting as a Master of Ceremonies on a bombing raid, while another story had him lost on a photo reconnaisance flight deep inside Europe when he was in a fight with enemy jet fighters. Either way the RAF lost one of its most unusual and effective pilots.

I had a normal dread of hospitals although during my two-month stay in various units I developed a great admiration for the doctors, orderlies, and in particular the hard-working nursing sisters. Whether close to the battle lines or far behind the front, the nurses worked long, exhausting hours, never sparing themselves as they tried to heal sick bodies and bring cheer to troubled minds.

On December 3 the doctors pronounced me healthy again even though my skin was still quite yellow. Feeling well and a little sad at the same time I made my way to Base Personnel Depot (BPD), Tunis. With so many tour-expired pilots around, some of them old friends, Christmas and New Year's were spent in drunken parties with plentiful food. On January 9 some of us were posted to BPD, Algiers, from whence we were to embark for England. As I proceeded by air to Algiers, our sky route took me over many of my old battlefields. The familiar sights brought back wonderful memories, which I longingly wished I might be allowed to experience again. We flew through the Souk valley where the sun always seemed to shine. There was our old campsite looking fresh and green, its beauty no longer marred by unsightly brown tents. There, as before, grazed a herd of single-humped camels, and as before, I puzzled as to what possible use their owners had for them. We passed Bône airdrome, still pockmarked with hundreds of old bomb craters. Tears came to my eyes in a sort of tribute to the memory of the brave men I had lived and fought with for nine months, many of whom had unselfishly made the final sacrifice.

The most fortunate of us boarded the S.S. *Elizabethville* on January 18. It was a small Belgian vessel of 9,000 tons, loaded with 1,500 troops and officers. We had cramped, overcrowded quarters but excellent meals to make up for some of our discomfort. Meals at sea were usually of a very high order, and the booze was plentiful as there were no American passengers on board requiring a "no liquor" rule. The nine-day voyage extended to seventeen days as our one-hundred ship convoy shunted about the Atlantic at slow speed to evade enemy subs and air patrols. I learned at this time that all of my belongings had been lost in Bari harbor early in December. Apparently during a night bombing raid on the harbor, the enemy made a direct hit on a tanker, which exploded, and the fire spread to two nearby ammunition ships, which also blew up. Before the raid was over, twenty-two of the twenty-four ships anchored in the harbor had been sent to the bottom. Our loss of life was enormous, and while the supplies and equipment could be quickly replaced, the loss of personnel was a serious and tragic blow. Much later I was to receive clothing coupons to replace my lost items and the lump sum of $140.00 to cover the replacement of my clothes and personal effects, a most modest settlement.

My cabin mate was Flight Lieutenant I.F. "Hap" Kennedy,[12] DFC, from Cumberland, Ontario. We had met a number of times while on operations, and we partied together as we awaited posting. "Hap" later became a squadron leader with a Bar added to his DFC. Tall and blond, with a perpetual grin that stretched from ear to ear, he was a very spontaneous and fun-loving person. Although a teetotaler at parties, he could give the impression that he had imbibed as much as any of us. He carried a small unused pipe which he placed in his mouth, upside down, to give the impression that he smoked, but it was never filled or lighted. Hap had encountered the enemy on nine occasions, firing his guns eleven times, producing a score of ten destroyed and one probably destroyed. Operating from Malta, he was awarded an immediate DFC, which he steadfastly refused to wear until ordered to sew the distinctive purple and white ribbon on his tunic. Hap's main and consuming interest, despite his carefree attitude, was to fight and kill the enemy.

We docked in England early in February, 1944, and the cold weather chilled our blood, thinned as it was by the semi-tropical heat of the Middle East. We proceeded to Bournemouth, which was the personnel reception center for Canadians returning from overseas as well as for those arriving from Canada. I met many old friends there, pilots I had trained or instructed with in earlier days. Some of them had been waiting as long as six months for a posting to an OTU. It was very discouraging for them as there were now far more pilots than there were job openings.

At the center the shabby, brown battledress, battered hats, and deeply tanned faces of us Middle-East veterans contrasted vividly with the young officers fresh from Canada, neat and trim in fairly new uniforms. They marched while we slouched; they appeared to observe rules and regulations while our scruffy bunch had long ago abandoned most military formalities. Our ragged appearance had one beneficial effect, however, for aside from dismaying air force officialdom, it did spur rapid processing of our papers, our food and clothing coupons, and our money and travel vouchers. We were as pleased to head for the sights and sounds of London as Bournemouth was to get rid of us.

I checked in at the Waldorf Hotel and soon made arrangements to visit ADGB (Air Defence of Great Britain) Headquarters to alert them of my presence and to learn what the future held in store. The adjutant there, Flight Lieutenant Haywood, promised that I would be sent to gunnery school on a course starting about March 15. In the meantime I was on my own, free to do whatever I wished as long as I kept him informed of my whereabouts.

That night I went to see the play "Panama Hattie" starring Bebe Daniels, and on the way back to my hotel, I stopped at a little fish and chip shop for a late-evening snack. My wallet was stuffed with two hundred English pounds in large five-pound notes, many weeks of food coupons, and enough clothing vouchers to replace totally my virtually non-existent wardrobe.

Pulling my wallet from my pocket, I took a large note to pay for my food, placing the wallet on a shelf below the counter. I pocketed the change, never giving another thought to the wallet, or to my money, coupons, and personal documents, and continued out the door to my hotel.

I awoke before dawn with a feeling that something was astray, but I was unable to put a finger on the cause for my unease. In my mind I traced the events of the previous day and finally, horrorstruck, realized what I had lost. At first light I went back to the food shop, where I learned they knew nothing of my loss. I next went around the corner to the Bow Street police station, where I received a sympathetic hearing along with assurances that I would not likely see my valuables again. Feeling foolish and dejected I returned to my room to figure what to do next. Then the phone rang. It was Flight Lieutenant Haywood. "Olmsted, did anything happen to you last night?" I related my sad tale until his chuckle stopped me. "I have it in my hands. My Women's Auxiliary Air Force (WAAF) secretary took your stool when you left and found the wallet, which she handed to me a short while ago. Come and pick it up."

What incredible luck! Only two men had any record of my being in England, the adjutant in Bournemouth and the adjutant at fighter headquarters and it was the latter's secretary who had found and returned my wallet. Its value would amount to a year's salary for the young woman. I told Haywood that I would like to reward his secretary suitably. He asked me to wait and in a few moments ushered me into the commander's office. Seated behind an enormous desk was Sir Roderic Hill, commander of the fighter defenses of Great Britain, appearing stern and resplendent in his bemedalled blue uniform. "Olmsted," he said, "I forbid you to reward the young lady. You should expect people to be honest, not pay them to be honest. Dismiss." I have never forgotten those wise but impractical words. In the end I was able to send a reward to the WAAF corporal, although we never met so that I could thank her personally.

My six-week holiday in London proved to be more of a change than a rest as I avidly took in every play and every movie and strove to increase the revenues of numerous quaint pubs. I ran into Winco Razz Berry who suggested it would be a good idea to take the esteemed fighter leaders course after completing the gunnery school course. I agreed that it was a fine suggestion, feeling, however, that I wanted to return to operational flying as soon as possible. I also met Squadron Leader Jimmy Walker, who was soon to be promoted to wing commander in charge of a Canadian wing. He promised to get me into one of his squadrons as soon as I finished my course. Jimmy introduced me to Bobby Page and his exclusive Kimmel Club on Burleigh Street. This was a favorite watering hole for the more distinguished pilots, both bomber and fighter, and I was often the only person in the small bar not wearing some sort of decoration. Famous names, famous pilots, recounted stories which I wish I had recorded at the time since these heroic deeds will probably never appear in print. Enjoyable as all this was, my funds were running low, and I longed to be back in the air.

My course at Central Gunnery School, Catfoss, located near Hull on the east coast, was an interesting and educational period, with plenty of flying, lectures, and training films. Wing Commander Al Deere, a noted New Zealand pilot, was our commanding officer for part of our course and then Wing Commander Winskill, a former CO of 232 Squadron, took over. Our course numbered sixteen pilots, including Hap Kennedy, Al Fleming, and a number of other friends, but the balance were pilots from other Allied and friendly nations. We worked well together, and I received some indication that my skill as a marksman was improving. I had been very critical of myself, knowing full well that my most serious drawback as a fighter pilot was my almost consistent inability to hit an enemy aircraft. By the end of the course I was confident this deficiency had been remedied.

My reward upon graduation from Catfoss was to be posted as gunnery officer to the Detling Wing, a huge grass airfield located near Maidstone in Kent. My duties included sharing the briefing sessions with the wing spy and setting up aircraft identification kits to help the pilots recognize all the various types of aircraft, Allied and enemy. I was also responsible for assessing the cine-films taken by pilots during combat. When the guns were fired a camera located in the wing was automatically activated, photographing the target as long as the gun button remained depressed. After a film was developed I could identify the target, the range, the angle of deflection, and the number of bullet strikes on various parts of the enemy aircraft, and from that make an educated guess as to the final result if the enemy did not blow up while being photographed.

Once I got my equipment and information organized and established, there was little for me to do. The four Spitfire squadrons forming the wing met little opposition on their sweeps over France, Belgium, and Holland, which meant that I had no film to assess. I therefore took the opportunity to roam the countryside, and I had to agree with those writers who said that Kent is one of England's most beautiful counties. I saw it during April and May and felt that the praises sung of England in the spring had not been exaggerated. The foliage was thick and green, and along the narrow country lanes which wound through lovely valleys and over rolling hills, the trees arched over the road forming shady bowers. Tiny fields bulged with young grain while clusters of daisies waved in the breeze. The charming thatched cottages looked exactly as they are portrayed in books and on postcards. Well-tended gardens were a riot of color and perfume and their bordering luxurious green hedges were trimmed to perfection. I often found it difficult to believe that the coast of France was only sixty miles from this blissful paradise. It was especially pleasant to stroll in the warm early evening to a nearby country pub to sip a few pints of bitter and to discuss events of the day with the "locals." They freely voiced their opinions, which I felt to be usually quite well-informed.

As May turned into June we all knew that D-Day, the invasion of Europe, was fast approaching. In my case, although I appreciated being closely associated with active fighter squadrons, I found it particularly frustrating to realize that I was only a supernumary at best, unable to participate in the daily routine of squadron life and, more important, unable to fly operationally on a regular basis.

Although I was technically on my rest period between tours, I pestered RCAF Headquarters by phone and personal visits several times a week to let me return to operational flying. The answer was a consistent "No!" Not until I had served my full period of rest. I asked to be permanently transferred to the Royal Air Force, without success, even though the British would have welcomed my services. Squadron Leader Stocky Edwards, the Canadian CO of 274 Squadron, personally pleaded my case to no avail. He was a superb pilot who had demonstrated great skill and daring in the Western Desert, earning a DFC, and a Distinguish Flying Medal (DFM) and Bar with some sixteen aircraft destroyed to his credit.

Our wing commander, E.C. "Hawkeye" Wells, DFC and Bar, tried to use his influence and charm to secure my posting to his wing. My keenness was rewarded by being allowed to fly from time to time with one or another of the squadrons on sweeps. On D-Day Stocky stood down one of his pilots, allowing me to fly as his number 2. In the squadron log I was listed as pilot X, which would have caused a great deal of trouble for him had I failed to return from a flight. Stocky understood my frustration and was willing to jeopardize his position by allowing me to cover yet another invasion, for which I remain forever grateful.

On another occasion while returning from a sweep over Brussels, I saw an example of the awesome power we had available to throw at the enemy. It was early morning and at twenty-thousand feet we passed a huge force of American bombers heading for Germany. Against a background of towering white cumulus clouds, the summer sun shone brightly, flashing off the silvery skins of the bombers. A parade of over one thousand Fortresses and Liberators stretched for miles and miles, and hordes of fighters flitted about, guarding their big brothers. Even as we sped by on a reciprocal course to that massive formation, it was a number of minutes before the final formations flew by. I reflected back a year to when we considered a big raid in North Africa to consist of fewer than two dozen bombers. How quickly our ability to wage war had increased.

It was about this time that one of the most fiendish weapons yet devised started to roar over the English countryside. It was the V-1 rocket, the "doodlebug" or "buzz bomb" as it was more often called. The V-1 was a small pilotless plane capable of flying at about 400 MPH at predetermined altitudes, most commonly fifteen hundred feet, and carrying an enormous explosive warhead. They were extremely difficult for our ack-ack gunners to hit, although our fastest aircraft did enjoy considerable success in shooting down these hideous weapons. They were usually targeted on London, and our Detling base was exactly under the course they flew from the launch sites in Europe. There were launches every ten minutes or so, day and night, and we frequently felt these noisy machines were flying right through our mess or barracks.

The V-1 could be heard a long distance away, its ramjet engine making a weird, unearthly, pulsating, thunderous sound. As long as we could hear the engine we felt some confidence. When the guidance system stopped the engine, it took the weapon some five seconds to hit the ground with a very distinctive explosive "crump." The damage from this bomb was caused by blast effect, and was very destructive and very powerful. One day when I was standing on a small hill watching a Tempest shoot down a buzz bomb, the bomb headed for me only to land in an orchard several hundred feet away. I threw myself to the ground, yet the force of the blast nearly ripped the shirt from my back. A thick green cloud arose over the orchard, gradually settling onto the trees and the ground.

I picked myself up and walked into the orchard to see what the actual damage amounted to. The hole made by the bomb was very small, being only a few inches in depth and not over ten feet in diameter. The whole force of the explosion was above ground. Several trees had been totally blown apart while, farther away, others were denuded of leaves and bark on the side facing the blast. The tree's foliage had been pulverized into a green chlorophyl-type paint which made the green cloud I had observed and had settled over the ground in a wet messy covering. Several featherless birds still clutched branches as they hung upside down, quite dead. Later I saw the damage resulting from buzz bomb explosions in builtup areas — the bomb would completely demolish several buildings in one blast. Truly a hideous weapon.

On June 5 news of the impending invasion was released to the forces. We were confined to camp while the groundcrews painted broad white and black bands on the wings and tails of the air-craft to identify them more clearly as friendly machines to the invasion forces. The atmosphere at Detling became tense as we paced up and down, awaiting our briefing session. Shortly after 11:00 PM we pilots formed a shadowy procession as we worked our way in the blackout over curbs and obstacles to the under-ground intelligence room. Once inside the brilliantly lighted buildings, we took our seats in a huge theaterlike operations room. Almost dazzled by the gigantic, gaily colored maps which covered three of the four walls, my mind returned to the briefing for the Sicilian campaign, which had taken place in a room barely capable of holding fifty people. At Milazzo before we embarked on the Salerno venture, we had been briefed at the edge of a landing strip amidst heat, flies, and dust. For this most gigantic under-taking we would have the finest of equipment and the best of facilities. The other invasions had been testing grounds where ideas and tactics were sometimes experimented with so that this great invasion could be assured of success.

Soon the wing commander, his intelligence officers, and his army liaison officers walked into the room with more rolls of maps and piles of books under their arms. Winco Wells mounted the dais and within seconds had a large map pinned to the wall displaying the Normandy coast. There was an audible gasp from the pilots. We had not considered Normandy as an invasion point; most of us had speculated that Dieppe would be the focus of the attack. Winco Wells turned to address us and for the next hour and a half he talked, unfolding the most stupendous, beautifully planned invasion yet devised.

At twelve minutes to midnight, the first troops were to be dropped by parachute onto French soil. The American paratroops were landing in the Cherbourg area while British paratroops were landing between Cabourg and Trouville, many miles to the east. The paratroops were to capture and hold certain strategic points and to disrupt the German communication system behind the beaches.

The invasion was supposed to have taken place twenty-four hours earlier, but a postponement had been caused by bad weather. It was to have been timed to coordinate with the offensive in Italy and in Russia, but the Italian offensive could not wait and General Alexander had to start his push several weeks before the Normandy invasion. Apparently it was all the Allied commanders could do to persuade Marshal Stalin to wait until June, for he wanted to launch his offensive in May.

Throughout the past few weeks the thousands of bombers that we had seen passing overhead had been engaged in an astonishing task. They had been attacking tactical and strategic targets in every part of German-held territory, paying particular attention to the area bounded on the south and east by the Loire and Seine Rivers. Prior to D-Day every bridge, both road and rail, crossing these two rivers had been bombed out of existence. This forced all German supplies and reinforcements destined for the Normandy front to be routed through Paris, causing a great deal of delay and trouble for the enemy. It also led to a build up of masses of rolling stock in the Paris region where they were later bombed by our waiting bomber forces.

The Allies had the staggering strength of ten thousand aircraft with possibly another four thousand in immediate reserve. It was estimated that the Germans had about one thousand aircraft, including bombers and fighters, to throw at our forces. Another thousand were deployed well inland and could be brought to bear against the western front within a few days, but this would divert them from their primary function, defending the German homeland. Our duty, as Spitfire pilots, was to cover the beaches and the shipping so that the German aircraft would be unable to bomb or strafe our troops at sea or on land. Later on, when airfields were built in France, we would operate from them, but in the meantime the short-range fighters were to fly from the south coast of England.

The invasion armada was made up of more than four thousand ships of all types with as many again held in reserve. We had several battleships and monitors as well as 150 destroyers, 100 cruisers, and a large number of submarines and lighter naval craft. The Germans were expected to counter-attack with their navy, which could muster five destroyers, about 200 submarines, and possibly 200 E and R boats, vessels very similar to our motor-torpedo boats.

Even as we were being briefed, one thousand Lancasters in ten waves of one hundred each were dropping 2,500 tons of bombs on the coastal gun emplacements along the invasion beaches. Deep behind this area a large number of Mitchell bombers were dropping flares along the roads and railroads to provide light for Mosquito bombers to bomb and strafe all moving transport. Further, there were standing patrols of aircraft over many of the enemy airdromes, ready to attack any German aircraft attempting to take off to try to run the gauntlet of our night fighters.

As I walked from the briefing room, I knew that the paratroops were already on their way down, and as I peered to the southwest, because of an unusual layered cloud formation, I could see the bright reflected flashes of our exploding bombs falling on the Normandy defences some 120 miles away. This was the stark reality of the gigantic events now underway.

The success of the D-Day invasion and the days immediately following have been told in hundred of books by authors who were there and by historians who were not. In an operation as large and crucial as the Normandy invasion, many things could and did go wrong, but overall, the faults and omissions were negligible. In my opinion, had Hitler thrown in the army he had waiting for a suspected landing in the Pas de Calais area, the outcome would still have been in our favor. The invasion front was too wide, our resources in manpower and equipment too great, and our reserves too plentiful to have failed. Rommel correctly predicted that if the Allies were not defeated on the beaches, the war would be lost. Added to this was our overwhelming air superiority, which was so complete and effective that German aircraft attempting to attack the landing beaches were literally flying suicide missions. The Luftwaffe could not afford to squander its diminishing resources in such a hopeless task, with the result that our pilots, much to their disappointment, saw very few enemy aircraft.

During the early days of the invasion I flew a number of patrols and sweeps with the Detling Wing while still trying on a daily basis to persuade RCAF Headquarters to post me to an operational squadron. Then, in mid-June when I visited our headquarters in person, a squadron leader stopped me in the hall.

"Olmsted? Are you Olmsted?" he asked. "Yes, Sir," I replied. "Where in hell have you been? We've been looking all over for you — you're to go back on ops immediately." There had been another foul up, with the right hand not knowing what the left was doing, but now I could care less, for my prayers had been answered.

The next day I presented myself complete with baggage to 83 Group Supply Unit (GSU), Redhill, in Surrey, and moved a few days later to Bognor, in Sussex. I drew camp equipment, a parachute, and flying togs from stores in preparation for a move to the continent, where the first Spitfire squadrons had just started to operate from hastily prepared flying strips in Normandy. A GSU is a station where large numbers of pilots and aircraft were kept in readiness to replace squadron losses with a minimum of delay. I was now part of the Second Tactical Air Force commanded by Air Marshall Sir Arthur Coningham, which included all the air elements assigned tactical tasks such as air-to-air combat and ground attack, as opposed to strategic assignments, the bombing of cities and major targets by heavy bombers in support of the continental British and Canadian armies. 83 Group, commanded by Air Vice-Marshal Harry Broadhurst, included ten wings which, in turn, included sixteen all-Canadian squadrons flying Spitfires, Mustangs, and Typhoons.

As happy as I was at this rather sudden turn of events, my pleasure was further heightened by the knowledge that I would once again be serving under the command of Harry Broadhurst. He had performed brilliantly during the Battle of Britain as a squadron commander and later as a distinguished wing leader. He was known to be a fine pilot and a remarkable shot, as proven by the number of enemy aircraft which fell to his guns. Later he had gone to the Desert Air Force, where his fighter pilot experience and innovative tactics were honed as he provided a new design for air support for the army. His concept of how a tactical air force should operate to best advantage, extending from the formation that a squadron should fly, basically a finger-four configuration, to having army intelligence officers working with our intelligence officers to ensure that our role and the army's were in harmony, became the model for other commanders. We were to support and protect the army, and under Broadhurst our flying reached the highest level of achievement and efficiency.

On the morning of July 2, I boarded an old Anson aircraft to fly to my new squadron, which had recently arrived in France. As I crossed the Channel, just skimming the waves, I tried to visualize what living and operating with Canadians would be like. Having done all of my operational flying with the RAF, I knew that I would miss my English friends and the RAF way of doing things, but I felt somehow that working with my own countrymen would be an exciting experience. The coming months were to prove that it was a privilege and pleasure, far beyond my wildest imaginings, to operate in an all-Canadian unit.

CHAPTER 11

FRANCE AND 442 RCAF SQUADRON

July, 1944

The Anson stopped at landing ground B-3, St Croix-sur-Mer on the Normandy beachhead. Unlike my posting to 81 Squadron in Africa when I was filled with uncertainty and some trepidation, on the present occasion I felt nothing but confidence, elation, and an enthusiasm which might have surprised seasoned veterans. My new home was 442 RCAF Squadron, commanded by Squadron Leader Dal Russel, DFC and Bar, forming part of the 144 Wing commanded by Wing Commander Johnny E. Johnson,[13] DSO and two Bars, DFC and Bar, the outstanding British pilot whose career was so closely linked with Canadian fighter pilots and squadrons.

To this point the squadron had enjoyed a brief but interesting existence. It originated at Station Rockliffe as Number 14 (Fighter) Squadron in January, 1942 with Squadron Leader Dal Russel as its first commanding officer. After spending several months on the British Columbia coast flying P-40 Kittyhawks, the squadron moved to the Aleutians under the command of Squadron Leader Brad Walker, DFC, to fight the Japanese outposts on Kiska for six months before returning once again to British Columbia. Early in January, 1944, the squadron embarked for England where it was renumbered 442 and joined two other squadrons, 441 and 443, also recently arrived from Canada, to form 144 RCAF Wing with Johnson as the flying winco. Equipped with Spitfire IXs the wing flew innumerable training exercises as well as a number of fighter sweeps over Europe, sometimes penetrating as far as the Ruhr. Then, in April, Dal Russel was once again made CO and the squadron sorties included dive-bombing bridges, V-1 sites, and other worthwhile targets of opportunity. The squadron relocated to Ford on the south coast to prepare for coverage of the landing beaches. Then, on June 16, it moved to France to become the first British fighter squadron to return to French soil since the fall of France in 1940. Despite the number of sorties flown since its formation in England, none of the pilots could claim an enemy aircraft destroyed until June 22. By the end of June, however, it was the highest-scoring squadron in the wing with fifteen destroyed.

After loading my gear onto a waiting truck, I stomped through mud and rain to Dal Russel's tent, where I had been directed to report, and hammered on his tent flap. A shouted "Come on in" welcomed me as I entered a dimly lit tent to see a tall, blond, handsome, and half-naked officer in the process of shaving. Shaking my hand, he bade me have a seat while he continued with his ablutions.

"You should know the history of the squadron, Bill," he said, "so that you know the problems we've had and why I asked for you." This last bit of information excited me more than a little.

He then proceeded to detail the squadron's story from its original formation in Canada under his command through to the present moment. He emphasized that all of the groundcrew were from the original group while most of the pilots had been with the squadron before coming to England as an autonomous flying unit. The pilots were keen, daring, and aggressive with many hours of flying experience, but with little operational experience to go with their flying ability. To offset this shortcoming, several experienced leaders had been added to the squadron strength, but it was still difficult to control the extremely spirited and intrepid pilots. Despite only six weeks of operational experience, the squadron was the highest scorer in the wing and, he added, "I intend to keep it that way."

With a twinkle in his eyes he concluded, "I feel that in order to get the most out of these keen pilots still more experienced leadership is needed. That's why you are here. You'll fly as a flight commander for a while, and I'd appreciate you passing on as much gen as possible to the fellows."

I was greatly impressed with Dal's presentation and even more so with the man himself. As one of the earliest RCAF pilots to go to England, Dal was among the few RCAF who flew fighter aircraft in the Battle of Britain. While with Number 1 Squadron he destroyed five of the enemy, for which he was awarded the DFC. Along with MacGregor and McNab, he was among the first Canadians to be so decorated. After completing his first tour, he returned to Canada, serving for a time as CO of the forerunner of 442 Squadron. Later he went back to England to complete a second tour with 411 RCAF Squadron, earning a Bar to his gong and promotion to the rank of wing commander, completing his second tour on October 18, 1943.

After another rest period he became one of the few Canadians successful in obtaining permission to fly a third tour of operations. To do so he had to accept a rank demotion to squadron leader in order to take over 442 Squadron. During the six months I was to serve under him, I watched and participated as he built the highest-scoring wing in the Second Tactical Air Force. Dal was a superb organizer, a fine pilot, and a great leader. I admired his understanding of human nature and how his personality inspired confidence and cooperation in every man who served under him. He was never too busy to talk to the most junior airman on the station or to pause and chat with some pilot who sought his advice or understanding. His open personality and friendly, spontaneous nature got the best, and the most, out of every man in the wing.

Within a week of my meeting him, Dal was posted to command 126 Wing which he had originally formed at Redhill in July, 1943. Our present 144 Wing was dissolved and Johnson moved to command 127 Wing. 442 Squadron was happily incorporated into Dal's new wing with Squadron Leader Harry Dowding taking over as my new CO.

During my months with the squadron, I learned more and more to appreciate the opportunity to work for Dal. He had an infectious laugh and a great sense of humor which we came to know well because he was constantly mingling with the pilots. His brother Hugh had been shot down and killed on June 16, which explained the dark circles around his eyes I noticed during our first meeting, but that was the only sign of the grief he kept bottled up within himself. Time and again I was to observe and even experience his compassion and understanding.

Within a week of our move into 126 Wing, I was given command of B Flight, with Flight Lieutenant Dean Dover in charge of A Flight. We lived entirely under canvas, as I had done so often in the past, and I was pleased to share a double tent with Harry Dowding, Dean, and our squadron medical officer, Flight Lieutenant Jack Whitelaw. What the men lacked in ops experience they more than made up for in a seemingly inherent ability to scrounge the amenities to make tent living more comfortable. It seemed as though they wanted the best of everything, and no effort was too much to acquire chairs, carpets, lights, and radios to make our quarters more home-like.

I was to learn that a Canadian squadron in a Canadian wing was a much more formal and structured organization than I had previously experienced. We had a patron, as did the other squadrons, ours being the City of New Westminster in British Columbia, and newspaper reports used that name as frequently as they used our squadron number. Each squadron had eighteen Spitfire IXs on strength, as well as twenty-six pilots, a commanding officer, an adjutant, an intelligence officer, a medical officer, and an engineering officer, who was in charge of approximately 115 ground personnel. This gave a squadron a total strength of 150 men.

126 Wing was commanded by Group Captain Gordon R. MacGregor, OBE, DFC, of Montreal, who had fought in the Battle of Britain and had received his decoration simultaneously with Dal. He had enjoyed an outstanding record as a civilian pilot and his wartime experience and accomplished administrative skills made him an ideal teammate for Dal and for the wing.

Our wing contained four fighter squadrons, 401, 411, 412, and ourselves, 442. Wing headquarters included over 300 men, including signals, motorized transport, kitchen, clerical, intelligence, and controller personnel, a senior medical officer, and a large section responsible for all major repairs and inspections of the aircraft. Each squadron carried out its own regular daily maintenance and minor inspections while the more extensive work was completed by the wing mechanics.

Each squadron divided its pilots into two shifts, One shift worked from noon one day until noon the next when the pilots were released to do whatever they wished, and the second shift took over for the next twenty-four hours. At the same time, it was arranged that there would always be two pilots on a week's leave in England, allowing each man a complete vacation once every three months. Quite frequently the returning pilots filled their ninety-gallon drop tanks with beer for the groundcrews, which guaranteed extra care on their part to execute perfect landings.

Each pilot was assigned a specific aircraft and in some cases two pilots shared the same aircraft. Each kite had its own rigger, fitter, and armorer, with assistance from squadron photographers, wireless experts, electricians, and chaps who ensured that the oxygen bottles were always full. This system promoted a good deal of cooperation between the pilots and the groundcrew to ensure that each aircraft was maintained at full serviceability. As I had been with the RAF, I was always proud of the dedication and expertise of the Canadian groundcrews. I knew that every time I flew an aircraft that it had been examined and cared for to the best of human ability, and I never flew a machine in Europe that malfunctioned because of sloppy maintenance. Words are inadequate to express my admiration for the hard working, dedicated groundcrew mechanics. Their abilities extended beyond servicing aircraft, for their drive and inventiveness allowed them to acquire or devise living comforts which were much better than what the pilots enjoyed. These comforts included much sought-after mattresses. They had a great advantage, however, for when we moved from airfield to airfield, they could always ensure that their acquired comforts were safely packed in the transport trucks, since they loaded these trucks.

When the wing moved to landing ground B-4, Beny-sur-Mer, just north of Caen, we settled in prepared for a lengthy stay. Dean Dover was promoted to squadron leader to take command of 412 Squadron with Flight Lieutenant W.B. Steve Randall taking his 442 Squadron A Flight. We rarely flew as a complete squadron since our protective patrol duties required only four or six aircraft in a sortie. As a flight commander, I could schedule myself to do as much flying as I wished. The result was that I flew more than the others and could watch the flying habits and skill levels of the other pilots, noting with pleasure their high degree of flying ability.

Throughout July we were plagued by an unusual amount of wet, cloudy weather which frequently rendered the airfield unsuitable for flying. When the sun shone the ground dried out rapidly so that the beachhead was frequently enclosed in a dusty haze. Our flying still consisted of routine patrols over the beachhead and our front-line areas. Occasionally we carried a 500-pound bomb suspended from the belly of the aircraft to attack specific targets requested by the army, or we might range further afield to attack and strafe targets of opportunity, usually moving transport of some kind. Very occasionally we made a sortie in squadron strength, which I led most of the time. Harry Dowding was nearing the end of his second tour, and had promised me the squadron, as had Dal, when he finished. His completion was delayed by various maladies, including dysentry, which attacked most of the personnel at one time or another, and prolonged his stay as CO. This delay did not bother me in the least since Harry had given up in disgust trying to control the amount of flying I did, finally allowing me to fly as often as I pleased. If there is a pilot's heaven, I felt I was there.

There were several very apparent differences in our flying in France when compared to my Middle East experience. Most of our flying was done at between 8,000 and 15,000 feet as compared to the 25,000 to 35,000 feet of earlier days. We also encountered flak on every trip, much of it being small calibre which you only noticed when an aircraft was hit. In addition we fired our guns on nearly every flight, not at enemy aircraft, for there were so few to be found, but at ground targets. This made every sortie seem worthwhile and productive, and returning pilots felt that they had done their bit for the day as opposed to just stooging around consuming fuel. Finally, the techniques of mobile controlling developed in the Middle East, coupled with superb equipment, allowed our air controllers to be extremely effective, an invaluable asset to the flyers. Squadron Leader John Edison, our senior controller, with his callsign "Kenway," had our complete confidence, and we knew that he would provide instant and accurate information, be it how to locate an enemy formation or a quick, direct course back to the safety of our base.

We lost pilots regularly, invariably from flak damage. We saw Flight Lieutenant Halloran go down twenty-five minutes into his very first operational flight. A few days later Flight Lieutenant Roseland went missing. In the same period our boys attacked and destroyed six midget submarines.

Anything behind enemy lines that moved, regardless of location, became a target for our guns. It was at times like this that I appreciated the aggressiveness of our pilots, and I am proud to say that while I was with them, they never hesitated to seek out and try to destroy every conceivable target. Dispatch riders on heavy motor bikes made wonderful targets as they zipped along a dusty road because the noise of their powerful bike engines drowned out the sound of our approaching strafers. A cannon shell striking the rider would explode with a bright green flash as the bike crashed into a ditch or a tree. Our intelligence information indicated the Germans felt that being a dispatch rider was about the riskiest business a soldier might be required to tackle.

On July 20 I had my first opportunity to check the quality of our air controllers and to test my air-firing ability. I was on a high cover patrol over the beaches with my number 3, Gerry Blair, an experienced pilot from Montreal, and two wingmen who were raw rookies with fewer than a dozen trips between them.

Kenway control called, "Hello Blue Leader. I have forty to fifty bandits not too far away. Are you interested?"

"Blue Leader to Kenway," I replied. "Sure am. Please give height and course to intercept."

We were at about 20,000 feet south-west of Caen. I ordered my section to use full throttle and start climbing. Kenway came back, "Blue Leader, steer 270 degrees. Bandits at 23,000 feet travelling north to south, right in front of you. You should see them now."

Sure enough, within a minute or so I picked out a stream of aircraft flying at right angles to my course. As I got closer I could see that they were an enormous gaggle of Fw 190s, some with the long nose which indicated a newer type of Focke-Wulf. I turned our flight 90 degrees to starboard, flying parallel to the enemy but going in the opposite direction. In a few sconds as the last 190 went by, I switched on my radio to advise Kenway that the enemy had been located and that I intended to attack. With a "Tally ho" I turned 180 degrees to port and fastened on to the last 190, which continued to fly straight ahead while the rest of the enemy split in half with one section turning to port and the other to starboard in climbing turns to come around and attack us from the rear. I suppose their delay in making this maneuver earlier must have been caused by their leader's doubting that four aircraft would dream of attacking his massive formation.

I felt an exhilaration I had never know before combined with a feeling of supreme confidence. This would be my first opportunity to practice the markmanship I hoped I had learned at Central Gunnery School. I intended to make the most of it.

I closed in on my target while still watching the other 190s sweeping around to attack from my rear. Squinting through my reflector sight, I drew a bead on my target and pressed the gun button activating only the cannon. My guns made a deep chattering sound with black smoke streaming over my wings, and the cockpit filled with cordite fumes. The cannon shells struck hard in the cockpit and wing root of the 190 with bright red flashes. Large chunks of metal flew off the stricken machine, with a quantity of the debris striking my aircraft and leaving dents in noncritical areas. The Fw rolled slowly to one side, streaming flames and, soon, exploding in a huge ball of fire. My total firing time was less than three seconds with the attack finishing off at less than 50 yards distance and some twenty-five degrees of deflection.

Even as I watched the other 190s lining up to dive on me, I was tremendously elated, realizing that at long last I was pretty certain of hitting any target I might aim at. My confidence soared and I looked almost disdainfully at the diving Fws. Confident or not, I kept turning my head making sure that no enemy was getting within range without my being aware of his position.

I decided to break hard to port and upward, into the attacking enemy. As they flashed by I completed a 360 degree turn and again fastened onto the last enemy as he flashed by. The pilot saw me on his tail and started to turn to port in a diving turn as he struggled to escape. Still turning, I fired from less than two hundred yards at twenty-five degrees deflection, closing rapidly to less than 75 yards. I thumbed the gun button and every cannon shell struck in the engine and cockpit with brilliant flashes. In a second the 190 exploded right in front of me, and again, flying debris struck my aircraft, but caused only minor damage.

With so many enemy and so few of us, in a strange way we almost had them outnumbered. With so many 190s flying around we could find any number of targets while they had to watch what we were doing and be careful not to run into each other. I had no idea where the rest of the aircraft in my flight might be, nor was I concerned. In the short time I had been with the squadron, I had made my position clear regarding the function of a number 2 or wingman, and I instructed all of my pilots that, once an attack had begun, every man was on his own.

Gerry Blair knocked one 190 down, with the pilot bailing out before his aircraft had been destroyed. Our wingmen were not hit nor did they fire their guns.

Suddenly, every 190 turned on its back and dived for a cloud layer lying at about 4,000 feet. It was remarkable to see so many aircraft do the same maneuver at the same time as they darted for the protective cloud cover. One minute the air was full of aircraft and the next it was empty! I dived after the 190s with my throttle wide open, but my Spit was left far behind. The 190 was such a superior machine in a power dive.

I called Kenway. "Enemy aircraft attacked and now diving. They seem to be heading due south." Kenway seemed to think they were heading east and was advising other squadrons in our area how and where to intercept the fleeing Hun. Hap Kennedy was in the area with his 401 Squadron, and he called me asking for directions on how to intercept. I replied over my R/T to Hap, "190s diving due south from Saint Lo, ducking into low cloud cover."

"Okay, thanks," radioed back Hap, and he was successful in finding some of the scattered enemy formation.

Back at base I gratefully accepted congratulations. I thought I could detect some incredulity in the pilots as to my sanity in attacking when so heavily outnumbered. Here again my experience had come to my rescue because I had encountered similiar odds during my first tour without worrying unduly about being outnumbered. Another factor in our favor, which I did not realize at the time, was that this strong Focke-Wulf formation was likely composed of fairly new Luftwaffe pilots led by a few very experienced German fighter pilots, possibly on some sort of a training flight. If they had been really clued up, aggressive types, they would never have let my flight get into a position to turn into them so easily and inflict so much damage in less than sixty seconds.

Upon examination we found that not one of our aircraft had been hit other than by the debris from the exploding 190s that had dented my aircraft.

Our intelligence facilities were far better and more complete than anything I had known before. We were a mobile wing, so organized that we could pack up and move, lock, stock, and barrel, by truck and aircraft, to a new location at a moment's notice, and we had, among our gear, two large intelligence vans. These were commonly set up side by side with enough distance between them to allow collapsible side arms to be raised providing a roof over the space between. With wall tarps and a cocoa mat floor this room became the centre of our operations, staffed by Flight Lieutenant Monty Berger, our excitable and energetic senior intelligence officer, his assistants, Flying Officer Don Stewart and small, quiet Pilot Officer Gord Panchuk, and an army liaison officer, Captain Bob Forbes. The walls were lined with maps of every description with special situation maps carefully marked showing in great detail the Allied and German positions. All known flak areas were clearly marked, and when new flak was reported by a pilot, it was added to the map. Since we were flying small formations to respond to the numerous army requests for our services, the intelligence officers were kept busy briefing the flights on each specific target in considerable detail, being just as careful in the debriefing when the flight returned to report the results. The army liaison officers were particularly useful in our support role, for they were able to emphasize the position and importance of each target. We learned some of the difficulties faced by the men on the ground and could appreciate more fully why our job was so critical. We frequently attacked small targets such as a particular farmhouse or a grove of trees at the edge of a woods, sometimes scant yards in front of our own troops. It is a great credit to the army liaison officers and to our pilots that to my knowledge we never inadvertently attacked our own men.

Our living conditions at Beny-sur-Mer were much the same as I had known earlier except we had no batmen to do officer's chores — the Canadian and English philosophies were directly opposite on the subject. Our food was of poorer quality, which may have been because the harsher living conditions in the Middle East were compensated for by more and better canned food stocks. We Canadians augmented our diet through the numerous and bountiful parcels we received from family and friends. These were generously shared with appropriate comments being made on the thought and care which went into the creation of each parcel. Every man did his own laundry, and while most of us were pretty good about the maintenance of our washables, a few of the pilots neglected this chore for long periods until forced by disparaging remarks to clean up or go.

Because our airfield was located close to the landing beaches, completely surrounded by hordes of soldiers and mountains of war supplies and equipment, the German bombers paid nightly visits. Sometimes they came in high, although usually they sneaked in low; regardless of the manner of approach, the noise of exploding bombs and of our anti-aircraft fire sent us scrambling for slit trenches, cursing as we stubbed our bare toes on unseen obstacles in the dark. The raids were quite effective, continuing until our forces broke out of the beachhead a month later. A few of the more industrious among us dug deep trenches in their tents into which they lowered their canvas cots, and over which they placed a metal roof for protection against flying shrapnel, thus ensuring their safety against everything but a direct hit. As noisy and frequent as the raids were, I don't believe we lost any men to them — only sleep.

I have always been a light sleeper, and I've always been able to get along on very little sleep, accustomed to arising, regardless of the hour, feeling, as the pilots put it, "disgustingly happy and energetic." When the squadron had to be prepared to fly at first light, I would make it my duty to waken the various pilots scheduled on the shift. As only one or two men might be required from each tent, I always tried to be quiet to allow the non-duty pilots to continue sleeping undisturbed. Almost without fail some of the pilots reacted to being awakened in exactly the same manner each morning, sometimes with amusing results!

H.F. "Hughie" Morse from Honey, British Columbia, was a young, handsome, and quiet youngster who had married shortly before joining the squadron. I would stroke his sleeping face gently to see a smile appear before he opened his eyes. I knew that he was dreaming of his wife as he woke up, and he would get up with a sheepish grin. Hughie was a fine, aggressive pilot, later awarded the DFC for his fearless flying. D.W. "Goodie" Goodwin from Maynooth was a constant problem on the ground or in the air. When I shook him he always responded quickly and pleasantly with a bright, "Yes, yes, I'm awake. Sure, sure, I'll be right up. Don't worry." And ten minutes later he would be saying the same thing. I could never be fully convinced that he did not talk in his sleep. In the air he would be diving to strafe a target before he would report his action over the R/T and request permission to do exactly what he was doing. Little "Goodie" had remarkable eyesight, which combined with his skilful flying and aggressive nature, eventually earned him the reputation as the top ground target scorer in the wing, winning him a DFC and Bar before his tour was over. "Goodie" was incorrigible, refused to be restrained, and was always ready to attack any target, anywhere, at any time. It was a miracle of good luck that he survived the war.

Neil Burns,[14] our youngest and biggest pilot, had played football in his hometown Toronto with a semi-pro team. The tiny Spitfire cockpit barely contained his huge frame, but he was an excellent, conscientious pilot who performed any task requested. Neil was a slow starter in the mornings, stumbling around half asleep for a couple of hours mumbling "Cruel world" or "Won't let people sleep." His first operational trip was as number 2 to Johnny Johnson, and Neil related later that he was so anxious not to screw up that he stuck indecently close to Johnson's ass. I flew a lot with Neil, knowing that I could always count on him, regardless of the situation, to perform his job. His skill and determination eventually won him a DFC. After I left the squadron and Neil had completed his tour, the squadron needed an extra pilot and asked him to fill in. He amiably agreed, and as so often happens, was shot down on his buckshee (extra) trip and taken prisoner.

Then there was "Bo" Middleton, whom I had instructed with in Canada and who was now getting his chance to fly operationally. He was massively built with powerful arms and heavy-lidded eyes which I always felt saw only part of what was taking place. Bo was not a good shot, but he made up for it by being very aggressive and a first-rate pilot. Once he went down to strafe a truck scooting along a road, which he missed, his bullets crashing into the woods bordering the road. The whole woods erupted in smoke and flame, for his cannon fire had struck an ammunition, petrol, and storage area, and burned for several days, finally revealing a large number of charred vehicles. You did not always have to be good — just lucky. Bo won a DFC for his accomplishments although I never gave him any marks for his wake-up performance. The first time I wakened him I received a right to the jaw. The next time and for ever after I shook him by the foot. His arms always flailed as he tried to strike his tormentor; I had learned the hard way to stay out of his reach.

While our major task continued to be the strafing of enemy transport and light armored vehicles, we did come across some different and more difficult targets. We frequently attacked German Tiger and Panther tanks, but their six-inch armour plating was quite impervious to our cannon shells unless we managed to score a lucky hit in the rear exhaust close to the fuel storage tanks. They were a piece of cake for the rocket-firing Typhoons, however. On one occasion while I made several attacks on two tanks in the Falaise area, I noticed a squadron of Typhoons circling above me waiting, it seemed, while I had my fun, after which they would show me how it is done. I made way and four "Tiffies" peeled off and dove on the targets. Eight rockets were loosed. When I dived down to have a look after their attack, there were only two blackened spots and some twisted debris — but no tanks. They had been blown to smithereens!

Strafing was a very dangerous, though thrilling, assignment and in the case of the Spitfire, a difficult one as the Spit was a very unstable gun platform. After a target was spotted the normal procedure was to detail two or more aircraft to attack while the remainder of the squadron hovered above at between five and eight thousand feet. The attacking aircraft would dive at a very steep angle until about seven hundred yards from the target, and clocking possibly 400 mph, when the pilot would decrease the dive angle to about twenty degrees. He would open fire at about four hundred yards, closing to one hundred unless his bullets blew up the target. In carrying out a full attack, the guns fired for only a second or two, and yet their effect could be devastating.

At first I disliked strafing because it meant frequently attacking a target in a heavily defended flak area. Eventually, however, I came to enjoy it, for the sense of accomplishment and the thrill of daring nearby guns made the task a grim yet exhilarating game. Very often when we attacked a truck, it would stop before we started to fire and a number of soldiers would jump out. By this time both the soldiers and the truck would be in the ringsight. The German soldiers obligingly stood stock-still in surprised poses of fear and dismay, the sound of the Spitfire having paralyzed their muscles. Then with a firm pressure on the gun button the truck would be blasted, and the soldiers would disappear in bright flashes.

In a strafing attack, a pilot sees the immediate results of his efforts. He can claim a damaged enemy truck or a destroyed vehicle, should it erupt in flames. Soldiers, gun positions, locomotives, and other targets vulnerable to cannon fire can be claimed in the same manner. After a day's flying, it was possible for a pilot, a squadron, or a wing to total all claims and publish an official damage report, which could later be confirmed by our cine-gun films.

In our role as dive bombers we were forced to use a trial-and-error method, for we had no special apparatus to aid us in aiming our bombs. The Spitfire carried a 500-pound bomb hung on a makeshift rack slung underneath the belly and later on in the campaign we added a 250-pound bomb under each wing. These ruined the appearance of the streamlined Spit, making it look like a fat ugly duck, overloaded and cumbersome, and greatly reduced our speed and maneuverability. But once the bombs had been dropped, the machine regained all of its great fighting qualities.

When we reached a bombing target, I would order the squadron into line astern. I would have the target sighted to slide under my port cannon and after it had disappeared for five seconds, I would peel off and dive steeply from 8,000 feet. With the target sighted in the firing ring I would release the bombs, pulling out of the dive at about 2,000 feet. Our bombing targets were often bridges, marshalling yards, or enemy supply depots where we would encounter heavy and accurate flak. Despite attacking such heavily defended targets, our losses were more often sustained during strafing attacks.

Flak is the one thing that pilots, be they fighter or bomber, fear above everything else. Flying along in formation a mile or two above the earth, it is possible to avoid flak by taking evasive action through frequent alterations of course and altitude, but once commited to a dive on a target, the pilot must press home his attack while shells and bullets of all calibres flash by. We were quite philosophical about flak, as much as we hated it, because surviving flak was strictly a matter of luck, and it claimed the best pilots as well as the poorer ones in time. The 88 millimeter shells and heavier calibre guns burst with a bright red flash surrounded by a large ball of black, wicked-looking smoke that hung lazily in the sky. At dawn or dusk, pink tracer shells were visible, a sight that fliers will remember for years. It was a horrible feeling to climb away from a target and watch the rosy balls of red-hot death streaming by, missing you and your aircraft by a very few feet. Then there was the reverse effect when you attacked a target, and the shells seemed to come up so slowly that you felt you were watching them for ages. Not until they were close did you get the full impression of their tremendous speed. It took steady nerves to carry on facing so many deadly messengers.

The German anti-aircraft gunners had their type of warfare

perfected to a very high degree. Several times we were called upon to supply area cover while hundreds of RAF heavies bombed German troop and supply concentrations in and south of Caen, which had very effective flak defences. We often saw horrifying examples of its accuracy. Big bombers with flames streaming from their engines would try to make our lines only a short distance away, the odd parachute appearing as a man drifted slowly to earth. Often there was a blood-red flash as an aircraft with bombs and petrol exploded, sending crew and machine to eternity in one brief second. I once saw a bomber blown into a screaming dive. There wasn't enough time for the crew to jump, and the pilot, unable to regain control of the aircraft, obviously pushed the nose of his bomber down into a steeper dive, ramming the target head on. As I watched in horrified fascination, I thought of the colossal courage and heroism of the seven men in that deathtrap, who, knowing that death was inescapable, had the fortitude to climax it with a final blow at the enemy.

I always liked to enter enemy territory by flying over the marshy ground just west of Le Havre. One morning while leading my flight over this area, we flew parallel but some distance away from a flight of twenty-four Marauder bombers escorted by a dozen Lightnings going in the same direction. Up came just sixteen rounds of 88 flak, destroying four bombers and one Lightning within the space of three seconds. I watched five aircraft containing twenty-five men plunge in flames to the ground, and it sickened me to such an extent I almost opened my hood to retch in the wind. It was an excellent example of the incredible accuracy the German gunners could attain. This accuracy was by no means an isolated instance, but one that was so graphic that I have never forgotten the hideous sight.

Throughout July and the first two weeks of August, the British and Canadian armies remained at loggerheads with the Germans in the Caen sector. Having captured the Cherbourg peninsula, the Americans concentrated on a breakthrough, which they accomplished at Saint Lo early in August. They were then able to capitalize on their penetration of the enemy defences by starting a wild rush to the south under General Patton, reinforced by vast quantities of men and equipment.

There were many schemes tried to assist the armies packed in around Caen in making a breakthrough to Falaise to the south, but no single assault was sufficient to penetrate the German armor and dug-in strength. We heard many stories of Canadian and British heroism and courage, and we knew the cost was high, for in the small Canadian cemetery close by our 'drome, new graves were added daily.

There were several very large bomber raids made at night against the defences in and around Caen. One clear evening a dozen of us travelled in a truck to a vantage point on high ground just north of the city to watch such a spectacle. We were well rewarded, for the night air gradually filled with a deep vibrating roar as the bombers in the first wave, bearing hundreds of tons of bombs, neared us from afar.

The night sky became a flaming mass of pathfinder flares and the quick-flashing fires of the devastating German anti-aircraft defences. The noise of the bombs bursting only a few miles away in the valley was like a thousand thunder claps mingling together and lasting for an hour. The harsh bark of the guns was drowned out by the steady rain of bombs landing in such a small, concentrated area. Occasionally a bomber, mortally hit, plummetted through the sky like a comet streaming long flames. Long after the last heavies had turned for home, the fires burned bright and clear. The night became so still in contrast to the din of a few minutes earlier that we found ourselves desperately wanting to shout to relieve the eerie, deathlike silence. As we bumped our way home, we were awed and thankful that we would never have to endure as devastating and terrifying a bombardment as we had just witnessed.

During the lull which preceded the armies' final push to Falaise, and just after the Americans had liberated the Brest Peninsula by the breakout at Saint Lo, Harry Dowding, Jack Whitelaw, Louis Cochand, and I decided to take a break to visit the west coast of France. Louis was the son of the owners of the renowned ski resort, Chalet Cochand at Saint Marguerite, just north of Montreal, and as he was perfectly bilingual, we wanted to use the talents of this tall and handsome fellow to ease our language difficulties. Louis was nearing the end of his tour and welcomed a break. We filled the jeep with petrol, cartons of cigarettes, and chocolates, and we set out on our 300-mile round trip.

The first part of our journey led through Tilley sur Seulles and the famous Villers Bocage. These two towns had been stumbling blocks for the British troops but, after several raids by heavy bombers, had been reduced to rubble filled with the cloying stench of buried bodies. In Villers Bocage the Germans had run their huge tanks through the walls into the basements of the buildings so that it was nearly impossible for our troops to knock them out. The bombers reduced the tanks to twisted wrecks at the price of obliterating the town.

From Villers the road led through glorious wooded countryside and pleasant farms which reminded me somewhat of Ontario. Along the side of the road were innumerable burnt-out enemy vehicles, and here and there a tank, pulverized by rockets, lay rusting in a field. Tiny graves, just rounded mounds and rough wooden crosses, were everywhere in their hundreds. Many were German but more were Allied. About the wreckage of a tank were the graves of its crew, buried only a few hundred yards from the scene of their destruction.

The stench at times became overwhelming, and in the American sector, where their army had so recently won a great victory, there were many bodies yet to be buried. We took time to examine a mighty Panther tank but were repulsed by the hideous sight of blackened corpses within the metal hull, and the smell emanating from them. The woods about Saint Lo were broken and shattered, and as we drove up the steep hill into the once-beautiful but now demolished town of Saint Lo, it was obvious that the Americans had paid heavily to capture that vital vantage point.

From Saint Lo the road wound down a gradual slope toward Avranches on the sea. The country was full of splendor and peace — the Germans defending this area had not fought, but retreated on the run chased by the relentless Americans. From across the bay we could see the magnificent church, Mont Saint Michel, with its spires pointing heavenward. We decided to cross the mile-long causeway linking the tiny isle to the mainland and visit the historic landmark. Driving through the ancient gates we parked the jeep in a secluded corner on the one and only street in the town.

We voted to spend the night at Poulard's Hotel, famous for its omelets. Monsieur and Madame Poulard were very gracious and took us to our rooms, which only a few days ago had been occupied by German officers; the hotel had been used as a rest center by the enemy.

That evening we enjoyed the famous omelets so wonderfully prepared that they fairly melted in our mouths, and over bottles of vin rouge, we gleaned the story of the island from a helpful guide. He told us that the first oratory had been established in the eighth century. Additions were built until, by the end of the fifteenth century, the fortress-abbey, constructed entirely of granite, towered high above the water. The medieval architecture was still in a perfect state of preservation.

The next morning, our guide showed us every part of this remarkable structure. Le Mont Saint Michel had been a sacred place from earliest times, and although the Germans seem to have respected its long history, they nevertheless left their mark. In the wide shallow stretches of water surrounding the Mont were thousands of mines and anti-invasion poles called "Rommel's Asparagus," strung with barbed wire and laced with dangling mines. Indignant civilians from the nearby farms had been forced to build these defences, but the inhabitants of Saint Michel must have profited from the German occupation, for they looked at us with sullen and unkindly eyes. Despite the beauty of the place, the atmosphere was so unpleasant that late the second day we once more loaded our jeep, this time with souvenirs, and started the long, rough trip back to the squadron.

As the month of July wound down, the pilots started running into small formations of German fighters, which meant that once again we started to fly in full squadron strength of twelve aircraft. The days of much larger formations were now gone, and during my second tour I never flew in anything larger than a single squadron formation. Squadron commanders were now the principal leaders; wing leaders received flying time only when they joined the squadron for a specific "do." This meant that each squadron was fairly autonomous, able to plan and organize its sorties within the overall wing schedule which, in turn, was frequently dictated by group headquarters. Within the overall plan it was gratifying to have so much control over our flying activity because it provided a squadron commander with the marvellous opportunity to put his experience and initiative to work and create a squadron roughly in his own image. As the senior flight commander and heir-apparent to Harry, I started early to mould the squadron into the fighting unit I thought it should be.

On July 27 I was leading the squadron for the second time that day on an armed recce south of Rouen. Dividing the squadron into two sections, I ordered green section to patrol the Lisieux area some thirty miles east of Caen while I took the remainder, yellow section, to patrol the Argentan area about ten miles south of Falaise. Each section began attacking ground targets when green section ran into a small gaggle of 109s. During the ensuing fight, Flying Officers Weeks and Morse each damaged an enemy before the 109s turned and fled southward. My section was thirty miles away, but I had received enough information to give an interception a chance. Opening my throttle wide, I flew what I judged to be an interception course.

Within a few minutes I spied a 109 some distance ahead and gave chase with everything my Spit could produce. Neil Burns was the only pilot with an aircraft able to keep pace with me, and the others soon fell well behind. Low rain clouds formed solid cover at 3,000 feet with side sheets of squalls forming curtains from the base of the clouds to ground level. The 109 was flying a straight, fast course, probably heading for his base, and although I lost sight of him in the squalls, by predicting his path I would catch sight of him again. Gradually the distance between us closed, and after a forty-mile chase, I finally got into firing position. The chase had to end quickly if we were going to have enough petrol to nurse our machines safely back to base.

At 300 yards I pressed my cannon firing button for two seconds. No results. At 250 yards I pressed the button again for one second. Again, no results. Suddenly I seemed to overtake the Me 109 rapidly as he started a gentle turn to port. At 150 yards I pressed the gun button a third time, only this time I used all my guns, cannon and four machine guns. A large number of strikes flashed in the cockpit and the wing root. Large pieces of metal flew off the enemy as a large brown cloud of smoke issued from the engine. He slowly rolled over, heading for the ground upside down.

As I watched what I presumed to be the death spiral of the 109, we suddenly broke into perfectly clear weather over the middle of Dreux airdrome, a large German fighter base. My surprise was compounded by the sight of some twenty Me 109s and Fw 190s buzzing around, obviously waiting for our appearance, having probably been alerted by my target 109. My last glimpse of him showed him still upside down at one thousand feet, heading for the ground, pouring smoke.

My more immediate concern was to get Neil and myself out of the mess we were in. I radioed Neil, "Stay with me as close as possible. I'm going to turn into each attack and try to get to that cloud layer each time I straighten up. The clouds to the north of us, Neil." Neil acknowledged. It wouldn't have meant anything to Neil, but something was worrying me. The 109s bore the familiar "Ace of Spades" insignia, which meant that the superb group I had met so many times in Africa was our foe.

As each German aricraft swooped in to attack, I judged my turn into the enemy so that none would get good shots at us. Each time the attackers broke off, I was a few hundred yards closer to the safety of the clouds. For some reason the Germans attacked in small groups or singly. I wondered why others would not attack while we were turning, coming finally to the happy conclusion that this mass of fighters trying to destroy us was not the experienced and daring Luftwaffe of old, thank goodness! Now a possible shortage of fuel was becoming our big problem. If we did not reach the clouds in short order, the enemy fighters would not have to shoot us down. We would crash for lack of fuel!

After what seemed an interminable time but was probably about six or seven minutes, having twisted, turned, climbed, dived and turned some more, we gained the cover of the low clouds. With a superb display of flying skill, Neil had stuck with me like a shadow. Our base was some one hundred miles northwest of

Dreux, and I felt we might have just enough fuel to reach safety if we slowed down and flew in as economical a manner as it was possible to fly in a Spitfire.

I soon discovered that our cloud cover, although dense enough to hide us satisfactorily, lacked depth. It was only about one thousand feet thick, and did not continue in the direction I wanted to go to get home. Every time I broke through the top of the cloud, the enemy was waiting, and when I tried below, more enemy fighters were waiting there. They did not have to be very clever to figure out where I was headed and thus could anticipate my course with great accuracy. I could only hope that we would not run out of cloud protection, for then we would have little change of surviving.

"Hello Kenway, Kenway control," I radioed. "Yellow Leader in trouble. On course 350 degrees for Rouen in cloud with Huns above and below. We are running short of fuel. Send help quickly."

Kenway acknowledged, and we contined our northerly course. As we flew farther north I found the cloud started to edge west, taking us a little closer to safety. At last, near Le Havre, our rescuers arrived, driving away our enemy shadows.

By a stroke of good fortune and wily fuel conservation, we landed safely at Beny. My engine stopped as I arrived at my dispersal bay — I had run out of gas. Even after numerous attacks by a determined but not very skilled enemy, our aircraft did not sport one single bullet hole. Lady Luck was still smiling.

My claim for an Me 109 probably destroyed was recognized but despite Monty Berger's recommendation that it be upgraded to a destroyed, it never was. Monty and I were both convinced my 109 had crashed very close to Dreux airdrome.

As July came to an end, I was surprised to find that I had flown forty-one sorties totalling forty-five operational hours, despite being plagued with rainy or foggy weather for much of the time. All round the squadron was in a good mood. The pilots were pleased with our operations since we were firing our guns so frequently. The groundcrews worked quickly to re-arm and refuel our Spits after each sortie, and the mechanics felt they were par-

ticipating fully with the pilots in our combined effort to destroy
the enemy wherever he could be found. It was a Canadian custom
to name squadrons after wild animals and we received the
nickname "Caribou" although our official crest design did not
arrive for many months.

As I became more familiar with the pilots, I quickly learned
to appreciate what a gung-ho bunch of fellows they were. Flying Officer Frosty Young already had two aircraft destroyed to
his credit and was to serve audaciously until shot down later at
Munster. Flying Officer Bill Weeks of Loggieville, New
Brunswick, was young, eager and individualistic, and won a DFC
for his aggressive flying. Another fireball was Flight Lieutenant
S.M. Stan McLarty, DFC, who was later killed in combat with
enemy aircraft. Flying Officer Jack Lumsden, DFC, from my
hometown of Hamilton, was a tall, dark, and handsome fellow
with a gentle and charming disposition. Jack was a superb pilot
and a deadly shot, and he pressed home every attack with such
determination that he frequently returned to base with foliage,
tree branches, or wire fencing caught in his tailwheel, caused by
pulling out of a dive at the last possible moment. He was shot
down once by flak, bailing out into the Channel where he was
rescued and returned to the squadron within a few hours. Flight
Lieutenant W.G. "Mac" Hume, a brother-in-law to Louis
Cochand, also took a spill into the Channel and remained there
for several hours before being rescued by a Walrus aircraft just
before the Germans tried to reach him. Mac was a gentleman
who enjoyed entertaining us with ditties as he strummed his
battered guitar. When the time came I was pleased to be able
to retire him and Louis simultaneously as tour-expired.

John Marriott had been in the army before joining the RCAF
and, being a horseman, he was quick to provide himself with a
great white beast which he kept tethered near our camp. Gerald
Blair of Montreal, W.B. "Barney" Sullivan of Vancouver, and
Glen Millar from Winnipeg were pilots with considerable flying
experience, all having been with the squadron in Canada. Not
all of our replacement pilots were so fortunate — young Len
"Willie" Wilson from Stratford for instance had a total of only

220 solo flying hours when he reported to us in France. His situation was typical of the few inexperienced pilots we received during the days of our very active and dangerous flying. I was very proud of all these young men, who bravely faced and endured great dangers.

CHAPTER 12

FALAISE BREAKOUT
AND CHASE

August, 1944

Falaise — the name conjures vivid memories for all those who were there, whether German, British, Canadian, or American. During the first week of August, the Canadian and British effort to break through the German defences at Caen started to show results, and the Canadians pierced the enemy positions during the night of August 7. General Patton with his Third U.S. Army was pushing rapidly northward and this left the Germans pressed on the north by the Canadians and British with the Americans to the west and south. On August 7, the German position within the Allied encirclement measured about sixty miles north to south by the same distance east to west. By August 16 the enemy was compressed into an area roughly forty-five miles east to west by about twenty-five miles north to south. The enemy-held territory projected thumblike into our positions, totally surrounded by our forces except at the base of the thumb. It was the Allied intention to cut across the base, trapping all of the German forces, which would then have to surrender or be annihilated. The escape route at the base of the thumb has become known as the Falaise Gap, and would be the source of much controversy in the years after the war. It is very easy to take sides in this controversy, blaming Montgomery or Patton or Bradley for failing to close the gap and allowing the remnants of the German armies to escape eastward.

Our understanding of the Normandy landing battle tactics was that General Montgomery was to hold the eastern invasion area, hoping to pin down the bulk of the enemy armored divisions, while the Americans, to the west and facing lighter opposition, would be able to break through to the south before turning east and then north to entrap the enemy. This is exactly what took

190

place, although with the passage of time, Montgomery is being blamed for the slowness of his breakout, despite facing seven German armored divisions while the Americans faced only one. One point in defence of the Allies is that the Germans, although decimated and badly understrength, were experienced troops, and when caught like rats in a trap, could be expected to fight ferociously and expertly, perhaps preventing the trap from being shut despite our best efforts. In the end, the Germans did escape in appreciable numbers, probably prolonging the war and thus denying the Allies an earlier victory.

Nothing, however, can be blamed on the Second Tactical Air Force, for we were given complete freedom to search out and destroy the enemy within the containment area, and we made the most of it. On August 8, our wing moved to a new airfield, B-18, Cristot, near Villiers Bocage, only five or six miles from the German positions. We had a clear understanding of the limits of the enemy lines with instructions to bomb and strafe everything within the containment area. It was like shooting fish in a barrel, for the targets were everywhere, unable to find cover from our aircraft. Between the time of their encirclement until August 19 when the gap was closed and the enemy was either captured or had escaped, our aircraft flew from dawn to dark and inflicted incredible damage, far beyond anything we ever imagined possible. With the closing of the gap, we still kept up a relentless pressure on the fleeing enemy, following him to the banks of the River Seine, the extreme range of usefulness for our aircraft.

Unfortunately for the enemy, the weather during this period was remarkably clear and suitable for flying with few clouds from which enemy fighters could attack us at propitious times. Our pilots piled up the hours; a number left after reaching their 200-hour tour quotas to be replaced by new pilots, who were, in most cases, very green to fighter operations.

I shall never forget those desperate days when every pilot fired nearly all of his ammunition on every sortie. On the peak days, I divided the squadron into pairs once a target area had been reached. Each number 1 would fire all his ammunition at targets of opportunity while his wingman provided cover. Then the wingman would take over until his ammunition was expended while his partner provided cover. Then back to base to refuel and rearm ready for the next trip. The targets were so plentiful that it was difficult to choose one over another, but the packed roads received the greatest attention. The attacks on escaping transport after the Mareth Line battle in North Africa were nothing compared with the devastation we created at Falaise. We were flying below five hundred feet over rolling, lightly wooded countryside where it was not uncommon to see miles of German transports, horse-drawn wagons and carts, and men on foot, all heading east. Interspersed among the enemy were civilian refugees, some in horse-drawn wagons but most on foot, clutching a few belongings. Because they were so closely packed it was impossible to discriminate among targets, and civilians were killed along with the Germans.

Our bullets were devastatingly effective against thin-skinned vehicles such as trucks and armored carriers, which we usually left in flames. Our massed gunfire proved to be especially effective against ground troops. Close to the ground we maintained a speed of about 300 mph, which gave them little advance warning, and we frequently caught soldiers by surprise. They would freeze for a shocked moment with eyes wide and mouths agape in their white faces. Before they could react our cannon and machine guns would mow them down with bright green flashes. Then, after a second or two, we would pass on looking for another target. There was little anti-aircraft fire because the enemy was fleeing too quickly to take the time to set up ack-ack defences. We did experience some damage from small arms fire, but since we could not see it, we really didn't worry about that danger.

It was particularly pathetic to have to shoot the horses, which were an important means of German transport, and watch the wounded beasts charging off the road, crazed with fear and pain, frequently dragging a blazing wagon behind them. I don't know how the other pilots reacted to the carnage, for we did not discuss it except in analytical terms of so many enemy vehicles or men destroyed, but it sickened me each time I saw it happen. Somehow, however, I was able to shut out the images and forget my revulsion when I returned to base. This was war and for a change everything was going our way, no matter how gruesome and cruel it may have been.

On readiness in our Paddington dispersal. Clockwise — Peppler, Gray (hidden behind), Colby, Hagger, Byford, Berry, and author with back to camera throwing the Liar's dice. Standing — Peart, Tasto, Young, and Anerk.

What we looked like when we moved to a new airdrome, before tents and shelters are erected.

Our open-air cookhouse, rain or shine. This is in Africa, but it could be anywhere it is so typical.

Olmsted, Peppler, and F/L Les Powell, Canadian Public Relations Officer. Paddington, April, 1943.

Tingley, March, 1943. "Lucky" Lucy just before being shot down.

Colin Gray at Malta with Wing Commander's insignia on fuselage.

Hap Kennedy and Steve Randall. Malta, 1943. Note Squadron scoreboard behind Randall's Shoulder.

Drying out after a wet night. Sicily, July, 1943.

Squadron Leader C.I.R. "Duke" Arthur, October, 1943, Italy.

442 Sqdn. Volkel, Oct./44. Top row — Smith, Burns, Doyle, Dunne, Olmsted, Mills, Lumsden, Schenk. Sitting on wing — Jowsey, Watkins, Keene, Francis. Bottom row — McLarty, Simpson, Dick, Ireland, Engineering Officer.

Normandy. Remains of Villiers Bocage after a bombing raid to neutralize enemy tanks shielded within buildings.

Engineers building a mesh landing strip on the Normandy Beachhead.

France, July, 1944. Olmsted returns after shooting up some Fw 190's. Note dent in front mirror and no goggles.

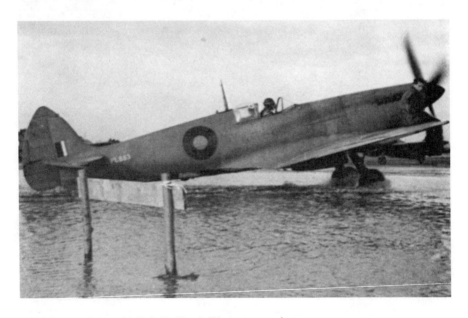

PRV Spit taxiing at Volkel, Holland. Water everywhere.

OPERATION OVERLORD AND FALAISE

GERMAN DEFENCE LINE   AUGUST 15 1944
JUST BEFORE CLOSING THE GAP

0   10   50 MILES

N

ENGLAND

LONDON

DOVER

SOUTHAMPTON

BRIGHTON

BOURNEMOUTH

STRAITS OF DOVER

CALAIS
BOULOGNE

PLYMOUTH

E N G L I S H   C H A N N E L

ABBEVILLE

DIEPPE

AMIENS
RIVER   SOMME

OVERLORD
LANDING
BEACHES

CHERBOURG

NEUFCHATEL
POIX

LE HAVRE

BEAUVAIS

BAYEUX   BENY
SUR MER

ROUEN

OISE RIVER

CARENTAN   CAEN

CABOURG
LISIEUX

RIVER SEINE

ST. LO   VILLERS

BERNAY

MANTES

BOCAGE   FALAISE

EVREUX

RIVER EURE

ST. MALO

VIRE

ARGENTAN

VERSAILLES   PARIS

MORLAIX

AVRANCHES

MORTAGNE

MONT
ST. MICHEL

ALENCON

CHARTRES

RENNES

LE MANS

F R A N C E

At base Monty Berger would ask during debriefing, "Well, how many troops did you kill this trip?" As if we knew! On a strafing pass of two or three seconds I might kill five or fifty — it was just impossible to gauge. It was enough to know that our efforts were highly effective and extremely destructive. Our accumulated scores of destroyed and damaged transport for the month were quite incredible. Our ace, Goodie Goodwin, had 101 vehicles, I had 89, Young 73, Middleton 71, Cochand 65, Morse 58, Miller 50, and Curtis 42 with the rest of 442 Squadron's pilots scoring somewhat less.

Flying so constantly over enemy territory meant we inevitably suffered losses of pilots and aircraft. Flying Oficer Campbell was reported missing and presumed killed. McDuff was shot down and captured by the Germans, only to escape and return to our lines eight days after going missing. Neil Burns was badly hit by flak twice in the same day, but managed a safe landing on each occasion. Randall and Goodwin, hit by flak, crash landed successfully behind our lines. The rest of us suffered minor hits which could be quickly repaired, and I received major hits on two occasions. We were all well aware that death could reach out for any of us at any time.

As we lost aircraft, replacements were immediately required and these were flown in by new pilots, who remained with us. New arrivals included Flying Officers Gary Doyle and Gordy Watkins and Flight Lieutenant J.E.G. Reade, who had instructed in Canada for three years but had no ops experience whatsoever. Other new arrivals included Flying Officers D.A. Brigden and W.H. Chappell, and Pilot Officers E.T. Hoare and E.J. Gosselin. Our adjutant, Flight Lieutenant Jack Brodrick, moved on to a higher position with group to be replaced by Flying Officer Stu Mills from Hamilton. Flying Officer A.F. Booth, an intelligence officer, was another new face filling the newly created position of squadron spy. Pilots were constantly leaving tour-expired, and in a few cases others were sent away after being judged unsuitable for operational flying. Having two pilots on constant leave sometimes meant additional flying for those in the squadron, and frequently the pilots returning from leave would be dumbfounded by the high turnover in personnel that had occurred during their absence. The constant demand for our flying services precluded training for the new pilots. They arrived, they flew, and they learned the hard way, through experience, on-the-job training with plenty of advice after each trip. It was very difficult for them, and I was proud of the enthusiastic way they responded. Low-level flying attacking ground targets was a much easier tactic to learn quickly than having to face enemy aircraft in combat, but in my opinion, much more hazardous.

Once the enemy escaped through the Falaise gap to flee eastward, our hectic pace slackened somewhat as we regrouped and attended to other neglected duties such as laundry, letter-writing, resting, and sight-seeing. One afternoon I took Dowding's jeep, loaded up with a few pilots, intending to reconnoiter the Falaise area on a souvenir hunt. Once in the killing ground we quickly lost our enthusiasm for acquiring mementos, for what we saw in terms of death and destruction would stay with us forever. The road sides were jammed with burnt-out vehicles of every description — half-tracks, tanks, wagons, and field guns — as well as dead and rotting horses and men. The stench was overwhelming; blackened, bloated carcasses seemed to move as maggots, huge flies, and incredibly vicious hornets moved over the remains. It was ghastly to view miles of destroyed equipment surrounded, in many cases, by the former occupants, stiff in death or burned to chunks of charcoal. Death had come in many ways, from bullets, bombs, being crushed under the wheels of a vehicle or tank, or being incinerated by fire. After a short time we left, too revolted to walk among the bodies to search for a Luger or a Mauser rifle or some insignia or trinket. We wished that we had not made the effort to view the death and destruction and were sincerely thankful that we would have no part in the burial and cleanup details.

Back at camp we had reminders of the horrors we had seen every minute of the day as the hornets invaded our tents and messing quarters in hordes, stinging indiscriminiately and with painful results. Drinking tea was a chore for you had to ensure a clear spot on the cup before putting it to your lips to take a sip. Toast and jam would support a dozen hornets and great care was required not to bite into one of the ornery critters. I could never

free myself from thinking about what bodies the hornets had been
crawling over before landing on my toast. Along with these vicious
insects came dysentry, which attacked us all and, in some cases,
required hospitalization. Even the milder cases meant many trips
to the bushes during the night and some very uncomfortable times
when strapped in the cockpit.

The enemy was retreating so rapidly across France, Belgium,
and Holland heading for the Rhine River that by August 22 they
were nearly out of our flying range. At the same time an extended
stretch of very bad weather kept us grounded. Finally group
ordered us to move to Evreux airfield some forty miles north of
Paris. Our advance party packed up and left for the new base,
but unfortunately the field was not ready for the rest of us. For
a week I slept on the floor of the intelligence van, loudly moan-
ing about cruel fate.

The move of a flying fighting unit required a great deal of additional effort from every person. Pilots had to pack their belongings, keeping flying gear separate, and strike their tents and other
equipment to be transported by truck. The mess tent, our intelligence facilities, the workshops and spare aircraft parts, ammunition, fuel, cooking equipment, and medical facilities all had to
be loaded onto trucks, driven to the new airfield, and then
unloaded and reerected. Our moves were usually well organized;
a refinement of the lessons learned in the Middle East.

We pilots looked forward to each move. It generally meant
that we would be operating from a captured German airfield with
a permanent flying strip. In this case, anything was better than
our Cristot dustbowl which could go from a desert to a sea of
mud after each rain. Every move also brought us closer to the
fleeing enemy, offering prospects of action in the air and against
the ground. Best of all, however, was the opportunity to fly over
new and strange territory and see new cities, new woods and
rivers, and indeed, whole new countries.

At Evreux all of the pilots and officers, except for me and a
couple of others, headed for the just-liberated city of Paris. As
the last vehicle disappeared down the road in dust, each man
dressed in his best blues, a signal arrived ordering us to move
immediately. In the next few days we moved three more times,

to St. Andre, B-24, to Illiers l'Eveque, B-25, and finally, to Poix, B-44, where we remained for four days. As we moved we went without baths and changes of clothing, ate cold meals from cans, and slept in our clothes on the damp ground or on hard floors in any kind of available building. It always seemed to rain whenever we changed locations, adding to our confusion and discomfort.

On September 5, Wing Commander Russel asked that I meet with him in his intelligence van. "Bill," he said with a very serious expression, "I've just had an urgent request to handle a dirty job. We have to provide two Spitfires to act as escorts to two photographic PRU Mustangs that have to take very low-level shots of bridges in the Arnhem area. The photographs are vitally important, and it is imperative that the Mustangs get back safely. The Spits will be required to do whatever is necessary to divert any enemy opposition. The Mustangs must get through."

He went on to explain why volunteers were required. Arnhem was 240 miles from our base at Poix with much more than half that distance behind enemy lines. Because of the speed of the Mustangs, we would be forced to fly at nearly full throttle to keep up, making it a certainty that our fuel would run out long before we could reach our lines on the return. This meant that the volunteers might have to crash land somewhere, possibly in enemy territory, with only a slight hope of escaping. "And the Mustang types will be here shortly to coordinate R/T channels and courses. This is a rush job and take-off is within the hour," he concluded.

I rounded up the duty pilots and explained the task. Jack was the first to volunteer to accompany me. We made our limited preparations before hustling over to the intelligence van to meet the PRU pilots.

They intended to fly on the deck which would place us behind and to one side, to keep them in view. They forecast a solid cloud layer at 2,000 feet, extending all the way to the target with rain squalls and patchy fog an additional probability. They felt they would have to make two or three passes over the target area, staying well away from any built-up areas, and would remain as low as possible to take the oblique photos. Radio silence was to be maintained at all costs. My heart sank when they added that they intended to fly at 320 mph indicated airspeed, which meant that our Spits would have only enough fuel to get us there with little left for our return flight.

We left Poix in a rainstorm and set about keeping the fleet Mustangs in view. The weather grew progressively worse with the cloud layer lowering to only several hundred feet above the fairly rugged terrain. On we droned, until one Mustang waggled his wings, made a sharp 180 degree turn, and headed back to base. We learned later that his radio had failed. When we were nearly halfway to the target, the clouds and rain now right down on top of the deck, the remaining Mustang waggled his wings, turned 180 degrees, and also headed back for Poix. Jack and I breathed separate sighs of relief. Saved by the bell! Or the weather!

I learned upon landing that the last Mustang pilot felt that he could not take acceptable pictures under such foul conditions at such a ridiculously low altitude. Rather than further jeopardize our lives and possibly compromise the secrecy of his objective, he decided to scrub the mission. Sometime later I was to learn that General Montgomery's staff wanted the photographs to assist in making their final plans for the airborne operation "Market-Garden,"[15] the Arnhem operation.

As often as we moved forward with our wing to a new location, we could not catch up to the army. They continued to move eastward with astonishing speed, leaving us nearly one hundred miles to the rear. Over this distance, carrying bombs, our duration over enemy territory was limited to about twenty minutes and afforded little time to locate and destroy targets of opportunity. Additionally, because of the speed of the army advance, especially of their forward elements, we had to take care that we did not mistakenly attack our own forces.

Poix airfield was a barren, desolate grass strip with no redeeming features. Close to Amiens of World War I fame, the area had once again been savaged by warring armies. Thankfully we were to remain for only a few days, but our stay allowed us to catch our breath before moving on. The only excitement we encountered when flying was on several occasions when we saw a V-2 rocket flash by a mile or two in front of us. As the monster spiralled skyward, we were close enough to fly through the trail of smoke and crystalline particles created by its engines. Search as we might, however, we were never able to locate the launch vehicle, even though we would be over the launch area within two minutes of the rocket's being fired. Time and again the Germans proved themselves to be masters in the art of camouflage. My years of searching for golf balls in woods and rough had prepared me to detect hidden objects and I was usually better at this than the other pilots, but try as we might, we never did discover a V-2 site.

I normally cruised the squadron at 210 mph to conserve fuel. This would put us at a considerable disadvantage if and when we met enemy fighters that regularly patrolled at speeds in excess of 300 mph, but since we encountered fighters so seldom, I never considered the speed differential a problem.

It was at Poix that I started an instructional program for all of the squadron pilots. Originally I felt it would be a method of filling in an hour or so of our time after our evening meal, but it was so well received that I continued the program, having a session every four or five days. During these bull sessions, we discussed all aspects of our flying tasks, whether they related to offensive flying or to just improving every possible safety precaution. It was a training and learning experience for everyone: no single person was the teacher, and each pilot contributed suggestions based on his own flying knowledge. The result was that we ended up with a consensus on such important topics as how best to bail out of a disabled aircraft or the best strafing techniques or how to get better results in our dive-bombing. We discussed air-to-air firing, deflection shooting, formation flying, and what emergency procedures to follow in every possible sort of trouble. I felt this helped us to become a much more efficient and high-scoring squadron and served to create an aggressive spirit combined with a sense of camaraderie that was not equalled by any other squadron.

CHAPTER 13

BRUSSELS—THE BELGIAN INTERLUDE

September, 1944

On September 6, the wing moved to Brussels-Evere airdrome, B-56, snuggled in the northeastern outskirts of the city. Here our pilots were to experience a most remarkable outpouring of enthusiasm and gratitude from a liberated people. And it was here that I would be exposed to events and circumstances that have kept memories sharp and produced many a satisfied chuckle in later years. I know that most other pilots and airmen have similar feelings.

Prior to the war, Evere had been the main base for the Belgian national airline, Sabena, which meant that the airport buildings and hangars were well designed, well equipped, and plentiful. These had sufficient facilities to provide us with comforts and conveniences we had not known for many months.

We landed in early afternoon on the large L-shaped grass airdrome, amidst hundreds of joyous and hysterical Belgians who had come to welcome us. They flooded the field, making it difficult to find a clear space to land each aircraft. Ignoring the whirling propellors, some tried to climb on the tail assemblies for a ride as we taxied to a parking area. As soon as the engines were switched off, they clambered all over the Spitfires, shaking our hands, patting heads, and even kissing the aircraft. The genuineness of their demonstrations was touching. After much gesticulating and badly phrased French, we managed to impress upon our enthusiastic welcomers that it was fine to admire our aircraft from a distance, but close inspections and handling were forbidden. But their feelings were understandable: we were their heroic "liberateurs." We were the first air force in Brussels, and for the next few weeks, we were to be feted as if we were the only air force in existence.

Thrilled by our warm reception the majority of us decided to visit the city, but not until we had organized and formed our operational plans for the morrow. Having done this, thirteen of us piled into Harry Dowding's jeep and bumped our merry way toward the center of the capital. Somehow we all managed to hang on to the tiny vehicle as it traversed the uneven wooden block roads. The jeep's seats were filled, some sat on the hood and others stood on the back end hanging on desperately to the spare tire. In appearance we resembled a gang of desperados — we were unshaven, grimy faced, and sweatstained, our clothes were dirty and dishevelled and our flying boots caked with mud, and most of us wore heavy, fleece-lined Irvine jackets. But our appearance failed to worry us in the least, and spirits were high as we clung to the jeep while Dowding tried to establish a new speed record between the 'drome and the city.

As we moved closer to the city core, the people in the streets became both more numerous and more boisterous. We reached a point where we could barely move because of the massed humanity. Those who did not try to jump on to the jeep endeavored to tear us away in order to have an airman for their own. When further progress became imposible, we sought to escape by diving into an open bar. There the patrons clapped, and within a minute our hands were full of glasses of beer, on the house or on the people. It was good beer, not unlike our own Ontario brands, and most unlike the weak English war varieties.

After chatting with the patrons, we learned that we were still some distance from the center of the city, where we were advised to proceed for our best welcome. A few of the pilots stayed because they had met families who refused to let them go. The rest of us piled into the jeep and slowly made our way to the main street, Boulevard Max, and Anspach Square.

After parking the jeep and removing the distributor rotor to immobilize the machine and prevent theft, we separated into groups of two and three, carried along by the milling celebrants, who, in a riot of enthusiasm and happiness, almost tore our clothes from our backs. Anything for a souvenir! Within minutes three of us were propelled through an open doorway into the large beer garden beside the Metropole, Brussels' largest hotel.

The beer garden was an enormous place, seating over a thousand people. It was jammed to capacity and dozens of white-coated waiters carrying tall tumblers of beer and bottles of wine strove to slake the unquenchable thirst of the patrons. The noise and activity were at their height, and yet, when we were pushed through the entrance, we seemed to attract the immediate attention of the entire gathering. Instinctively and in unison, the huge crowd stood up and for ten minutes clapped and cheered as the three of us, dirty, poorly dressed, and flushed with embarrassment, were dragged to the center of the room. Many eyes were filled with tears of gratitude and joy. The fourteen-piece orchestra on stage at the rear of the beer garden, sensing that a decisive moment had arrived, stood and played the Belgian national anthem and then "God Save the King." It was played and sung with a spirit of reverence and meaning that I had rarely heard before.

The Belgians had suffered five years of cruelty and hardships imposed by the Nazi occupation. Their relief at being freed from constant threats and terror became a spontaneous outpouring of genuine gratitude and generosity, now lavished upon us and all the other airmen in the city. Many times we were told that they wished they could celebrate with every fighting man in the Allied armies; as we were the first on the scene, we received the full measure of their jubilation.

We spent several hours in the Metropole beergarden, and the beer and champagne flowed freely. We were pushed and pulled from one group to another and from table to table to be praised and welcomed, by rich and poor alike, for they were all there that night. The only answer that I could give to the people who thanked me so lavishly was to say that it was worth four years of service on my part to be able to spend four such wonderful hours with them. That statement usually brought tears to their eyes, and at times I, too, had tears in mine. I remain convinced that the time I spent in the air force was more than repaid by those hours I spent in Brussels during the first days of the liberation.

Because it was getting late, we finally bid goodbye to our friends, but not before promising faithfully to return the following evening. Once more we boarded the jeep and, after being lost for more than an hour in the blackout, eventually ended up at the 'drome, there to collapse thankfully on our canvas cots.

The citizens of Brussels declared a ten-day holiday to celebrate their liberation, which also gave them the opportunity to host the airmen and soldiers stationed in the immediate vicinity. As air force, I suppose we were viewed as rather glamorous warriors, for we found it impossible to move around without signing for autograph hunters which, while flattering, became a bloody bind after the first few days. Once we were stopped to sign a book, others immediately gathered clamoring for "un souvenir." Another part of our appeal to the citizens was that during the long years of the occupation, the only visible sign of the Allies' continuing to fight was the frequent appearance over Brussels of our bombers and fighters. Hence nearly every airman, regardless of rank, was adopted by a family to be entertained in a generous and even lavish manner.

Harry Dowding, Jack Whitelaw, Neil Burns, and I were adopted by three very wealthy families, who ensured that we never wanted for attention or companionship. We were invited to the most exclusive clubs, to golf, ride horses, swim, or play tennis, with clothes and equipment provided. By late afternoon, we would retire to a cabaret on the Avenue Louise to drink champagne and later dine at an expensive black market restaurant night club. Money was no object, and these demonstrative people would not allow us to spend our own funds.

During our more sober moments, we were shown some of the impressive points of interest in Brussels, including the Bourse and the Palais de Justice, which had been deliberately damaged by the Germans during their hasty pullout. We visited the Royal Palace with its beautiful park, the Hotel de Ville, and the Palais Legislatif, where in 1915 a German tribunal had sentenced Edith Cavell to death. Visits to the homes of our friends, to theaters, and to parks gave us an insight into the Belgian way of life. We followed a tree-lined highway to beautiful Louvain, the cathedral city of Belgium, and south to the battlefield of Waterloo.

The continuing liberation festivities disrupted the routine of both pilots and groundcrew and affected their motivation. To reimpose some order we introduced a system whereby the maximum number of men could be in the city at all times with their new-found friends but operations were not neglected. Our operational efficiency improved while we all had the opportunity now and again to live a few carefree, luxurious hours far removed from the tense and often strained squadron atmosphere.

Our new airdrome had been an important German bomber base up until D-Day, when fighters started to use it. The Belgians told us that the Germans had flown over the city in spectacular formations to impress the populace, continuing to operate until the day before we arrived. The 'drome was filled with evidence of their hasty departure: we found aircraft in some of the hangars, tables set with partially consumed meals, unfinished drinks in the bar, and lockers that had not been emptied of personal belongings.

As I explored the 'drome I could only marvel again at the ingenuity of our enemy. It was surrounded on three sides by factories, apartment buildings, and smaller dwellings, and in an effort to save the hangars from the ravages of our bombers, the Hun had cunningly camouflaged the hangars to look like the surrounding buildings. The hangar walls and doors were decorated with windows, doorways, stairs, fences, and even lush green foliage all of which, from a short distance, made them resemble the nearby civilian structures. Because some buildings were undamaged, I felt that the success of the camouflage could not be doubted. There were camouflaged dispersal pens too, which even when viewed from the ground, looked like nothing more than natural bumps or irregularities in a normally flat terrain. Cleverly constructed fake aircraft of several different types were parked in likely places, and I was surprised at the thoroughness of the workmanship which had gone into them, even though they were nothing more than dummy targets for our bombers. Although flimsily constructed of wood, they bore a remarkable likeness to the aircraft they were meant to represent.

Our task during this period was to fly offensive fighter patrols behind enemy lines. The main problem we faced was that the Huns to the north were forty-five miles away, on the northern outskirts of Antwerp, and to the east, over sixty miles away, close to the Maas River. In order to extend our patrolling time over such distances, we found it necessary to once again use the dreaded long-range fuel tanks.

When plotting our courses to and from targets we rarely included wind speed in our calculations, since, in clear weather, ground features allowed us to pinpoint our location at any time. We just ignored windspeed, even on take off, although we usually tried to land into the wind. Meteorlogical information beyond our airfields was limited to occasional reports from recce aircraft which became rapidly dated and were effectively useless. Flying over solid cloud cover presented another problem, one that rarely bothered me, for I had a very good native sense of direction that rarely let me down. One day, however, I was flying a front-line patrol with the squadron high above a solid cloud layer, which extended as far as the eye could see in every direction and, for some reason, I had the uncomfortable feeling that I was lost. Suddenly there was a small break in the cloud cover immediately over the towering spires of a huge cathedral, which I recognized. Speaking slowly and clearly in my usual drawl, I radioed to the rest of the pilots. "Anybody know where in hell we are?" Complete silence. After a few seconds I returned. "If you guys look below at the cathedral you will always know when you are over Cologne, in the Ruhr valley. Out." The 100 mph upper winds had blown us more than forty miles off course.

Soon after arriving in Brussels the Allied armies stopped rolling forward, for a very good reason: they were out of gas, literally. Then for ten days some five hundred Dakota aircraft flew steadily to Evere, bringing the precious fluid, each aircraft loaded with thousands of pounds of highly flammable gasoline stored in four-gallon cans. It was not uncommon to see three Dakotas at a time rolling to a stop on the runway while others waited to take off and thirty or more circled around waiting an opportunity to land. The hordes of parked aircraft offered a tempting target for an enemy bomber, but none came. The roads in the direction of the front lines were bordered with Jerry cans of petrol, stored in the open, providing another target which was ignored. While this very necessary activity was going on, it was impossible for us to operate, and since there was no enemy air activity, we were ordered to stay on the ground, ready to scramble at a moment's notice should danger approach.

By early September, the Allied forces on the continent consisted of twenty American divisions, twelve British, three Canadian, one French and one Polish, supported by over 6,500 Allied aircraft including 1,500 light and medium bombers and 5,000 fighter aircraft. Air and ground support was provided by more than 2,000 transport aircraft and innumerable supply trucks. Until a large port such as Antwerp was captured, however, all fuel, ammunition, and supplies had to be trucked from the original Normandy beach landing areas and it finally proved impossible to supply the armies' needs fully during the five-hundred mile dash across Europe. Had it been possible by some miracle to keep adequate supplies flowing when and where needed, it is very likely that our armies could have caught and crushed the enemy, thus ending the war months before the actual day of victory. Our short pause to resupply gave the Germans the time required to reequip and regroup, and form new defences along the Siegfried Line and the Rhine River.

Air Vice-Marshal Harry Broadhurst paid us an inspection visit one day, arriving in his captured German Fiesler Storch aircraft, which had accompanied him from the Middle East. He was obviously annoyed at the airdrome crowding as the constant traffic made it extremely difficult to operate a wing of Spitfires from the shared facilities. After ordering us totally grounded until further notice, he arranged that we move to a new location, Le Culot, B-58, situated near Louvain, some twenty miles east of Brussels.

Our wing completed the move on September 21, four days after General Montgomery's assault on Nijmegen and Arnhem in his ill-timed Market-Garden operation. The 'drome had been under construction by the Germans when our armies' advances halted the building in final stages of completion. Had we arrived two weeks later the Germans might have been able to complete the small village they were building to house their troops and which we now took over.

Hardly had we settled in at Le Culot and begun carrying out long patrols as we attempted to cover the early stages of the

Arnhem-Nijmegen assault, when my career received a boost. One day after I had led the squadron for two hours in abortive weather over Nijmegen, Arnhem, and Wesel, Wing Commander Russel was waiting at the dispersal when we landed. "Bill," said Dal, "I've got good news for you. Both you and Goodie had just been awarded DFCs. Congratulations." Goodie and I were delighted, naturally, as we accepted approving comments, mixed with a few raucous remarks, from our friends.

After the initial excitement subsided, Dal continued. "Squadron Leader Dowding is now tour-expired, and I'm giving you command of 442 Squadron as of now. Congratulations again, Bill. I know you will do a good job and I wish you the best of luck."

Sorry as I was to see Harry Dowding leave, I was thoroughly thrilled at the prospect of leading the squadron on a regular basis. The $1.25 increase in daily pay that came with my promotion to squadron leader helped reduce the pain of my bar bill, which grew enormously as I treated the pilots to celebrate the occasion properly. Harry was my tent mate during his second tour, which provided an opportunity to study him as a man and a personality. Flying was a different matter, for as his B Flight commander, I rarely flew under his leadership. On the few occasions when I did, I realized he was a born leader, who led the squadron well and for whom the pilots had great respect and loyalty. He accepted my eagerness to fly constantly and was gracious enough to not pursue the futile task of restraining my keenness. He had a sharp and dry sense of humor and could be very critical in a kindly manner, never creating resentment or hostility. He had flown 327 ops hours in two strenuous combat tours, for which he was awarded the DFC and Bar. With Dal, Harry had built a tremendous spirit of confidence and efficiency in the squadron, and I fully appreciated the great responsibility he had passed on to me.

There never was any doubt in my mind about my ability to lead the squadron effectively, since nearly all of my operational experience came as a flight commander, and even then, I was leading a squadron much of the time. What I had done for a flight I could now use as the basis for combining the effectiveness of two flights. I now had the job for which I felt qualified and which I thought the finest in the air force — commanding officer of a fighter squadron. That seemed to be what flying as a fighter pilot was all about. No major changes were needed, just some fine tuning. Flight Lieutenant Stan McLarty took over my flight and deputy flight commanders were appointed for each flight. This gave the squadron five qualified leaders with other pilots recognized as very capable of leading four or six aircraft on any specific duty. I continued to hold regular bull sessions where we exchanged ideas seeking to improve our effectiveness both as individuals and as a flying unit.

Once Harry had departed I did not try to fill his tent space with another pilot, as Jack Whitelaw and I had put the extra space to good use. In any case, all the pilots were bunked in with comrades they would have been reluctant to leave. Jack was a quiet, freckle-faced, intelligent, and soft-spoken medical officer who worried constantly about every man in the squadron and watched over us with a motherly eye. I frequently caught him staring at me as though trying to read my innermost thoughts. He had a fulltime job watching the pilots for signs of the "twitch," or operational fatigue, and he certainly worried far more about us than we did about ourselves. Jack was a close and dear friend whose attention and professionalism contributed in no small way to my eventual survival.

CHAPTER 14

ARNHEM—WE FINALLY CATCH UP WITH THE ARMY

September, 1944 – November, 1944

In late September we were ordered to exchange our Spitfire IXBs with 125 Wing for their Spitfire IXEs, which proved to be very battered and neglected aircraft. The Spitfire IXE wing was designed to carry two cannon and two .50 Browning heavy machine guns, which would greatly increase our effectiveness while strafing. The heavier machine guns had much more hitting power than our four lighter .303 guns, and I was particularly pleased at this improvement in our armament. Each wing also had a special bomb rack, capable of carrying 250-pound bombs, which doubled our bomb load. It was obvious that our role as ground support aircraft was being reinforced and would be our steady diet from then on. It was comforting to know that once we had delivered our bombs the IXE was just as good as the IXB against enemy aircraft.

After our move to LeCulot, the army won enough territory to warrant our move to a new airfield, Rips, B-84, some twenty miles south of Nijmegen and extremely close to the German lines to the east. As an airfield, Rips was a disaster, being typical low-lying Dutch farmland, which responded to the wet weather by becoming a soggy, muddy lake, severely curtailing our operational ability. Our eastern boundary was flanked by dense woods held by the Germans, who actually captured two of our airmen who were out hunting for firewood. In order to escape Rips before we became mired in for the winter, temporary metal tracking was hastily laid so that we could leave for Volkel, B-80. On October 14 we moved to our new 'drome located some fifteen miles north of Eindhoven, where the wing was to spend its most difficult and probably its most glorious period. Bomb-cratered by many Fortress raids, Volkel had formerly been an enormous German bomber station. A small-gauge track encircled the 'drome, forming a miniature railroad system which the Germans had used to transport bombs and equipment from their stores to the aircraft. The runways and taxi-strips were made of small wooden blocks and had kept a large maintenance gang of enslaved Dutch laborers hard at work throughout the German occupation. Being so little above sea-level, Holland had few sites suitable for airdrome construction, which meant that all existing airdromes were crowded with Allied aircraft of every description. Volkel had four wings flying Typhoons, Tempests, and Spitfires along with communication and transport aircraft, all adding up to nearly four hundred machines, which virtually blanketed the grass surface. The volume of traffic caused long delays before take-off and landing because we had to await our turn. Operating under such crowded conditions was a far from ideal situation.

We continued to live in tents, which were becoming quite tattered and were unable to hold out the wet weather and collapsed whenever the wind blew anything stronger than a breeze. The situation finally became untenable, forcing the squadron personnel to jam into a small schoolhouse in Mille, a couple of miles from the flying field. Here, at last, although very crowded, we were warm and dry and relatively content during the remainder of our seven-week stay.

Volumes have been written about the Arnhem or Market-Garden plan proposed and developed by General Montgomery, and rightly so, since it was one of the most daring military operations ever conceived. However, little mention of the air force support effort has been made in the accounts that I have examined, which is unfortunate, for our Spitfires performed magnificently, doing everything that was expected of them and more.

At the time of the attack on Arnhem on September 17, the Allied armies held nearly all of Belgium with the British and Canadian forces on the Dutch border while the American armies to the east were roughly ten miles from Germany and the Siegfried Line defences. It was Montgomery's belief that he could force a rapid thrust through the Arnhem-Nijmegen sector in southern

Holland, which he felt was lightly defended, and then sweep to the right, or east, into the northern plains of Germany. This would cut off the important Ruhr valley and open a path for a quick drive on Berlin. His plan assumed that he could demolish what he considered light German defences around Arnhem with paratroopers in short order, with his support forces arriving by land to reinforce his airborne divisions.

The British 1st Airborne Division was to drop around Arnhem, the American 82nd Airborne Division was to drop in and around Nijmegen, and the U.S. 101st Airborne was responsible for the Eindhoven area. General Dempsey's Second British Army, some sixty miles south of Arnhem, was to advance along a major road system to extend like a finger into enemy territory to link up with the airborne troops, thus creating a path to allow our main forces to flow into Holland and Germany. Crucial to our success was the preservation of the bridges at Nijmegen and Arnhem which spanned the lower Rhine and Waal Rivers. As flyers our task was to prevent enemy aircraft from bombing the bridges and to search out and destroy all enemy road and rail traffic outside the defence perimeter. As the only Allied fighters within operational range of the bridges, our wing along with Johnny Johnsons's 127 Wing carried an enormous responsibility.

General Montgomery's plan immediately ran into two major obstacles. The first was that the Arnhem area was defended by massive formations of elite German troops. Our intelligence had detected these but their advice was ignored by Montgomery. The second obstacle was the horrible weather, over which Montgomery naturally had no control. This limited his ability to fly in badly needed reinforcements and supplies but made it possible for enemy fighters and bombers to hide in the cloud cover, and pop out at convenient times to bomb and strafe our positions.

For the first two weeks following the airdrop, the weather remained abortive and made our task extremely difficult. Sometimes we covered the area by patrolling above the solid cloud cover while at other times we operated below the cloud base at an altitude of 6,000 feet or less. We saw enemy fighters infrequently, and when we did, they usually escaped in the cloud cover.

The battle areas were clearly marked on our maps before each flight to ensure that we attacked only the enemy. We saw the ground littered with gliders which had been towed to release positions by Dakotas and other transport aircraft. Some were crashed, some were burned out, and others were spread irregularly over the flat countryside. Thousands of parachutes sprinkled the ground like lonely snowflakes, clearly indicating where our troops had landed. From the air the ground looked almost serene, making it difficult to believe the intelligence reports about the very desperate struggle taking place below.

One of the greatest feats in the history of the wing was achieved while we were covering the great Arnhem-Nijmegen-Eindhoven airborne landings. In the space of only a few days the wing destroyed more than one hundred enemy aircraft and damaged many more. It was a stupendous triumph. Our losses were slight, which was amazing because the enemy attacked with large formations, frequently numbering one hundred machines. We were always outnumbered, but in every case, whether the odds were twenty-five to one or four to one, our Spitfires attacked, destroying some enemy craft and sending the others racing for home. Aces were born overnight. Flight Lieutenant Don Laubman, DFC and Bar, destroyed eight enemy aircraft within two days to bring his score to thirteen destroyed. Squadron Leader R.I.A. Smith, DFC and Bar, claimed six Huns to bring his score to thirteen destroyed. Many others registered two or more kills and the wing's scoreboard could scarcely be kept up to date so quickly were the successes being reported. I had originally felt that my greatest strength as CO of 442 Squadron would be in directing the squadron in battles with enemy aircraft, but now I had the misfortune of never being in the air when the enemy could be caught; it was just not my luck to be in the right place at the right time. Further, I was grounded, unable to fly, during the period of the most intense activity.

One evening while in the little red schoolhouse in Mille, I was having another bull session with all my pilots, discussing the ways to successfully abandon a Spitfire in trouble. During the exchange of ideas, I was called to the phone. It was Dal Russel, who explained that he had been ordered by group headquarters, presumably Air Vice-Marshal Broadhurst, to see that I recommend eight pilots for decorations in recognition of our outstanding success against ground targets. I was grounded until I had written up the various citations. Naturally I was flattered that our work was being recognized beyond the wing organization and I felt that very few squadron commanders had ever been ordered to recommend men for decorations on such a large scale. I related in vague terms the gist of the message to the pilots, without mentioning any names. Up to now our morale had been superb. This news seemed to elevate us to an even higher plateau of enthusiasm.

I was disappointed at being grounded but realized that in addition to having to compose the citations, a short rest and change of pace would do me a world of good. Accordingly, Jack Whitelaw and I took off to Brussels for relaxation. In the few weeks since we were there last, great changes had taken place. While the Belgians were under German domination, the black market had carried on a flourishing business, and the Belgians, in a way, were thankful for it. The poor did not get a great deal to eat, but at least their money could buy the bare essentials. The wealthy, on the other hand, were able to buy almost everything they needed and lived quite well, although at great expense. The Germans had imposed a curfew which started at eleven o'clock at night and lasted until five the following morning. Those who wished to spend an evening at a nightclub started their parties before curfew hour and stayed until the curfew was lifted the next morning. That arrangement seemed to have been satisfactory to both the Belgians and the Germans.

When the Allies arrived, they abolished the black market, but omitted to bring in the food which the black market had ordinarily supplied and which the population had relied upon. Thus the city began to go hungry as it never had before. The curfew now didn't begin until midnight, but all nightclubs and cabarets were ordered to close at half past ten and to ensure that they did, the electricity was turned off. This forced the clubs to carry on with candles because they were unwilling to close that early. As a result, the nightclubs were raided nightly by the Belgian military police, who forced the patrons to leave. What might have been an indignity became a common occurence in Brussels, because the Belgians were a gay people who like to wine, dance and romance in their city's many smart cabarets and luxurious nightclubs.

In order to smash the black market, all money used during the German occupation was made worthless after a suitable warning period, each individual being allowed to cash or exchange a relatively small amount of the old money for the new Belgian currency. This move produced the desired result, although it caught many whose small fortunes plummeted rapidly in value. Despite these strict measures, the Belgians did not grumble, although they might have preferred a little less Allied control. They obviously accepted the measures as the necessary medicine for the restoration of Belgium.

Brussels became a rest center for the British and Canadian twenty-first Army Group and for all the RAF and RCAF stationed in Belgium and Holland. Hotels, cinemas, restaurants, and cabarets were commandeered by the Allies, and the city soon became one massive stronghold of troops on furlough. All passes for leave in Brussels were issued with a special pamphlet devised and issued by Army Welfare Services and Education Branch, Headquarters Brussels Garrison, containing much useful information and a variety of restrictions. Each of us required a special Leave Scheme Pass, all cafes were to be emptied by 2300 hours, curfew was in force from midnight to 0500 hours, and all brothels were out of bounds to service personnel. We also had to be suitably dressed, were not allowed to carry personal firearms, and were required to salute senior officers as well as the tomb of the Belgian Unknown Soldier. We could not change money for civilians or speculate in currency and we had to vacate our hotel rooms by 1100 hours on the day of departure. Among the general notes was a warning not to talk about or identify our unit, nor were we to discuss equipment, losses, or battle experiences: "The people of Brussels are very hospitable and will do all they can to make your leave enjoyable. Enjoy yourselves with them but do not tell them anything." We were also told of the high prices of casual refreshments, and informed that we must not buy food in civilian restaurants. The pamphlet included a large-scale map of Brussels clearly indicating the hotels, bars, theaters, and points of interest.

Our leave lasted only a couple of days, of which I retain one memory. One afternoon as Jack and I were sitting in a popular cafe enjoying a drink, a waiter approached with a message that a lady and her granddaughter would like to join us if it was not inconvenient. More out of curiosity than the need for companionship we agreed. Soon a magnificent creature, like a ship in full sail, marched up to our table accompanied by a very shy young girl. The lady was something from a different era, dressed totally in black in a very ornate dress which I guessed was high fashion before World War I. Wearing an enormous black hat, smoking a cigarette through a long black holder, she used her cane as if it were one more ornament. I felt this imperious person was in her late seventies and she exuded an air of confidence, although I thought I could detect a slight nervousness. In broken English she introduced herself as Madame Spaak and the twelve-year-old girl with her as Catherine. After ordering ice cream she got around to inviting us for dinner that evening to their home on the Avenue Louise. We politely refused, pleading previous engagements, something I have since regretted, for her son, Paul Henri Spaak, became prime minister of Belgium and the young girl achieved international recognition as the movie star Catherine Spaak.

One night back at camp while chatting with Larry Robillard, a very experienced pilot with 401 Squadron, I heard an interesting story. I always enjoyed Larry, for he was a great conversationalist who could relate his many varied experiences in a most amusing and fascinating manner. He had been shot down in France over a year earlier and being perfectly bilingual and a devil-may-care type, he evaded capture successfully. Eventually he joined a resistance group with whom he operated for some months, and then, becoming bored, he returned via an escape route to England. He was allowed to fly operationally again, knowing that if he were shot down, captured, and his previous experience came to light, he could be shot as a spy. We were discussing the situation of Flight Lieutenant J.N. Dick who a few weeks earlier had chopped off the tail of a Fleet Air Arm pilot who was flying with the squadron to gain some combat experience. Coming home from a sortie the squadron was ordered into close formation which prompted the accident. I never condoned close formation flying or aerobatic displays after a sortie for many reasons. The pilots were not accustomed to tight formation flying where every man must be keenly aware of his abilities and the location of the other aircraft. Further, on the return home after a sortie a man may have been experiencing all sorts of different emotions, from release of tension to excitement, fatigue, or relief at having survived another flight. With twelve men in twelve aircraft the range of emotions would be great and in my opinion not the time to try some fancy flying. Lastly, even if no action had been involved, a pilot could not always be sure that he had not unknowingly picked up a stray piece of flak which might have damaged a vital control.

I had sat on the board which examined Dick's role in the mishap causing the death of the Navy lieutenant commander. The verdict was that it was an accident and that Dick should return to England for further flying instruction. Larry related how Dick could see aircraft through clouds and on several occasions demonstrated his remarkable eyesight by directing 401 Squadron onto enemy aircraft that no one else had seen. His ability to detect aircraft consistently was uncanny and a most valuable asset for a pilot. All this had been unknown to me until know. Thanking Larry for the information I sought Dal Russel. I explained to Dal how extremely valuable a man Dick was and said that it was a waste of talent to leave him in England. Could Dal arrange to have Dick posted to 442 Squadron where I would fly him as my number 2? Dal agreed with my argument and within a week Dick joined our squadron, where he proved that his eyesight was as remarkable as had been suggested. Unfortunately, his eyesight did not prevent him from being shot down and killed several months later.

As suddenly as it had begun, Operation Market-Garden finished. Nijmegen, on the southern bank of the Lower Rhine, was ours at last, but the majority of the heroic troops in Arnhem were lost. For weeks after, we patrolled the vital Nijmegen bridge, which the enemy tried desperately to destroy in order to isolate our troops on the northern bank. The Germans had bombed it day and night and swimmers had floated downstream intending to blow it up, but all attempts failed and miraculously the bridge stood.

On September 27, I had half the squadron on a high-level patrol when I spotted what appeared to be two Fw 190s carrying large belly slung bombs. They were at our altitude of about 25,000 feet, making a large orbit with the obvious intention of dive bombing the important Nigmegen bridges. I reported to our Kenway controller that I was about to make contact and gave chase with my engine wide open. Since I had guessed their objective, I made to cut off their position and prevent them from attacking. I cut my circle tight but I made no gain on the aircraft, which were flying a considerably wider circle. I was amazed! "Kenway, Caribou leader here. I'm chasing these bastards, I've got 420 mph on the clock, I'm flying a smaller circle than they are, and I'm not getting an inch closer. What the hell are they?" My astonishment must have been apparent, but up to this time I had never seen an Me 262, the new enemy jet-propelled aircraft.

Kenway control replied, "Can't help you any. Stay with them and keep us informed. Out." Much easier said than done. I finally got a clue about what they actually were other than Focke-Wulfs. I radioed the rest of the pilots, telling them that we were going to start diving now, hoping to intercept the 262s over the target, or least prevent them from making an accurate and damaging attack.

At full bore I dived toward a spot I thought would intercept the enemy as they dove. I was doing better than 450 mph, but the 262s were probably clocking 650 mph — no contest. At a difficult and acute angle I fired, with no observable results. I continued to follow the enemy as they scooted over the target and headed for safety. I got in another shot and saw a puff of black smoke, but concluded that I had not hit him since I was at least six hundred yards behind and the smoke probably came from some throttle adjustment he had made. I followed him for some thirty miles as he jinked one way and then the other, and he very definitely seemed to slow down. The excitement of the chase slowly cooled as I realized the 262 was playing with me. His jinks were made to allow him rear vision to see exactly where I was and his slower speed was to entice me to follow until I was easy prey for him or whoever he called for help. Assistance was sure to come, for we were heading straight for his airdrome at Rheine. I gave up in disgust, without waggling my wings goodbye. I later learned that I had done the right thing, for all of the 262 pilots were extremely experienced men, the very best the Luftwaffe could muster, including General Adolph Galland, head of the fighter section of the Luftwaffe. The Allies were very fortunate that the German discovered the possibilities of this remarkable aircraft so late in the war, before it could be produced in significant numbers; otherwise the outcome of the air war might have been very different.

With the Arnhem defeat the battle lines stiffened and remained relatively static until spring. Our flying emphasis changed from patrol and defensive work to attacking a great variety of targets in Germany and German-held territory, with special emphasis on rail interdiction. This included attacking marshalling yards, rail junctions, tunnels, bridges, embankments, and rolling stock. We also started to carry a 250-pound bomb under each wing in addition to the 500-pound bomb slung under the belly of our Spits. I felt like crying when I first saw the aircraft loaded down with these extra ugly appendages. We started diving at a steeper angle, almost to the vertical, which improved our bombing accuracy if frequently resulting in aircraft damaged by having their wings rippled by the force of the pullout from our dives.

With such a volume of flying activity, we faced increasingly difficult problems. Our experienced pilots rapidly became tour-expired and were replaced by new, operationally inexperienced men. Goodwin, our leading ground attacker, completed his tour with a score of 180 vehicles damaged and destroyed, Middleton left with 130 vehicles destroyed, Blair left, as did O'Sullivan, with 39 transports, an ammo train, and 8 locomotives destroyed, and one aircraft probably destroyed in 198 ops hours. In addition, we were losing pilots to enemy action as our dive-bombing and stafing in heavily defended areas exacted a heavy price in pilot lives. We lost Costello, who bailed out after being hit by flak and was last seen running into a small woods. Curtis dove straight into the ground. Millar was killed by ground troops while descending by parachute. Nearly everyone was hit at least once by flak. A note in my log book dated November 1 indicated that in seven weeks I had gone through seven Spitfires — they were not destroyed, but damaged seriously enough that in each case a replacement was required.

Our days at Volkel were filled with drama, pathos, tension, danger, and horror. Our flights to targets involved flying fifty miles or so behind enemy lines through flak-defended areas, and we were fired upon frequently even when not attacking specific targets. Being close to the Ruhr, only forty miles away, damaged bombers sought our field for safety. One day while waiting at the end of the runway to take off with my flight an RAF Mitchell bomber circled the 'drome firing distress flares, obviously badly shot up. Knowing that he wanted to land on our runway, I turned our flight around to taxi back out of the way. In came the bomber intending to make a wheels-up crash landing. When only one hundred feet up, someone jumped from the aircraft and hit the ground with a sickening thud, landing where my aircraft had been before moving out of the way. The body bounced six feet and thudded back to earth. Ten feet off the runway another man jumped out, to be dragged to his death. The aircraft finally stopped, blocking the runway as ambulances and firetrucks rushed to the rescue. The airman near us was a frightful mess, with every bone in his body smashed and bone fragments piercing his flying clothes from head to foot. It was tragic because they could have survived had they remained in the aircraft. We surmised that at some point the pilot had instructed his crew to bail out and either had not rescinded the order or his radio failed and he was unable to issue further instructions to his crew. Obviously blind panic had taken over, which wasted two lives needlessly.

On another occasion a battered B-17 Flying Fortress circled our field with one wheel down, the bomb doors open, the nose shot off, two engines stopped with the propellors frozen, and a parachute streaming from the tail. Somehow the pilot made a perfect belly landing. An 88 millimeter shell had scored a direct hit on the aircraft while it was bombing in the Ruhr, blowing off the front six or eight feet of the nose. Thrown into a vicious dive, the pilot had ordered the crew to jump, but the wind howling through the open nose blew his parachute pack away, leaving him no opportunity to escape. He fought to recover, finally regained control, and was able to limp the short distance to Volkel with no electrical system and no radio. When we examined his machine, I could only marvel at how this terribly battered machine was able to stay aloft as long as it had. The interior was covered in blood and a foot, without sock or shoe, lay jammed in the controls at the pilot's feet. it was a horrible and depressing sight, reinforcing our opinion, so strongly held, that we were fortunate to be flying single-seat fighters rather than such large, cumbersome monsters as the B-17.

During late September and early October, we noticed that the ground features of parts of Holland were changing — rivers became lakes and low-lying land areas became large, deep marshes. The ruthless enemy had been busy destroying dikes and pumping stations, allowing the North Sea's salty waters to flood deep into the Dutch hinterland in a desperate, and successful, effort to slow the advance of the Allied armies. This affected us favorably as it meant that German traffic was now concentrated on fewer road and rail lines, actually increasing our chances of locating worthwhile targets.

Lest the reader conclude incorrectly that I led all the sorties, I hasten to emphasize that we relied on other leaders in the squadron to share the responsibility. We might send four aircraft off on a specific target, then four more a half hour later and perhaps the final four still later. This meant that we really had three offensive units in the air at the same time pursuing different objectives. I felt all of our section leaders were capable and aggressive, able to lead missions that would bring recognition to the squadron. The leaders had proven themselves time and again, shown that they could find an elusive target, exercised good judgment, and earned the trust and confidence of their fellow pilots.

The weather worsened steadily with the approach of winter, and the sky, rarely clear of clouds, was often a solid gray blanket of ice, rain, and danger. Under such adverse conditions, flying in small, compact formations became a virtual necessity to ensure that no one would get lost. Navigating accurately in poor weather was always a problem, especially since the metal in our bombs caused our compasses to read incorrectly by as much as forty degrees.

I remember only one pilot being lost to enemy action because of bad weather. I had sent Flying Officer Al Hoare to Brussels to pick up a replacement aircraft. On the return flight he missed our airdrome, and ended up in the middle of the Ruhr in exceedingly bad weather. He was shot down, apparently, but at the time we only knew that he was missing. Prince Bernhardt was asked to see what his sources of information behind enemy lines could uncover. He reported that Hoare had been killed, which meant that we had to pack up his kit to be returned to his family. I needed a shoe polish brush and helped myself to his. Some twelve years later at a fighter pilots' reunion in Montreal a short, slim chap came up to me saying, "I'll bet you don't remember me." Without hesitation I replied, "You're Al E. Hoare, regimental number C35274. You're supposed to be dead." His eyes widened and his mouth fell open as complete surprise took over. I explained that his shoe brush with his name and number stencilled thereon was mine, and that I used it regularly and therefore was familiar with his vital statistics. After a long talk I added that he could not have the brush back.

Each time someone shot down an enemy aircraft, it became an occasion for the squadron to celebrate. Enemy aircraft were seldom seen and never by me. McLarty had success, as did Wilson and Costello. Frosty Young was in ecstacy after shooting down two Focke-Wulfs on the same trip. Jack Lumsden, so deadly on ground targets could scarcely speak after destroying his first enemy aircraft. It produced a very different feeling, shooting down an enemy aircraft, for that was the traditional role of the fighter pilot. While we relished shooting and bombing ground targets, knowing that we were helping to win the war, it could not compare with the satisfaction derived from shooting down an enemy fighter.

Young, Costello, Millar, and Curtis were all close friends, having joined the air force at the same time and having been with the squadron since its inception. Three of them were lost to enemy action, leaving only Young. His face grew long and dark, and black circles formed under his eyes, and I rather sensed that he knew his days were numbered. Seeking vengeance, he attacked targets with a determination and courage that were even greater than he had shown before. He grieved silently for his friends and nothing that any of us could say would cheer him up. Even the award of the DFC did not raise his spirits.

Fate intervened a few hours before "Frosty" Young finished his extended tour. We were beating up a locomotive in the Munster marshalling yard. I had attacked first, my cannon shells causing great clouds of steam to erupt from the boiler. Frosty, eager and confident, was immediately behind me. He gave a long, accurate burst with every bullet striking telling blows to the engine. Even from a few hundred feet away, I could see a massive fire building beneath the boiler and shouted a warning to Frosty over the R/T, but I was too late. Just as he was over the engine, it exploded in a cloud of flying debris, carrying his aircraft five hundred feet up in the air as if it had been a feather. The Spit immediately began to pour black and white smoke as a long, wicked-looking flame sprouted from the engine cowling. The plane slowly started nosing toward the ground. I yelled frantically over the R/T, "Frosty, Frosty, get the hell out. Hurry. Hurry."

The aircraft started heading straight down. Somewhere, somehow, in those few brief seconds while the Spitfire was in its death dive, Frosty got out, his chute opening a bare second before he hit the ground. His aircraft exploded into pieces within thirty yards of him.

We felt that he would have survived, and a month later our feelings were confirmed when he was reported a POW. Frosty had landed in the midst of the German anti-aircraft gunners defending the marshalling yards, and we wondered how he fared in their hands, landing so close to where he had blown up a locomotive. Later we discovered that the gunners had beaten him severely. He was one of the finest pilots in the squadron, a marvellous shot, and always keen to engage the enemy, regardless of the danger or the odds.

That left Stan McLarty as the only surviving member of the original squadron and he was killed two months later. Red-headed Stan was a real fireball and probably the pilot most eager among us to succeed. He was a fine leader, brave to the extent of being reckless, a beacon for others to follow. An example of the depth and range of the squadron spirit, nourished by men like Young and McLarty, showed up during the Seventh Canadian Victory

Loan drive. We were encouraged to participate further in the Canadian war effort by buying Victory bonds, with a squadron quota of $3,100.00. We led the wing by raising $6,800.00 or 213 per cent of our target.

Two experienced pilots arrived to bolster our dwindling pilot roster, Flight Lieutenant N.A. Keene, DFC, and Flight Lieutenant M.E. Jowsey, DFC. Among the green pilots arriving were Warrant Officers C.B. Simpson, Al Bathurst and J.G. Livingstone; Flight Lieutenants W.V. Shenk and D.M. Pieri; and Flying Officers J.A. Cousineau, R.B. Barker, R.C. Smith and J.P.W. Francis, who shot down a Fw 190 on his first operational trip. The poor weather persisted so we continued to fly flights of four and six aircraft, feeling that such small groups were more managable in poor weather and yet sufficiently strong to combat successfully any enemy fighters which might be encountered.

Sometimes when chasing enemy aircraft, they seemed to disappear into the ground in a bewildering manner. We had heard that they had landing strips covered with camouflaged netting, which would have accounted for their sudden disappearance. Not many subscribed to that theory, however, and I never did discover the secret of their magic act. When I discovered a new German airfield which had not been previously reported, I therefore felt we might attack it with encouraging results. Unlike the Americans, however, we were forbidden to attack enemy airdromes since it was thought that our potential losses would not offset the damage we might inflict on the enemy. I reported to Dal my views on how the 'drome, just outside of Dorsten in Germany, could be attacked successfully, and I pleaded with him to give our squadron the opportunity. Finally, reluctantly, he agreed, with certain provisos. We would have to attack in early morning when there was a heavy ground haze and the sun was behind us so the German gunners would be facing the bright light. We were to make only one pass with bombs and guns.

After carefully briefing the pilots we became airborne at first light en route to our target some one hundred miles distant. Leading the Spits in a wide sweep up-sun I radioed "Tally ho" and put the nose down in a moderate-angle, high-speed dive. The attack plan was perfect and it was only as I neared the 'drome that I realized the thirty Me 109s scattered about the surface were all dummies! And I felt like the biggest dummy of all! We pasted the field, shot up the flak towers, destroyed fifteen dummy aircraft, and not a shot was fired at us. We took our disappointment out on rail traffic before returning to Volkel to report the results. There was much laughter there, which did not improve my disposition. That airdrome proved once again the ingeniousness of the enemy.

From the day we moved to Volkel to the middle of November, the "City of New Westminster" Squadron displayed a spirit and an ability greater than it had shown before. Our days were long, starting with the predawn armed weather recce and ending with a late show at dusk. Each trip tried the nerves of the pilots as they had never been tried before, taking on a danger and grimness that had been unknown in the past. Each pilot made several sorties daily, and on each trip, he was obligated to attack some heavily defended marshalling yard in a city such as Munster or Dorsten at the eastern edge of the Ruhr or Dusseldorf in the heart of the Ruhr basin. Rarely was there a sortie where one or more aircraft was not hit by flak, and all too often one of our machines failed to return. It was at Volkel that the true temperament and grim determination of the pilots was revealed. Flying an aircraft that was never built for dive-bombing, an aircraft that would stand very little punishment from flak, attacking the most heavily defended targets in the world, operating under the worst possible weather conditions, but displaying an inexpressible keenness and a desire to do a successful job, they never failed to earn frequent commendations from Air Vice-Marshal Harry Broadhurst, Air Chief Marshal Sir Arthur Tedder, and other Allied commanders.

Daily it recorded more motor transport demolished, and more locomotives and railway cars destroyed and damaged than any other squadron in the wing. Anything that walked or moved in Germany was a target for our guns and did not escape our eyes or our aim. Wherever we went, wherever we attacked, death and destruction to the enemy always resulted.

Train busting became a particularly rewarding occupation for our pilots, although it was extremely dangerous. When we first started to attack trains in Germany, we had a great deal of success because of relatively minor opposition from flak. About the Ruhr and to the north trains were plentiful, and in the cold air their smoke and steam were visible for miles. As the war progressed and the enemy began to respect the damage we could inflict, he began to arm each train with three or four flak cars, making our job more difficult. Finally the wily enemy must have installed radios in the trains, for frequently as we approached, the train would race for the nearest flak-defended area along its route. If the locomotive made the defended area in time, it would stop and blow off clouds of steam to lure us into attacking. Such tempting targets were generally attacked and invariably we met a warm reception. At other times locomotives would go puffing merrily along completely oblivious to any danger from the air until our bullets caused great clouds of steam to gush from the cannon-riddled boiler. Very often the engineers were killed and the train would keep moving engulfed in steam, until its momentum died and it finally stopped. At other times they would stop, shut off their steam, and hope that we had lost sight of them.

The damage inflicted on a locomotive was easily assessed. Thick gushes of steam pouring from both sides of the boiler — our cannon shells could completely penetrate the machine — enabled us to claim a damaged locomotive. About one in forty would blow up, and we then claimed a destroyed. Why so few blew up I cannot say, but when they did it was a most satisfying sight. Nor were the cars and trucks drawn by a locomotive forgotten or left untouched — they were attended to once the engine had been disabled. We managed to catch a few ammunition trains leaving the Ruhr, which would explode when hit and burn for a whole day. Attacking oil tankers involved a special procedure since they had to be destroyed from a distance. When hit, they threw up a wall of flame two to three hundred feet high, quite capable of engulfing an unwary pilot with fatal results.

Troop trains were recognizable because the soldiers' carriages were generally located immediately behind the locomotive, and they were always well-defended with flak cars. It was necessary in most cases to first silence the flak cars, which the pilots did with little regard for their own safety. They had a job to do:

destroy the enemy wherever he could be found. Every man in the squadron and the wing could tell exciting and scarcely believable stories about just that. These were related casually with no reference to the number of dangerous dives made in the face of strong flak positions or the number of times that a train exploded just far enough away to grant another day of life.

On October 28 I asked Steve Randall[16] and Jack Lumsden to accompany me on a "rhubarb," a low-level search-and-destroy flight, along the northern border of the Ruhr. Steve was a very different breed of fighter pilot nearing the end of his second tour. Stocky and well built, with a craggy face usually lit up in a smile, hair which grew straight up, a soft, raspy voice, and a marvellous sense of humor, he loved to play his battered guitar as he sang his own witty compositions. He enjoyed life, loved people, and was easily the most popular man on the squadron. Added to this was his particular skill as a leader in the air with a record of always returning with all his aircraft from each mission. The men preferred his leadership over that of most of the rest of us, a compliment which was richly deserved.

Rhubarbs were rarely flown, but I felt we might be able to surprise an enemy aircraft or perhaps locate some unusual target. At zero feet we skimmed over the woods of Germany, along tree-lined roads, by peaceful farms, and over minute villages without seeing a solitary person. Other than thin wisps of smoke seeping upward from isolated dwellings, there was no sign of life, although we were nearly one hundred miles behind enemy lines. Finally a locomotive was spied which we attacked and damaged. Another and yet another came into view and fell to our guns. While we were attacking the third train, Steve was attracted by some aircraft tied down on the flat cars and he attacked them several times from an altitude of less than one hundred feet. Satisfied with the destruction we had created, we turned away to attack another locomotive. Then Steve reported that his engine temperature was rising alarmingly. I immediately ordered him to head for base with Jack and me acting as escorts. Steve knew he would never make our lines, yet his voice was calm and cool as he talked over the radio. Within a matter of minutes a large white blast of glycol left his aircraft, and he announced that he had "had it." Staying some distance away we watched while he glided over a large wood near Wesel, where he planned to bail out. Over the R/T came his last message in an unperturbed voice. "Thanks a lot, Bill. I'll be seeing you. So long, fellas." A few seconds later his parachute opened, and he descended exactly as he had planned. Tears came to my eyes as I watched him float earthward. Then sorrow changed to anger and I was ready to do almost anything to avenge the loss of my friend, my ablest flight commander, and one of the best-liked men in the wing. The rest of the wing who had heard his final words over the R/T were deeply touched by his calmness and perfect procedure. He had certainly shown us how to go down like a man, and for the squadron, it was the gloomiest of gloomy days.

In a queer sort of way, Steve had actually shot himself down. The coolant radiators on the Spit were large air scoops located on the underside of the fuselage, positioned to allow our speed to force cooling air through the light grillwork. During a strafing attack bullets could strike a hard surface in such a manner that the bullet fragments ricochetted in random directions, often colliding with our fast-moving aircraft. When the vulnerable glycol cooling radiator was struck, the liquid coolant poured out, usually in the form of white smoke, and a Spitfire so damaged could not stay aloft for long. The flying time left an aircraft depended on the size of the hole in the radiator, but when the coolant was gone, the engine ceased to function and generally burst into flames from overheating. Steve's luck had run out, doubly so as we learned later, for the Germans were waiting in the woods and denied him any opportunity to escape.

On October 29, the day after losing Randall, I ran into some tought luck as well. On my second sortie of the day, I was leading the squadron to dive-bomb a large railway bridge on the southern fringe of Münster. As I peeled off the target in a gradual turn to port, I saw a string of large tractor-trailer trucks proceeding south on the autobahn paralleling the Dortmund-Emms Canal. I decided to attack.

My rule had been that after each bombing attack, all aircraft should be checked for bomb hangups before further action was considered. I broke my own rule, this time unaware that the 500 pound belly bomb had not released. Our bomb racks were originally designed for bombs to be dropped from level flight, and since nothing else was available, we had to use them for dive-bombing. In a dive speed of 450 mph, the force exerted by speed and pressure on the rack was often too strong for the electrical system and the release hook would fail to open. Hangups or the bomb's failing to drop would result. This happened to me. I failed to notice the weight since my speed and a good pullout, combined with a turn without skidding or slipping, fooled me into thinking the aircraft was bomb-free.

Attacking the first lorry I opened fire at three hundred yards in a medium dive. The vibration of my guns shook the bomb free, so that it struck the truck when I was less than fifty feet above the vehicle. It blew the truck to smithereens, knocked me unconscious, and blasted my aircraft several hundred feet upward. My Spit slowly rolled onto its back, and when I regained consciousness two or three seconds later, I was heading for the ground upside down. Death was only seconds away, although I was too dazed to think clearly. The trees below looked enormous. Suddenly, instinctively, I moved the control column hard and the aircraft righted itself, pulling out of the dive just above the tops of the trees.

In a few moments I realized that my plight was desperate. I wondered whether or not I should bail out while I still had an opportunity or try to fly back toward base. Then I found that there was no choice, for struggle as I might the coupe top would not open.

Setting a rough course for Volkel, I surveyed the damage from the cockpit. Both wings were badly buckled from the force of the explosion and had been blown or bent upward an extra foot and a half. Every panel in the aircraft had been blown off, with the ground clearly visible through great empty holes in the wings. Pieces of brown canvas from the covering protecting the truck cargo were streaming from the jagged metal pieces of my aircraft, and the fuselage was buckled and twisted while the tail unit fluttered and vibrated, threatening to break off. Both ailerons were sticking almost straight up in the air. While I was subconsciously recovering from the dive, Providence had made me move the control column the only way it would work. The cockpit had been badly stove in and none of the cockpit instruments read correctly. The radio and oxygen equipment, normally situated behind the seat, were rattling on the floor of the Spitfire, completely shattered. Some of the control cables had been completely severed; there was no elevator control, and the rudder remained the only control which worked normally. It took both my hands, one foot, and all my strength on the control column just to prolong what little flying capability remained.

Using full engine power I staggered through the air at 140 mph and climbed about two hundred feet per minute. From Münster to safety was almost one hundred miles. I was certainly on my own, for though the pilots herded about me, without a radio I had no idea what was happening other than my own immediate problems. Several lifetimes seemed to pass before my derelict aircraft crossed our lines at some 15,000 feet.

Upon reaching the comparative safety of friendly territory I thought that since I would have to bail out, how clever it would be to jump right over our field and save me a long walk home. That opportunity disappeared because the smashed coupe top would neither open nor jettison. I released the control column so I could use the strength of my back and legs for added leverage against the confining cover. At last it released and blew away. Now there was the question of how best to exit from the machine. All the methods of abandoning an aircraft flashed through my mind; diving over the side while flying as level as possible finally won out.

Before I could make the final decision, the engine apparently ran out of oil. It was making strange noises as it lost power, indicating that it might blow up at any moment. At the same time the tail assembly started to flutter and vibrate so violently I thought it would fall off. With the loss of engine power the Spit became totally unmanageable and it entered a steep spiral dive. With helmet already off and straps released, and radio and oxygen lines unhooked, I pushed myself headfirst through the side door, into the slipstream.

The Spit's dive was now so steep that the pressure on me meant

I was stuck, pressed against the plane's metal skin, staring at the tail. The fuselage was rippled and bent horribly. How did the machine ever fly, let alone last for one hundred miles? I had a few moments to think of these things, for I was completely stuck, unable to move. Then, after a seeming eternity, the rapidly increasing wind pressure suddenly plucked me from the side of the aircraft, flinging me free. For a silly moment I felt that I was being chewed up by the propellor, a totally impossible act since the engine was pointing down and I was well behind it. This ridiculous impression was to invade my dreams for years afterward.

Hurtling through the air at nearly 300 mph, staring alternately at the sky and then at the ground, I thought it a wonderful feeling to be free, with no sense of falling or of speed. The gentle, almost somersaulting motion of the fall allowed the air to fill my clothes and dry my sweat. It felt as though my whole body was being caressed with velvet — soothing, peaceful, wonderful.

After dropping free for several thousand feet, allowing my rate of descent to decrease somewhat while the various thoughts had raced through my head, I looked down to my left side, saw the D-ring of the ripcord, and pulled it. I looked at the metal ring, thinking what a queer-looking object it was, and since it had done its job, I threw it away as being of no further use. There was a sharp jolt as the pilot 'chute caught in the air, pulling out the main canopy with a force which jarred every bone in my body. I must have been falling at great speed to receive such a jolt when my downward momentum came to a shuddering halt. I felt angry and helpless drifting down and extremely weak from having fought the controls of my aircraft for so long. I was completely drained. I watched with no emotion as my aircraft crashed in a tiny Dutch field, but later I would thank that remarkable aircraft for lasting long enough to bring me safely home.

My worries were not yet over, for I was a mere two miles from the German lines, toward which a very brisk wind was blowing the parachute at a good rate of speed. With thousands of feet still to drop there was a very real chance that I could still end up in enemy hands. My recourse was to pull the shrouds of the chute to speed up the rate of descent as well as counter the wind drift. Tugging desperately on the silken cords, I pulled down the edge of the canopy and the rate of descent increased dramatically. Below was a small village that had a church with a wicked-looking spire, and I could imagine it spearing me, bottom first. I could see people, small as ants at first, running from every direction to converge on my probable landing site. Cars, trucks, and jeeps twisted through tiny lanes, each trying to be first to reach me when I finally landed.

Too late I released the shrouds to slow my rate of descent, starting a violent swinging motion which I did not have time to stop. Although I missed some tall trees I was hurled against the side of a sloping slate roof, with the lower half of my body smashing through it as easily as if bursting a paper bag. Within a minute a crowd of Dutch civilians gathered about the building, curiously watching a helpless airman stretched flat on the slope of the roof. The owner and his wife had been eating lunch when I smashed through their roof, but they seemed to accept this as an everyday occurrence!

A short, stocky British army captain succeeded in rescuing me, giving me and my rolled up 'chute a seat in his jeep while the escorting Spitfires flew low and dipped their wings in a farewell salute. My landing site was the tiny village of Veghel, only six miles past our base. Arriving at the captain's mess, he urged half a bottle of Scotch into me and as the liquid warmed my body, aches and bruises seemed to disappear and muscles and nerves relaxed. I was safe, unhurt, and life seemed very, very sweet.

Meanwhile Dal Russel and "Doc" Whitelaw were searching the Dutch roads for a squadron leader who might be trying to hitchhike north with a heap of white silk tucked under one arm. Dal's concern proved once again his considerate nature. He and Jack had dropped everything, including lunch, to search for me, a gesture I appreciated.

My misfortune proved something else to me, something I shall never forget. When I returned to the squadron many of the men had tears in their eyes. I had always known that there was great comradeship among the pilots and groundcrews, but I had never imagined that the depth of feeling was so great that it could find expression in open tears. I was overwhelmed and resolved to work harder than ever for the welfare of everyone in the squadron in whatever ways I could.

I wanted to fly the following day. Weather grounded all flying, but I did the only flight, a weather recce. It seemed important to me to see if I felt as keen and capable after my escapade as I had before and the only way to test this was to fly. To all outward appearances I was none the worse for my experience.

Within a few days of bailing out I began to feel quite strongly that my incredible good luck was starting to run out. I still flew and attacked as I had before, using the same judgment and determination to obliterate any target selected. As leader I could not avoid or lessen the risk on any sortie nor could I show any lessening of enthusiasm. It was my responsibility to set an example for all the pilots, to continue to prove myself, all the while realizing that my skill and experience counted for very little in the long run because the law of averages and luck would catch me again, and soon. In over 490 operational hours I had never been nicked by a bullet fired from an enemy aircraft, and my kites had received relatively few flak hits until recently. Now my aircraft was being hit on nearly every sortie. While most of the hits were minor, I had to face reality: going from very few hits over a long period of time to being hit on nearly every trip did not bode well.

Over seven weeks we had lost six pilots shot down, missing, or killed, with another seven posted tour-expired. The most experienced pilots had departed, to be replaced by equally keen but usually inexperienced men. We were like a football team which had been deprived of a dozen of its first-string players. As we were now flying small formations most of the time, it was imperative that the squadron have very experienced, capable section leaders. We did have a number, but the strain of constant flying was too much to ask of them.

In desperation I asked Dal for help. As usual, he came through, sending Flight Lieutenant E.G. Ireland, a member of 411 Squadron to us while we sent Flight Lieutenant MacLean to them. "Irish" Ireland was a quiet chap, short and stocky, with a shy smile and a quiet chuckle, exactly the kind of pilot and man we needed, and he fitted in perfectly right from the start. It is very disruptive for a pilot who has become an integral part of one squadron to transfer to another in mid-career, but I know he was reassured by our warm welcome. Irish continued in the service after the war until retirement, later becoming recognized as the finest precision pilot in the RCAF.

CHAPTER 15

TIME RUNS OUT

November, 1944 – December, 1944

The wing had organized ten-day refresher courses in England for each squadron. Our turn in the rotation came on November 14 when our fifteen Spitfires, with bomb racks removed and replaced by long-range fuel tanks, took off for Warmwell, in Dorset, some fifteen miles west of Bournemouth on the south coast. While technically regarded as a training course in air firing and dive-bombing, we treated the change as an opportunity to relax, to enjoy warm beds with sheets, to explore nearby pubs, and to savor the excellent meals and the marvellous hospitality offered by a station that catered to operationally tired pilots. At the same time we found it useful to practice our attack procedures without the distraction of guns firing back.

I spent some of my time recruiting several new pilots to bring our roster up to its full complement, with emphasis on men about to start their second tour of operational duty. As a result Flight Lieutenant "Mitch" Johnson from Selkirk, Manitoba, Flying Officer Max Perkins, and Flight Lieutenant D.C. "Chunky" Gordon from Vancouver joined our ranks and later proved the value of their previous experience. My faith in the ability and aggressiveness of experienced operational pilots was repaid many times over because the requirements of military flying could only be learned under actual combat conditions. Aerial warfare was the most effective teacher, brilliantly highlighting unforgettable successful survival techniques.

After a day's delay because of terrible weather, we left Warmwell on November 25th with twenty-two new aircraft and thirty-two new pilots. Our ranks had been further increased by two operationally inexperienced pilots, Flying Officers D.J. Jeffrey and A.J. Urquhart. I protested, without success, that I was not

interested in first tour types who put us well over our establish-
ment of twenty-six pilots. Despite that, we were refreshed and
a new sense of purpose and dedication pervaded our ranks. We
were ready and eager to fight again.

From Volkel we ranged far and wide, searching for German
targets. Often our objectives were dictated by the dangerous European weather, which prevented us from hitting our intended
targets and forced us to select alternative locations to dive-bomb.
Every aircraft flew loaded with three bombs, which we were
anxious to release as early in each mission as possible so that we
could assume the role we more properly felt was ours — being
fighter aircraft. On the few occasions German aircraft were encountered, the pilots acquitted themselves extremely well, adding
to our squadron score. My own success at finding enemy aircraft
remained pathetic, and I never saw anything I could catch, only
the speedy Me 262.

We rarely saw the Me 262 in groups larger than three aircraft
and mostly we spied only single aircraft. The 262 carried a formidable armament of two or four 30-millimeter cannon, and
despite being twin-engined, was only a little larger than a Spitfire. Many were reconnaisance aircraft fitted with cameras only
but we could never distinguish these from the fighter version
during an encounter. On occasion, single 262s would overtake
us from behind, forcing us to break our formation or take defensive action while the German pilot proceeded blithely on his way,
probably chuckling at his apparent invincibility. Despite their
superiority, they rarely seemed prepared to mix it with us, and
destroyed very few of our fighters.

In the 262 the Wehrmacht possessed the spying camera eyes
it had lacked even before the Allies landed on the Normandy
beaches. Because of our stupendous air superiority, the German
generals had had to do without a great deal of the vital information that photographic and reconnaisance aircraft could supply.
But with an aircraft such as the 262, they were able to get coverage
and reports in a quantity they had not enjoyed for many months
and they began to forecast Allied plans as they discovered the
movements of our supplies and armies. In addition, the 262 was
used as a bomber; repeatedly when they attacked our 'drome,

the bombs were dropped without our seeing what had dropped them. The more we were exposed to it the more angry and helpless we felt, for there was absolutely nothing that we could do to counteract this new menace. Our main hope was that we might never run into a large formation of 262s willing to stay and fight it out. We would have a bad time of it.

The industrial area of the Ruhr valley encompassed an enormous area roughly seventy miles north to south by the same distance east to west. Within this heavily defended area, our daily targets included Munster, Dortmund, Munchen-Gladbach, Dulmen, Krefeld, Bochum, Gelsen Kirchen, and Essen. Once we had dropped our bombs on some important target, we ranged the roads and railroads, searching for targets that could fall prey to our guns. The flak had intensified, and although we suffered numerous hits, for some reason the damage did not seem as serious as during the earlier period. The cities bombed so often by day and by night by the heavies seemed lifeless, with great blocks of destroyed buildings showing gaping black holes where once there had been roofs. The countryside seemed dead as well. Farm livestock was practically non-existent, and it was difficult to find people or vehicles moving along the roads, which forced us to look long and hard for targets to strafe. Nevertheless we rarely returned without having fired our guns, and we continued to lead the other squadrons in the wing by a wide margin in ground targets destroyed.

Early in December the winco called me to his office to outline a new type of sortie. In the early evening I was to take the squadron on a blind bombing mission, the first time that Spitfires had been requested to perform such a task. The army had instituted forward controllers who could pick up our plot on radio tubes which would indicate our position relative to the ground. Then, by giving us directions over the R/T, they could deftly maneuver us to a predetermined point and tell us when to release our bombs. All I had to do was fly a steady course at a constant height of 10 000 feet and maintain a constant airspeed with the other eleven aircraft huddled up in close formation. If we obeyed directions perfectly, all our bombs would fall on the target, the town of Heinsburg, reportedly jammed with German troops. I followed the directions, releasing our bombs upon command although the ground below was totally obscured by a dense cloud layer. Later on we were informed by the army that all our bombs had fallen in the target area. This was my first and only experience with "juke-box" bombing, an exercise we enjoyed because we attracted no flak, and we visualized the surprise of the Germans when bombs rained down accurately even when there were no aircraft in sight.

One of the problems of operating in a Canadian squadron in the most successful wing in the Second Tactical Air Force was the amount of publicity which regularly appeared in the newspapers back in Canada. From war correspondent's reports, my family was able to keep track of my activities with alarming accuracy. They knew how much I was flying and the hazards involved, which prompted increasing requests from Mother to pack it in and return home. In my letters I admitted that I was tired and experiencing the first recognizable signs of operational fatigue or the "twitch." But I kept stalling the family by writing that the weather was poor most of the time, severely curtailing our flying, and that I had only a few more trips to go before I would be finished. I stressed that my experience had honed my skills to the point where it was possible to minimize the risks of operational flying. This was plain malarkey for the most part, for no amount of experience would save an aircraft from a flak hit, but it sounded great on paper. Even so I had been juggling my flying hours so that I reduced somewhat the actual hours spent flying operational sorties.

I was still keen and eager to attack anything and everything, no matter where the target might be. In my heart I knew that my time was limited, and that my fantastic luck was running out, a thought I obliquely admitted to Doc Whitelaw but concealed from the pilots. Had they suspected that my zeal was flagging or that fear was becoming my copilot or that I was losing some of my ability to motivate, squadron morale would have suffered immediately. My sleeping habits were poor, and remain so even to this day, but as my roommate, the Doc observed me closely and eventually weakened enough to prescribe nightly sleeping pills to allow me to get some badly needed rest. I became increasingly conscious of his eyes studying me as he kept tabs on my mental and physical condition. I have no doubt that some of his concerns were transmitted to Dal.

On December 6 the wing moved to Heesch, B-88, an ideal airdrome from which to operate, situated ten miles southwest of Nijmegen. Built by the Royal Engineers, it was located on the highest piece of land in that section of Holland, which we guessed to be less than two feet above sea level. We inherited an appreciable number of wooden buildings, which had formerly housed a Dutch youth labor organization and converted very comfortably to our requirements. We acquired stoves and fuel and were able to enjoy warmth and comfort without the crowding we had known for so long.

Our comfort was offset by the winter-dreary Dutch landscape, which became increasingly inhospitable as the lowlands continued to flood. The Rhine River, normally averaging about a half mile in width, in many locations now spanned ten miles. The twelve-mile stretch of ground between Arnhem and Nijmegen was almost totally submerged. Emmerich had water lapping at the roof eaves, and Wesel was surrounded by a huge, formidable moat. Soldiers suffered through wet and cold for long periods, and we were pleased to entertain grateful army officers in our luxurious mess, to which they returned as frequently as they could. Heavy fog, sullen clouds, and depressing cold rains all seriously interfered with our flying programs, and the pilots found solace in reading, sleeping, writing letters, and playing cards.

As I have stated elsewhere a fighter squadron was largely a self-contained unit. It derived much of its drive and enthusiasm in the air from the sense of cooperation and comradeship displayed on the ground, where we lived together in relatively confined quarters. We shared our parcels from home and listened and commiserated with men with minor problems. Unlike my days in the RAF, we had no batmen to do our chores, which meant that we always had laundry to wash or clothes to mend. With so many different personalities living together, each responding in his own hidden and different ways to the strains of operational flying, I was gratified that we survived as a large, contented, and effective family, little realizing that the relationships we developed under wartime conditions would remain treasured memories for life.

With the end of my tour in sight I had been helping Milt Jowsey[17] to position himself to assume command of the squadron when I left. Milt, who was the most operationally experienced pilot in the squadron, constantly displayed a confident and knowledgeable attitude, and was well able to lead the pilots aggressively and intelligently. I felt that he would maintain the record of excellence which we had achieved. His future record proved the wisdom of that belief.

As for the rest of the pilots, I felt we had excellent section leaders, capable of taking command of two aircraft or twelve with equal effectiveness. Not all pilots were equally aggressive and determined, but those that were far outnumbered the remainder. Some men seem to emerge as natural leaders while others, less aggressive perhaps, were content to be led. Despite these natural variances, I did not feel that we had a single weak link, and I never felt anything but tremendous pride in my pilots, one and all.

Shortly after moving to Heesch, Dal told me one day that I was through with operational flying. I was somewhat shocked, for although I knew my time was nearly up, his abruptness caught me unprepared. In my most eloquent manner I pleaded with Dal to allow me a short extension, ostensibly to train Milt more fully to take over the squadron. He finally agreed to letting me fly ten more hours, fewer if I were hit by flak. Dal later may have had second thoughts about granting my request, although he stuck to his bargain. For my part I tried to make every sortie as rewarding and devastating as I possibly could, knowing that this experience would never be repeated. My plane was knicked once or twice by flak, but the damage was so minor that it was not reported, which allowed me to approach the ten-hour limit imposed by the winco.

On December 14 the weather dawned clear for a change, bright and cold, and the prospect of a clear day allowed us to plan a full flying program. I led the first sortie with eight aircraft to dive-bomb the rail marshalling yards at Coesfeld. With one section of four Spits, we got four rail cuts, destroyed a locomotive, and damaged fourteen rail cars. We then turned westward and I used the top section of aircraft to bomb another marshalling yard, where a large fire was started amidst a number of railway carriages. With our aircraft now free of bombs, I regrouped the fighters to start a search for targets to strafe.

A few minutes later I spied a train heading at top speed for the large Dutch city of Enschede pulling eight passenger cars. I ordered my section to follow as I dived on the engine, determined to stop its rush toward safety. My bullets were on target and crippled the engine, forcing it to slow down. Because there were flak cars interspersed among the passenger cars, I felt the train was particularly important and radioed the pilots to blast the flak gunners.

Soon the flak wagons, manned by gray-uniformed men, were clobbered, completely silenced. Then my first impression of the importance of the train was confirmed as streams of Wehrmacht soldiers jumped from the cars, seeking protection in the railroad ditches and low scrub vegetation. We then strafed the ditches, flying parallel with the tracks while our targets, fully armed, bravely returned our fire.

Suddenly Kenway controller interrupted. "Caribou leader, we have some bogies southwest of your position. Are you interested?"

"Kenway. Caribou leader here. Very interested. Please give course and distance. Out."

"Caribou leader, Steer 270 degrees. About twenty miles at angels ten [10,000 feet]."

"Roger, Kenway. We're on our way."

"Caribou squadron," I radioed, "Buster. Steer 270 degrees and climb."

Opening the throttle wide, I pulled the aircraft up from the last dive and headed due west, climbing as fast as the Spitfire could go. I took a quick glance to the left to see how the rest of the planes were doing, and then a quick glance to the right for a final assessment of the damage done to the train. As I swung my head, I just happened to glance at the radiator temperature gauge located on the lower right side of the instrument panel. The needle flicked from a normal 90 to 140 and back to 90 again in the flash of an eye, at exactly the instant I looked at it.

HOLLAND, BELGIUM
AND THE RUHR

0 5 10   20   30   40   50 MILES

GERMAN DEFENCE LINE DECEMBER 1944

N
O
R
T
H

S
E
A

N

HOLLAND

AMSTERDAM

HENGELO
DEVENTER
ENSCHEDE
APELDOORN

THE HAGUE
ARNHEM
ZUTPHEN
LOWER RHINE RIVER
ROTTERDAM
COESFELD
WAAL RIVER
NIJMEGEN
BOCHOLT
MAAS RIVER
EMMERICH
HEESCH
GERMANY
WESEL
'S HERTOGENBOSCH
DORSTEN
GELSENKIRCHEN
RIPS
ESSEN
BOCHUM
EINDHOVEN
DUISBURG
RUHR
VALLEY
VENLO
KREFELD
MÜNCHEN-
GLADBACH
DÜSSELDORF

OSTEND
BRUGES
GHENT
ANTWERP
BELGIUM
COLOGNE
LOUVAIN
YPRES
BRUSSELS
AACHEN
DÜREN
WATERLOO
LILLE
LIEGE
BONN
NAMUR
DOUAI
MONS
REMAGEN
FRANCE

MOSEL RIVER

I normally never glanced inside the cockpit or checked my engine instruments. The feel of the aircraft — the sound of the engine or the touch of the controls — was almost all I required to know that my machine was functioning properly. I had been trained to look outside the cockpit, to swing my head constantly from side to side, determined that no aircraft would sneak up behind me. Our instructors had always warned, "It's the Hun you don't see who will get you."

Fate had willed me to look at the temperature gauge at the very moment it made the short, severe swing. I knew immediately that I was in serious trouble. Even though I seemed to go numb, my hands and head reacted instinctively. "Kenway, Caribou leader here, Mayday, Mayday. Aircraft hit and in trouble. Give me vector for our closest front line. Mayday, Mayday. Caribou leader. Out."

"Caribou leader. Steer 200 degrees. Nijmegen is your closest landfall. Steer 200 degrees. Good luck." All this was done in a quiet, unexcited manner. The voice, probably that of Squadron Leader John Edison, our senior controller, had a calming effect as my brain and my experience started to make the necessary preparations for whatever might develop.

I rammed the throttle forward to emergency power, pushing it through the wire restraining gate, and the engine responded well. I needed all the altitude I could get before the engine seized up. Climbing at over 5,000 feet per minute, the Spitfire grabbed for height until at 13,000 feet it started to vibrate violently. The end was not far off. To prevent the engine from bursting into flames, I switched it off and moved the propeller lever to coarse pitch. Just as I completed this setting, the connecting rods broke through the engine block, severing oil and glycol lines. This allowed the hot fluids to pour out, and covered the aircraft and me with a sticky, inflammable mixture.

I radioed the escorting Spitfires: "Caribou leader. I am unhooking my straps, jettisoning my hood, and getting ready to bail out if a fire starts. Will leave the radio plugged in for guidance instructions since I can't see forward. Thanks, fellas." With that I trimmed the aircraft to glide deadstick at exactly 132 mph, which was my assessment of the optimum speed needed to cover the most possible miles starting from the height that I had.

All straps were undone, the side door was open, and the hood was jettisoned. I could not see forward through the oil-covered windscreen. The silence was nearly complete; only the wind made a whistling noise as I glided toward our lines. For once I wished I had worn goggles, knowing that if a fire broke out there would be an explosion rather than a slow burn. There was plenty of fuel still left in the fuel tank located at the rear of the engine, which was right in front of my eyes.

When the engine gave up, safety was about twenty-five miles away, on the south bank of the Rhine River. The last fifteen miles would be over territory manned by fierce Hitler Youth troops who reputedly took no prisoners, a most distressing proposition.

Each second was filled with racing thoughts as my Spitfire seemed to lose height without much appreciable forward movement. I thought of the seven unopened letters I had just received from home before taking off for this flight. I thought of the telegram I had sent Mother over a week ago saying, "Finished ops now. No need to worry anymore." What a gross lie! What a hell of a mess! Gliding with a bullet-ridden radiator behind enemy lines with no engine. I thought of home and of previous good times while Jack Lumsden calmly ordered me to turn a little bit left or a little more to the right, ensuring that I stayed on course. I was very dependent on Jack to steer me home.

He kept repeating the distance I had to go: twelve miles, eight miles more, five miles, three miles. It seemed as though I was just skimming over the German troops. Only the presence of the rest of the squadron flying on all sides of my machine prevented the enemy gunners from directing concentrated fire at my machine alone. The courage of the pilots, exposing themselves at this low altitude and at slow speeds to heavy enemy fire, was incredible. They performed a brave yet foolhardy diversion and certainly made it possible for my aircraft to glide so far without being hit again by ground fire. Or perhaps the Germans felt I was going to crash anyway since my crippled aircraft was streaming a long tail of black and white smoke.

The Rhine slipped below my wing at last, posing another problem. Should I stay with the aircraft and crash land or jump? Both alternatives were decidedly risky. To crash land a Spitfire without my Sutton harness being tightly buckled was almost certain suicide and there was no time left to refasten it. Therefore I would have to jump, but would I have enough height? The Irving Parachute Company did not guarantee a parachute opening safely under eight hundred feet whereas I would have only five hundred feet of height and probably less. Feeling quite committed to jumping as soon as the river bank appeared below, I pulled the nose of the Spitfire up to slow it down to 100 mph, while at the same time gaining a life-saving two hundred extra feet of height. Grabbing the sides of the door hatch with both hands, I hurled myself out, head first. One tumble and I pulled the ripcord to open the parachute. There was a gentle tug as the 'chute opened, and I had a few seconds in which to watch my smoking aircraft dive vertically into the ground, exploding in a mass of flaming wreckage.

Gently my feet touched the soft, mushy ground with no more force than landing on a soft mattress from a two-foot jump. I bent my knees, then straightened them immediately, safe at last and completely unhurt. Waving to my escorts, I gathered the parachute into a silken bundle and headed for a small group of soldiers running to my assistance.

Within minutes the Canadian soldiers guided me towards the road, where a waiting jeep hustled me to our base only a few miles away. I actually arrived in time to put the finishing touches on the operational summary of our sortie, gleefully mingling with the pilots as we rehashed the successes for our spy.

Dal Russell invited me to his caravan for a drink, and I willingly accepted the offer. In his warm, brightly lighted office he poured two stiff drinks from a bottle of Scotch. Raising his glass, his face and eyes unusually serious, he said, "Well, Bill, this is the end of the road. You've had your last trip."

"I'll drink to that, Sir," I replied. I was smiling, in a rare and carefree mood.

The glasses were raised and emptied.

EPILOGUE

Experience had proven that it was difficult to obtain a posting to an operational squadron. Now I was to learn that it was also difficult to leave. Records had to be completed, which would take a week or so. All my flying clothes had to be returned to stores with explanations of why I had so few remaining of the many signed for over the years. "Lost due to enemy action" satisfied the stores officer as he signed off my equipment, including "Pistol, revolver," "Jacket, Irvine" and "Mae West." The finality of the procedure seemed prophetic in a way, for I realized that I was through with operational flying forever, that an important stage in my life was complete. The war would undoubtedly end in a few months, and I desperately wanted to return to Canada, to resign from the service, and to return to civilian life.

Like most pilots, I was a fatalist, living every day to the full for tomorrow might be the last one. To hell with the past — nothing could be done to change it. It was understandable, I think, for the pilots to live as they did, to be so exhuberant and demonstrative, for death was squarely faced on each sortie. Had we been flying as I had during my first tour, when we fought mainly opposing aircraft, one's life expectancy could be quite good, for survival depended largely on one's own personal skills. On the other hand, flying over heavily defended Germany, the situation was totally different, and survival was mainly dependent on luck. Skill was required, of course, but was not nearly as significant as luck. I had always felt that the survival equation was sixty per cent luck, twenty-five per cent skill, and fifteen per cent guts for Spitfire pilots engaged in attacking ground targets. Flying against and meeting enemy aircraft, the skill factor in the equation would rise dramatically while the luck factor would decrease.

I decided to visit Brussels for the last time while I awaited my clearance papers. I had barely unpacked my bags when pandemonium broke loose. Early in the morning of December 16, German General Gerd von Rundstedt began the so-called Battle of the Bulge by launching three armies through the hilly Ardennes Forest to penetrate the American-held positions. The suddenness, the massiveness, and the viciousness of the attack, aided by incredibly bad weather which kept our aircraft grounded, caught the Americans completely off guard and enjoyed immediate success. I had no prior inkling of the attack and was startled and dismayed by the Belgian refugees who started pouring into the city, creating a panic atmosphere. The size and range of the German thrust took the population by surprise and they remembered vividly the enemy advance of 1940. Despite the Allied effort to calm and reassure the Belgians, there was extensive fear. I became caught up in the worry and decided to return immediately to the squadron. The journey by truck eastward along the Maple Leaf Highway was a nightmare as troops and equipment were being rushed along it to reinforce the front, only to be hindered by literally thousands of refugees fleeing in the opposite direction, quite convinced that the German advance would encircle Brussels.

At the wing there was no sense of panic or confusion. For more than a week, the Germans continued to be favored by the weather — low clouds and zero visibility effectively kept our air forces grounded. Intelligence then confirmed that the enemy thrust had been blunted by our forces.

My last few days of waiting seemed interminable. It was difficult to accept that I no longer had a position of command, with duties to perform that required concentration and action. By December 22 I had received all of my clearance documents,[18] said final goodbyes, and trudged out to the waiting Anson aircraft for the trip to England. Within minutes the lumbering Anson circled the 'drome and then set course due west for the three-and-a-half-hour flight to Tangmere. Much further west lay Canada and home, but strangely that knowledge did not prove very comforting. I knew that I was leaving a way of life that I would never know again, the struggle for survival that few would understand except those who had lived it, and it was tearing me apart. But this was a finished chapter in my life, finished just as suddenly as I would close the cover of a book after reaching the last page of the final chapter.

The pilot flew low over the flooded fields of Holland, the muddy green quaintness of Belgium, and the more majestic beauty of France, on across the gray English Channel and over the rolling English fields toward Tangmere. With my face pressed against the plexiglas window, I watched the countrysides I had known so well roll past. As in Africa just one year earlier, I was again leaving my heart behind in strange lands to which I might never return. The old battlefields were now only memories, but those memories would always be brighter because of that last poignant glimpse.

After a few days in London, I received notification of the award of a Bar to my DFC, which I celebrated with a double Scotch without bothering to secure the rosette that signified the extra gong. Then, on January 10, 1945, I boarded a train to report to Number 3 Repatriation Depot, Warrington, on the English west coast. This was to be my final overseas posting before boarding the liner *Ile de France* for the return trip to Canada. After a few days the station commander, Group Captain Denton Massey, called me to his office. Shaking my hand he roared, "Congratulations, my boy. You're improperly dressed, y'know. Find yourself some DSO ribbon. And come over to the mess tonight for a drink. Congratulations."

And so I learned of my DSO, the only one given to a member of 442 Squadron. Then and now I have never viewed it as a personal award, but have always felt that it was given in recognition of the outstanding accomplishments of the squadron. Since squadrons do not earn medals, I was the fortunate pilot selected to represent the rest. Throughout the war the pilots of 442 were awarded three bars to their DFCs, which went to Dowding, Goodwin, and myself. We also received ten DFCs, eight of which I recommended — Young, McLarty, Middleton, Lumsden, Morse, Weeks, Goodwin, and Burns — with the other two being me and

Gordon, who won his a month later. None of us could boast an appreciable number of enemy aircraft destroyed, for our medals were earned, in my estimation, the harder way, through attacking heavily defended ground targets. There was little opportunity to build up large scores of enemy aircraft destroyed, for they appeared so seldom that even finding them was a moment of rare good luck. We did what we were ordered to do, to attack and destroy the enemy wherever he could be found, and we found him on the ground.

While awaiting my embarkation order, I spent a good deal of time reflecting on and trying to make sense of the past two years. I tried to find explanations for certain actions I took at one time or another, for the results achieved, and for other perplexing questions.

I never felt any bitterness toward the enemy, although many did. I respected him; I hated him. But in shooting down an airplane or destroying a truck or an engine, you never thought of the man in the cockpit or at the controls of an engine. You thought of the target as a plane or a locomotive, an inanimate thing, without ever a thought for the lives involved. And so when we were hit, it wasn't a man who got us, it was a gun, something you could hate and fear without a thought for the operator. If we had thought about the lives we took, our own personalities and attitudes could have been severely affected. I am sure that some thought of death and destruction in more humane terms, which may have made them a little less aggressive or caused them to shoot a little wide of a target. I was never aware of such a situation, but I realize that there were some who felt less sanguine than the majority of us. Similarly, when we lost a pilot, outwardly he was quickly forgotten, which was made easier by there being no body to bury or funeral to attend. Had we brooded over the inhuman aspects of killing, we would not have been airmen able to continue in combat.

In the three months following my departure, another thirty percent of 442's pilots were lost as they continued to war against the enemy. Jowsey I have already mentioned and Neil Burns, both of whom survived. Those lost and reported missing included Brigden, Urquhart, Doyle, Cousineau, McLarty, Pieri, and Dick with the phenomenal eyesight. We had paid an enormous price for our part in the illustrious history of 126 Wing.

From Monty Berger, the senior wing intelligence officer, I have gathered interesting statistics covering the wing from D-Day to the final capitulation of Germany on V-E Day. The wing moved three more times to end up at Wunsdorf near Hamburg. It consumed 2,789,804 gallons of aviation fuel, all manhandled in about 700,000 four-gallon Jerricans. The wing expended 3,422,527 rounds of ammunition and lost 325 Spitfires and seventy-nine pilots, of whom twenty-one escaped or became prisoners of war. In 20,000 sorties our loss was one pilot for every 250 trips flown. 126 Wing flew more sorties than any other wing in the Second Tactical Air Force with a top-scoring record of 360 enemy aircraft destroyed, fifteen probables and 153 damaged. On the ground the pilots destroyed and damaged 4,468 enemy vehicles, blew up or disabled 496 locomotives, rendered 1,569 rail cars useless, and made 426 cuts in rail lines. Every 126'er should be proud of that remarkable record.

Every pilot wanted to prove, either to his comrades or to himself, that he had the skill and courage to carry on. We all felt lucky, or invincible, or both, and without such an optimistic outlook even our youthful exuberance would not have sustained us. We all had confidence in our abilities as pilots, although some of us probably overestimated our skills. I know that I considered myself a good pilot, experienced on many different types of aircraft, but really good pilots, much better than I, existed in fair numbers. The difference between a good pilot and an exceptional pilot was a quantum leap in excellence. In my view, the Germans probably produced more superb fighter pilots than we did, partly because they had more opportunity to fly offensively to perfect their skills.

Our greatest deficiency seemed to be the lack of emphasis on and training in improving our shooting skills. Some pilots were naturally excellent marksmen who rapidly built scores that attested to their shooting proficiency. A fighter aircraft was designed basically to shoot down other aircraft and having a pilot who was a poor shot through a lack of adequate training or natural ability was almost a waste of a man and an aircraft. If I harbor any regrets about my past, my lack of shooting skill would be high on the list.

I thought of the comrades I had known and flown with, who helped me to survive. I would never forget those with whom I had fought against desperate odds when only cooperation and mutual courage allowed us to live to fight another day. The chances we took and our resulting successes will forever be like vivid postcards flashing before my eyes whenever I chance to daydream or encounter old friends. It was a wonderful life while it lasted, and we crammed a hell of a lot of living and dying into short, tumultuous careers. I knew that I had lived and enjoyed each day to the full and if young enough, I would not hesitate to do it all again.

My success related directly to the quality of the commanders I had been privileged to work with, men such as Colin Gray, who led and taught by personal example; Razz Berry, with his cherubic expression and wild mustache, who obtained results by individual achievement and a soft voice; or Dutch Hugo, who was so accomplished, so modest, and so responsive to every mood of those men under his command that he remains an outstanding personality in the memories of the men who knew him. Duke Arthur, a special man able to fight through the entire war and survive, understood my restless spirit, allowing me opportunities to lead and learn that many other squadron commanders would have forbidden. Much the same can be said for Harry Dowding, who also allowed me exceptional leeway in leading and designing my own tactics. And of Dal Russel, whose deep understanding of men and their attitudes was directly responsible for the remarkable spirit of 126 Wing, which compiled such a momentous record. To Dal I owe the greatest debt, for he allowed me full rein, checking me only when necessary so that I was able to point the squadron in the direction I thought we should travel. From the start of my operational career these men nurtured me, carefully corrected my mistakes, and added to my responsibilities as they saw fit. I owe them a great debt of gratitude and happily, they all survived the war.

At last as I awaited my turn to climb up the gangplank, of the *Ile de France*, an old friend discovered me amongst the group waiting to board. "Hey, Bill, did you hear about the squadron?" "No," I replied, "I haven't heard a thing in over two weeks."

"Well, y'know on Near Year's Day when all the Huns pulled off the surprise 'do' with hundreds of fighters hoping to catch us on the ground with hangovers, Smitty had himself a ball. He was returning early from a patrol with a bad engine when over Eindhoven he saw more than one hundred Fw 190s and Me 109s beating up the 'drome. All on his lonesome he attacked and squirted at ten or twelve different enemy, staying until he ran out of ammunition and fuel. He landed safely back at Heesch, dead-stick, and made no claims on the enemy. The best part was that the A.O.C. Harry Broadhurst and lots of other big-wigs were on the 'drome, hiding in slit-trenches, watching the whole thing. They phoned later to say that Smitty had shot one down and damaged another. Not bad, eh? One guy against a hundred?"

Sixty percent luck, twenty-five percent skill and fifteen percent guts. I wonder.

GLOSSARY

A/A	ack-ack, antii-aircraft gun
ABC unit	Automatic boost control
A/C	Air Commodore rank
Ace	a pilot credited with 5 destroyed aircraft
A/C 2	Aircraftman Second Class
AFC	Air Force Cross decoration
Ammo	Ammunition
AVM	Air Vice-Marshal rank
Bail out	To abandon an aircraft, usually by parachute
Bank	To turn involving raising of one wing
Beat up	To attack a target continuously or put on a low-flying display
Bind	To perform a monotonous or distasteful task
Black out	To lose consciousness due to centrifugal force
Blower	Supercharger on aircraft engine
Bogey	An unidentified aircraft
Boost	Amount of power given to engine by throttle setting
BPD	Base Personnel Depot
Briefing	Instructions given to pilots before a sortie
Buster	To move engine throttle rapidly to maximum power
Buckshee	Extra or free
Carabiniari	Italian policeman
Cine-gun film	See below
CFI	Chief Flying Instructor
'Chute	Short name for parachute
Clock	Often refers to airspeed indicator

252

CO	Commanding Officer
COTC	Canadian Officers Training Corps
Crate	Slang for an aircraft
Dead stick	Without engine power
Deck	The ground
D/F	Direction finding to locate aircraft
DFC	Distinguished Flying Cross
DFM	Distinguished Flying Medal
Do.	Dornier-German aircraft maker
Dog fight	Aerial combat
Drogue	Target towed by aicraft for air firing training and practice
Dual	Flying with instructor or student
Duff gen	Incorrect information
EFTS	Elementary Flying Training School
Erk	Any groundcrew airman or technician
ETA	Estimated time of arrival
Flak	Anti-aircraft gun fire from the ground
Flamer	Aircraft or vehicle on fire
Flat out	Maximum speed — as fast as possible
F/L	Flight Lieutenant rank
Flight	Less than a squadron — can be 2 to 6 aircraft
F/O	Flying Officer rank
Fuselage	The body of any aircraft
Fw	Focke Wulf — German aircraft maker
Gaggle	A group of enemy aircraft
G/C	Group Captain rank
Gen	Pukka gen — any information, pukka if true
Gong	A decoration or medal
Group	A grouping of a number of squadrons or wings
Had it	Finished, washed up
HE	Heinkel, German aircraft maker
HMT	His Majesty's Troopship
Hun	Any German fighting man or machine
Intercom	Intercommunication system within or between aircraft
IO	Intelligence Officer or "spy"
ITS	Initial Training School

Jerry	A German, any German
Ju	Junkers, German aircraft maker
Kite	Any aircraft
LAC	Leading Aircraftman rank
Let down	To lose height or altitude gradually
Line astern	One aircraft lined up behind another
Luftwaffe	The German Air Force
Mae West	Slang for inflatable life jacket
M and V	Meat and vegetable — standard meal fare
Mayday	Universal distress call
Me	Messerschmidt — German aircraft maker
Mission	Same as sortie, trip, do
MT	Motorized transport
Nacelle	Engine cowling
Oleo	Shock-absorbing aircraft landing gear
On the clock	On the airspeed indicator
Orbit	To fly in circles
Ops room	Operations room to gather and disseminate information
PDC	Pilot Disposal Center
Peel Off	To break away from a flying formation
Pitot head	A tube mounted externally on aircraft to give airspeed
P/O	Pilot Officer rank
POW	Prisoner of war
Prang	Slang for crashed or damaged aircraft
PRO	Public Relations Officer
PT	Physical training
PRU	Photographic Reconnaisance Unit
RAF	Royal Air Force
RCAF	Royal Canadian Air Force
Recce	Armed reconnaisance
Rhubarb	Low-level, search-and-destroy flight
SFTS	Service Flying Training School
S/L	Squadron leader rank
Slip stream	Air stream created behind spinning propellor
Spinner	Propellor boss or nose

Spitfire gunsight	See below
Sprog	Inexperienced pilot
Sten gun	British light machine gun
Stooge	To fly around rather aimlessly
Strafe	To attack ground targets with cannon and machine gun fire
Summerfelt matting	British system of wire netting laid on ground to create runway
Tallyho	Signal given by leader to attack
Tannoy	The loudspeaker address system
Through the gate	To open throttle fully for maximum power
Undercarriage	Aircraft landing gear
USAAF	United States Army Air Force
Vector	To direct an aircraft in the air to a specific target
Vic	A V formation of aircraft
WAAF	Women's Auxiliary Air Force
W/C	Wing commander rank
Winco	Wing commander
Wing	A number of flying squadrons (between two and four)

Due to lack of film and film developing equipment, we rarely used our cameras in the Middle East. However, in Europe, we used film everytime our guns were fired. A wing's exposed film would be strung together and about every two weeks was shown as a movie night to the pilots. These were fun nights, for the results revealed on the films were frequently hilarious, such as a blank film forcing the guilty pilot to describe what he was shooting at. Or a target might appear to be bobbing all over the place which could indicate a nervous or inexperienced attacker. Many pictures were quite spectacular, proving the audacity and aim of a pilot, whether depicting an attack on an aircraft or a ground target.

For most of the war our Spitfire gunsights consisted of an orange-colored ring which appeared on the front inside of the windscreen when the on-off switch was operated. The center was an orange dot while at either edge of the ring a horizontal orange bar could be adjusted by twisting the throttle grip. The aiming theory was to adjust the side bars to the wingspan of the enemy aircraft as it appeared at your predetermined firing range. As you approached the target you made certain that the deflection allowed ensured that the target flew towards the center dot and that the wings appeared to just touch the horizontal bars. If a pilot was flying properly, if all his guns were working, and if he had made all the right calculations, he might hit the enemy when he pressed the gunbutton.

By August, 1944, our replacement Spitfire IX's started arriving equipped with a new gyroscope gunsight which some pilots found to be deadly accurate, permitting a few sharpshooters to run up impressive scores. Instead of a ring, a series of small adjustable bars could be quickly arranged by twisting the throttle grip to fit the wingspan of an enemy, in any attitude, and if the centre of the sight was positioned on the target, your bullets should strike the enemy.

I had two reservations about the new sight. First, it took time to adjust the target requirements which forced a pilot to keep his head in the cockpit long enough to allow a wily and undetected enemy to attack. Second, since the sight worked on a gyroscopic principle, after even mildly strenuous flying maneuvers, it toppled or tumbled and required precious seconds before it settled down to become useful again. This could mean the loss of a firing opportunity. For these reasons I usually had the gyrosight removed if my machine was so equipped. Johnny Johnson, the Allies leading ace, also declined to use the new sight and kept the old ring and bead.

NOTES

1. Squadron Leader Donald C. Laubman, DFC and Bar, p.5
   Don served a lengthy time in Canada as an instructor before
   finally joining a fighter squadron overseas where he became
   the leading Canadian scorer with fifteen confirmed victories.
   He was shot down by flak in April, 1945, and taken prisoner
   for a month before being rescued with the surrender of Germany. He remained in the service and rose to be one of the
   most highly respected and competent generals in the Canadian Armed Forces.
2. Squadron Leader Albert U. Houle, DFC and Bar, p. 5
   Bert spent much of his operational career in the Middle East,
   Malta, Sicily, and Italy, ending his operational career on Spitfires as CO of 417 RCAF Squadron. He remained in the
   RCAF until retirement with the rank of Group Captain, the
   end of a brilliant military profession.
3. Flight Lieutenant L. "Cap" Foster, DFC, p. 10
   Cap spent years in Canada instructing before reaching a Spitfire squadron in Europe. His operational experience earned
   him the DFC, but a more memorable exploit was his looping
   the loop under the Rainbow Bridge at Niagara Falls. This
   feat was even more amazing since there was a net hanging
   under the bridge to protect workmen carrying out
   maintenance repairs. This left little room between the net
   and the angry gorge waters.
4. Penalty Period, p. 14
   In order to discipline a pilot instructor who refused to succeed or who committed unauthorized flying disdemeanors
   to improve his chances of obtaining a posting to a more en-

joyable task, he was frequently sent to a bombing and gunnery school. Air force authorities felt that after a suitable penalty period in that position, the pilot could eventually get his ultimate wish, a posting overseas for combat duties.

5. Pilot Officer Chalmers "Smiley" Goodlin, p. 22
   He survived the war and after OTU soon transferred to the U.S. Army Air Force. He later gained renown as a test pilot in the era when Chuck Yeager broke the sound barrier for the first time. Smiley had the nickname "Slick" by then.

6. Flying Officer Geoffrey Page, p. 33
   Geoff finished the war as a decorated Spitfire Wing Commander whose recently published autobiography, *Tale of a Guinea Pig,* relates his full and interesting story.

7. Group Captain Petrus H. "Dutch" Hugo, DSO, DFC and two Bars, p. 38
   Hugo was born December 20, 1917, in South Africa. As a wing leader in Britain he achieved success in antishipping strikes, a most hazardous occupation. He survived the war with twenty-two destroyed, and many probable and damaged to his credit as well as shipping and ground targets. He was a superb marksman and one of the most understanding and approachable men I was to meet.

8. Wing Commander Ronald "Razz" Berry, DSO, DFC and Bar, p. 39
   He survived the war ending up with seventeen confirmed victories.

9. Wing Commander Colin F. Gray, DSO, DFC and two bars, p. 44
   Colin and his twin brother Kenneth were born November 9, 1914, in New Zealand. Colin finished operations with twenty-eight and a half destroyed, which ranked him amongst the top dozen highest scoring allied pilots. He remained in the service after the war and eventually retired to his homeland. His brother, a bomber pilot, won the DFC, and was killed on a bombing raid over Germany.

10. Squadron Leader C.I.R. "Duke" Arthur, DFC and Bar, p. 95
    Duke finished the war with the third most operational hours

among Canadian fighter pilots, behind Stan Turner and George Keefer. He remained in the RAF until retirement, when he returned to Canada. He is currently living in Vancouver.

11. Flight Sergeant King, p. 125

   King's fate was a mystery, for there is no record of him after we loaded him into the ambulance. Pep and I speculated that he had a concussion, had passed out and died from it in hospital, and that somehow his body was never identified.

12. Squadron Leader I.F. "Hap" Kennedy, DFC and Bar, p. 154

   Hap was posted to 401 RCAF squadron in Europe a couple of weeks before I got my posting to France, by which time he had been made CO of the squadron. On July 26 I was in the air when I heard Hap notify his squadron in a calm voice, "I've been hit and will bail out. Take over Charlie. Don't follow me down. Lots of luck. Cheerio." He evaded successfully to return through our lines a month later. This finished his flying career. He returned to Canada to complete his education, finally graduating as a doctor of medicine. He is still the modest, almost shy person that he was in the air force.

13. Wing Commander J.E. Johnny Johnson, DSO and two Bars, DFC and Bar, p. 166

   Born in England in 1915, Johnny finished the war as the highest scoring allied pilot in the European theater with thirty-eight enemy aircraft to his credit. He was very much an individualist, although a fine leader. He had remarkable eyesight, so necessary in a fighter pilot, as well as an uncanny ability to find the elusive Hun. Being able to find the enemy is partly luck, but Johnny had an extraordinary understanding of the enemy under almost all conditions and so became a very successful hunter. His experience and clever tactical ability proved that he was the complete fighter pilot, a fine shot, and a great leader.

14. Flying Officer Neil Burns, DFC, p. 177

   Neil was released from a POW camp at the end of the war and remained in the service until forced to leave at retire-

ment age. After Neil read this manuscript he commented,
"When I arrived at 144 Wing I was interviewed by Johnson
in his trailer. He pointed to the wall behind his desk which
contained photos of all the pilots on the wing. He then said,
one, get your picture taken for my gallery and, two, you will
be flying as my number 2 tomorrow. If you lose me, you'll
be sent back to England." Small wonder he was anxious!
Neil added a further observation. Just before Christmas,
1944, he remembers looking around at the pilots during a
squadron briefing and realized that in just seven months he
was the only one left from the day he joined the wing at airfield B-1.

15. Market-Garden, p. 198
    This heroic and ill-advised action has been described many
    times with one of the better accounts being Cornelius Ryan's
    A Bridge Too Far.

16. Flight Lieutenant W. Bruce "Steve" Randall, MID, p. 226
    In my opinion Steve deserved a DFC, but the best I could
    do was to recommend him for a Mention in Despatches. He
    was a POW until the end of the war when he returned to
    Canada and civilian life.

17. Squadron Leader Milton E. Jowsey, DFC, p. 239
    Milt proved to be a very capable squadron commander. His
    aggressiveness led to his being shot down in Holland, where
    he evaded, being looked after by Dutch civilians until our
    advancing armies overran his hiding place on April 3, 1945.
    He returned to civilian life and is now a very successful con-
    sulting mining engineer living in Sudbury.

18. Clearance documents, p. 246
    Dal's remarks on the "Pro forma for disposal of aircrew
    on completion of operational tour" read, "S/L Olmsted is
    a most able and daring squadron commander whose leader-
    ship has been outstanding. He has turned his squadron into
    the most aggressive ground attack squadron in the Wing.
    He has completed 517 operational hours and has expressed
    his desire to return to Canada where he wishes to obtain his
    discharge and go back to college to finish his education. It

is requested that he hold his acting rank of squadron leader."
Air Vice Marshal Harry Broadhurst wrote, "This officer has
given a grand tour of operations and I agree that he should
be repatriated for a rest."

ROYAL CANADIAN AIR FORCE
CERTIFICATE OF SERVICE

ISSUED TO OFFICERS

This is to Certify THAT (Rank) *Acting Squadron Leader* (Number) *Can J 5125*

(Name in full) *William Alfred Olmsted*
was appointed to Commissioned Rank

in *the Reserve, Special Section, General List, Pilot Branch*

ROYAL CANADIAN AIR FORCE on the *Twenty-third* day

of *April* 19 *41*

and was STRUCK OFF STRENGTH on the *Sixth* day

of *April* 19 *45* by reason of *Retirement on completion*
of a term of voluntary service during an emergency,
and was transferred to Class "C" of the General
Section of the Reserve

PARTICULARS OF SERVICE

Countries: *Canada - 31-8-40 to 5-9-42 and 22-1-45 to 6-4-45*
England - 6-9-42 to 20-1-43 and 4-2-44 to 2-7-44 and 22-12-44 to 22-1-45
Africa - 21-1-43 to 3-2-44. Europe - 2-7-44 to 22-12-44.
Served in the ranks in Canada from 31-8-40 to 22-4-41
Orders, Decorations, Medals, Mentions and Commendations *Distinguished Service Order,*
Distinguished Flying Cross & Bar, 1939-43 Star. Canadian
Volunteer Service Medal & Clasp.
Wounds *Nil*

Dated at *Toronto, Ontario* this *Sixth* day

of *April* 19 *45.*

for Chief of Air Staff

R.C.A.F.—R. 188
80M—11-44 (4851
H.Q. 885-R. 188

CANADA

MINISTER OF NATIONAL DEFENCE FOR AIR

Mr. and Mrs. R.I. Olmsted,
15 Chedoke Avenue,
Hamilton, Ontario.

OTTAWA
February 23, 1945

Dear Mr. and Mrs. Olmsted:

Once again I would like to express the feeling of extreme pride with which all ranks of the Royal Canadian Air Force join me in extending most sincere congratulations to you and your family on the additional honour and distinction earned by your son, Squadron Leader William Alfred Olmsted <u>DSO</u>, <u>DFC</u> and <u>Bar</u>, through the award of the Distinguished Service Order.

The citation on which this award was made reads as follows:

"This officer has led the squadron on very many sorties during which great loss has been inflicted on the enemy. Much of the success achieved can be attributed to this officer's brilliant leadership, outstanding skill and courage which have inspired all under his command. Squadron Leader Olmsted himself has been responsible for putting out of action a large number of mechanical vehicles, numerous locomotives and coaches and much other equipment. He has also destroyed four enemy aircraft. His determination to harass the enemy on every possible occasion has been worthy of the highest praise."

Your son's outstanding Service record is one of which we may all feel justly proud.

With kindest personal regards

Yours sincerely,

Acting Minister of National Defence for Air